Nathanael Burwash

A Handbook of the Epistle of St. Paul to the Romans

Based on the revised version and the revisers' text

Nathanael Burwash

A Handbook of the Epistle of St. Paul to the Romans
Based on the revised version and the revisers' text

ISBN/EAN: 9783337006112

Printed in Europe, USA, Canada, Australia, Japan

Cover: Foto ©ninafisch / pixelio.de

More available books at **www.hansebooks.com**

A HANDBOOK

OF

THE EPISTLE OF ST. PAUL

TO THE

ROMANS,

BASED ON THE REVISED VERSION AND THE REVISERS' TEXT,

FOR THE USE OF STUDENTS AND BIBLE CLASSES.

BY

N. BURWASH, S.T.D.,

Professor of Biblical and Systematic Theology in Victoria University.

TORONTO:
WILLIAM BRIGGS, 78 & 80 KING STREET EAST.
1887.

PREFACE.

THE present work is the result of special studies commenced some seventeen years ago. During that time it has been the duty of the writer to examine the Epistle to the Romans critically with successive classes of students. This class-room work has doubtless left its impress on the form of book which is now offered to the public. In this joint labour of teacher and students four leading hermeneutical principles have guided us:—

1. In dealing with the work of an author of the literary rank of St. Paul we have assumed that there is no mere verbiage, that every word and every grammatical construction has its reason in the living thought and mental processes of the author. To ascertain what that reason is, *i.e.*, to reproduce to our own consciousness this living thought and these mental processes, has been our first aim. For this purpose we have had constant recourse to the Grammar, using Winer, Buttmann and Kuehner; to the Lexicon, using especially Grimm and Cremer; and above all, to the Concordance, tracing words, phrases and constructions through the entire writings of St. Paul, and endeavouring thus to secure more exact definition of the thought which such terms connoted in the apostle's mind. We hope that here and there serious difficulties in interpretation have been removed by the light gained in this way.

2. It has further been taken for granted that, especially in St. Paul's writings, a perfect logical sequence is maintained. Perhaps no other writer, either ancient or modern, places us so fully under the obligation of this principle as does St. Paul. He is pre-eminently a perfect logician. He has also his own forms of

logical connection, with which one must become familiar in order to avoid mistake. His use of connectives is therefore a study of prime importance, and his methods of grouping the various elements in his argumentative process must be carefully noted. His rhetorical methods are also at times of very great importance in following his line of thought. By such helps as these it has been our aim to follow from point to point the logical movement of the thought of the writer; and we feel, after years of study in this direction, fully justified in saying that he is never incoherent, and that he never palms off upon his readers mysticism, allegory or rabbinical fancies for argument; in fact, that the demands of the most perfect science are satisfied by his logical method. This especially appears in his use of proofs from the Old Testament scriptures, which he never cites after in an irrational, unhistorical, or so-called spiritual fashion. His spiritual meaning is always true philosophy, the elucidation of moral principle. We have therefore proceeded upon the principle that Paul's work admits of a thoroughly rational interpretation throughout, and have sought to find such a sense to every passage.

3. We take it for granted that a mind of the logical power and matured thought of St. Paul held a perfectly defined conception of the whole sphere of truth with which it had to deal; that not only were the great fundamental points of truth, such as man's responsibility, the principle of faith, God's sovereignty, etc., clearly defined, but that they were so harmonized and articulated as to form in his own mind a self-consistent system of moral and religious truth. While the present Epistle does not formally propound such a system it gives abundant evidence of its existence. Such a mind as St. Paul's, engaged for twenty-five years or more upon the work of making clear to others the great truths of Christianity, could not fail to have framed them into a coherent, systematic conception; and certainly must have clearly defined to itself the individual elements of truth. We have therefore had recourse at every point to the study of the important parallel passages. In the Epistles to the Galatians,

Corinthians, Ephesians, Philippians, etc., we have found abundant materials for the more perfect definition of doctrines, arguments, and even illustrations, which have been presented in our present Epistle in more summary form. The apostle has thus served as his own expositor, and has left us no room to doubt as to his true meaning. Perhaps no hermeneutical principle has been more fruitful of light and help, both in the definition and expansion of the apostle's thought, than this. It is a great boon that we enjoy in the possession of so many works from the pen of this great Christian founder, and that so many of them are written from a point of view which throws light upon the contents of this his greatest work.

4. We have taken it for granted that Paul's system of religious truth had its natural genetic relation to antecedent and contemporaneous thought and religious life; that it is a part of a history, governed by the laws which obtain in the history of the spiritual life of humanity. In saying this we do not exclude the supernatural. We believe that the supernatural is involved in, or perhaps we should say links itself on to, the very laws of our spiritual being; that it is not a magical interference operating from without, but a divine power working from within. So we believe revelation itself has its laws of development, in which, as in nature, God hath unfolded his plan. In fact, Paul himself boldly affirms this, and regards himself as a minister in this process of development. We have therefore felt justified in using to the fullest extent possible the historical method. We are well aware of how vast, how impossible to human knowledge or skill, is the task thus attempted. Who has the power to trace the birth and perfecting of thought in his own mind? Who then can understand its life-long process in the mind of another? But though a perfect mastery of this science of genetic interpretation lies almost infinitely beyond us, yet even its elements are so full of help in the task of apprehending the thoughts of a great mind that we have made what effort in this direction lay in our power.

In conclusion, we can assure our readers that the hours spent in communion with St. Paul in this Epistle have been hours of the most blessed satisfaction. While dealing more directly with the intellectual aspects of this great book we have not lost sight of the fact that intellect is quickened into its highest life by the profoundest emotion, and that he who would understand Paul aright must feel with him. Not for ourselves alone but for our readers as well have we prayed for this gift, the gift of perfect sympathy with the clear moral conviction, the lofty faith, the boundless enthusiasm, the unfaltering trust, the patient, consecrated love of Paul. Without this all attempt at understanding him must fail. May God grant that in this spirit we may all abound yet more and more!

N. BURWASH.

VICTORIA UNIVERSITY,
    COBOURG, ONT., *March 21st, 1887.*

INTRODUCTION

TO THE

EPISTLE TO THE ROMANS.

THAT this Epistle, as stated in its opening sentences, was written by St. Paul has never been seriously doubted in the church. From the days of Irenæus downward there is an uninterrupted consensus of testimony, besides clear references to the Epistle in the apostolic fathers.* The internal evidence also, whether drawn from the tenor of doctrine or from the incidental allusions, is complete. A comparison of ch. xv. 25, etc., with ch. xvi. 1 and 23, shows that it was written from Corinth, just before the journey to Jerusalem with the alms of the churches of Achaia and Macedonia, *i.e.*, in the spring of A.D. 58. It is worthy of note that the Epistles to the Corinthians were written twelve and six months prior, and the Epistle to the Galatians probably within three months of the date of this Epistle.

Of the origin of the church at Rome, and of its condition at this time, we know but little beyond what is contained or implied in the Epistle itself. It was essentially a Gentile church (ch. i. 13; xi. 13), with some Jews (ch. ii. 17; iv. 1), though this last point is not so clear. Many of its members were personally known to St. Paul (ch. xvi. 4, etc.); some of them former fellow-laborers with him (vv. 4, 9); one (v. 5), and it may be more, among the converts of his former ministry. It is not impossible that the church had been founded or largely built up by the labours of these associates and converts of Paul, and was thus founded in *that type of Christian doctrine* which Paul preached. But as a whole this church did not

---

* See Irenæus, Adv. Haer, L. v., Clem. Ad. Corinth I. ch. 35, etc.

stand in any such relation to him that he could assume authority over their faith or intermeddle with their internal affairs (ch. i. 11, 12). In seeking, therefore, for the historical occasion of this Epistle with a view to determine its scope, we require to study not so much the internal state of the Roman church at this time as the relation of Paul to the entire Christian world at this juncture in his ministry.

THE OCCASION.

It is evident from the Epistles to the Corinthians and Galatians, as well as from various allusions in the Acts, that, at this time, the character of Paul's work and teaching, and also his apostolic authority, were seriously called in question by an active, a large, and a somewhat successful party in the Christian church. Now, the very fact of such a question having been raised must have rendered Paul anxious—

1. To set himself right with his old friends and fellow-workers by placing his complete doctrine of the gospel fairly before them.

2. To place his position rightly before the church at Rome, which he intended shortly to visit.

3. To anticipate and prevent any injurious influence which the false teachings of his opponents might exert here as already elsewhere.

The second of these motives is seemingly most prominent, though all three are secured in the same way, *i.e.*, by a full argumentative exposition of the entire doctrinal system, or, as he calls it, "the gospel," which he preached as opposed to the "other gospel" which taught, "Except ye be circumcised after the manner of Moses, ye cannot be saved." This accounts for the peculiar form of controversial style adopted in this Epistle—a form which has led all expositors, ancient and modern, to the view that Paul has in mind an unnamed or an ideal antagonist in many of the most animated parts of the treatise.

WHO WAS THIS ANTAGONIST?

Three answers have been proposed:

1. The unbelieving Jew.
2. The adherent of the original form of Christianity as preached by Peter.

INTRODUCTION. 11

3. The pseudo-Christian Jew who meets us in the fifteenth of Acts, and in the Epistles to the Galatians and Corinthians.

This last we take to be the true view. In a letter to believing Gentiles why should Paul defend his doctrine against unbelieving Jews? On the other hand, we must consider the position of Baur, which identifies the original Jewish church with the pseudo-Christians, "false brethren," referred to, as altogether untenable. Paul's ideal antagonist, whose sceptical question he so frequently voices in this Epistle, is the Jewish Christian, who exalts circumcision above Christ.

THE SUBJECT

of this Epistle we thus take to be a complete exposition of Paul's doctrinal system as opposed to the spurious Judaizing form of Christianity; and we conceive that the most important introductory matter to the right understanding of this Epistle is a review of the entire controversy between Paul and his Judaizing opponent. In taking this position we do not for a moment admit Baur's theory that Ebionitism was the original form of Christianity, and that Paul's was a later antagonistic and supplanting system. On the other hand, the entire history of the case, as well as the study of this Epistle, will furnish evidence that Paul regarded the gospel which he preached as the true, original gospel of Jesus Christ. Nor do we admit, with Baur and the ancient Ebionites, that the preaching of Peter was in accord with the teaching of Paul's opponents. On these two points we ask the student to examine carefully such passages as 1 Cor. xi. 23; xv. 3; Gal. i. 6, 7, 11, 12; ii. 7, 8, 9 (See also Acts xv. 9, and x. 43.) It is further certain that in the days of Justin Martyr there were two schools of Jewish Christians who still reverenced and observed the Mosaic law. One of these showed no disposition to impose that law on the Gentile church, and these we take to be the genuine successors of Peter, James, and the elders and apostles at Jerusalem (see Dialogue with Trypho, 47.) The others "strove in every way to persuade other men, I mean those who have been circumcised from error by Christ, to observe the same things as himself, telling them that they will not be saved unless they do so." These we take to be the genuine successors of Paul's opponents.

THE EBIONITES.

This party, which appears so distinctly in Justin Martyr's time, about a century after the writing of our Epistle, can be traced down to the end of the fourth century with but little variation in their peculiar tenets. Their separation from the church as external sectaries dates from the time of Hadrian, about A.D. 130. But their doctrinal peculiarities were not the result but the cause of this. In A.D. 130 Ebionitism was a fully developed system of belief. What was this system? and to what extent was it already in existence in the time of Paul's conflict with the Judaizers?

In endeavouring to answer these questions we shall first borrow from Mosheim a synopsis of the doctrine of the Ebionites of the second century. "They supposed Christ to be an ambassador from God endued with divine power, yet they conceived him to be a man born in the ordinary course of nature, the son of Joseph and Mary. They maintained that the ceremonial law of Moses must be observed not by the Jews only but by all who wished to obtain salvation, and therefore St. Paul, that strenuous opposer of the law, they viewed with abhorrence. Nor were they satisfied with the mere rites which Moses appointed, but observed with equal veneration the superstitious rites of their ancestors and the customs of the Pharisees which were added to the law."

From this outline of Ebionitism, with which all our historians agree, we gather the following points:—

1. The essential principle of Ebionitism was a divergent view of the way of salvation. This was to be attained by observance of moral and ritual law.

2. This led to their regarding Christ as the prophet or teacher, but not as the *priest*, of his people.

3. As such lower faith in Christ did not involve his divinity, this was denied.

4. This legal view of the way of salvation involved no doctrine of the internal sanctifying work of the Holy Spirit.

5. It involved no deeply spiritual conviction of the guilt and power of sin.

6. It maintained in full the Jewish idea of their peculiar right to salvation by virtue of the covenant of circumcision.

These six points are, we think, fully borne out by the study of the Clementines, the most important Ebionitish work which has come down to our times, as well as by the remarks and references of the ancient historians and church writers.

Were these fundamental elements of Ebionitish doctrine already developed in the apostolic age? We think they were.

1. Three of the Gospels imply in their teachings some such form of opposed teaching: St. John in his entire doctrine of the incarnation and deity of the Word; St. Matthew and St. Luke in their explicit statement of the miraculous conception.

2. The Epistle to the Hebrews stands in antagonism to this teaching point by point.

(*a*) Ebionitism denies the divinity and pre-existence of Christ. The Epistle to the Hebrews opens with the most direct assertion and proof of this fundamental doctrine.

(*b*) Ebionitism clearly ignores or denies the priestly or mediatorial work of Christ. The "sum" of this Epistle is this: "We have an High Priest who is set on the right hand of the throne of the majesty in the heavens."

(*c*) Ebionitism sets forth a legal way of salvation. The Epistle to the Hebrews insists that in all ages "without faith it is impossible to please God."

(*d*) Ebionitism expiated sin by ritual offerings. This Epistle asserts that it is "impossible for the blood of bulls and of goats to take away sin," and everywhere exhibits the most deeply spiritual views of the guilt of sin.

(*e*) Ebionitism failed to recognize that deeper intent of the law so fully taught in our Lord's Sermon on the Mount, which requires truth in the inward parts and a righteousness only attainable by the regeneration of the Holy Ghost. But the Epistle to the Hebrews sets forth the Word of God as "quick and powerful, sharper than a two-edged sword, piercing to the dividing asunder of the soul and spirit, and of the joints and marrow, and a discerner of the thoughts and intents of the heart;" and it exhibits the work of divine grace as a *new* covenant, in which God "will put his laws into their mind and write them in their hearts."

Nor is this strongly marked antithesis of the great lines of thought in this Epistle to the fundamental principles of Ebionitism a mere accident. This Epistle was written to the Hebrews, but not to the unbelieving Hebrews, for there is no argument to prove that Jesus is the Messiah; that is taken for granted as a matter already believed by these Hebrews. But the very fact that the fundamental doctrines regarding the person, office and work of the Messiah required such extended exposition and demonstration indicates the existence of opposing tendencies.

3. Let us now fall back twenty years further to the date of the Epistle to the Galatians. This Epistle is not indirectly but directly opposed to the Jewish error of Paul's day, and hence that error is definitely described.

(*a*) Ebionitism presented a fundamentally different way of salvation —a legal and ceremonial righteousness. Paul's opponents preached "another gospel," a "perversion," turning men away from the *grace* of Christ. This "other gospel" was justification by works of law and not by faith.

(*b*) Ebionitism denied the divinity and mediatorial work of Christ. Paul thought it needful to assert that "in the fulness of time God sent forth his Son, made of a woman, made under the law, to redeem them that were under the law."

(*c*) Ebionitism held superficial views of the guilt and inward power of sin, and its idea of religion was external and ceremonial. Paul in this Epistle insists on the spirit of adoption, faith working by love, the fruits of the Spirit, not circumcision nor uncircumcision but a new creature, exposing the deep moral pollution of the works of the flesh.

Here, then, we have Paul contending with the essentials of Ebionitism, but not yet in their fully developed form. If the central principle of Ebionitism was a fundamentally wrong view of the way of salvation, then that wrong central principle is here most clearly discussed and opposed. That those who followed this wrong way lacked the deep, heartfelt conviction of sin, and the corresponding experience of the inward work of the Spirit, is likewise evident from the tone of the Epistle. But it would seem that they had not yet so far consciously developed their beliefs as to deny the divinity of Christ and his mediatorial work; hence the apostle touches these points less fully and professedly than the author of the Epistle to the Hebrews. He perhaps merely anticipates that which he saw clearly involved in the system. Ebionitism may have been as yet practical rather than speculative.

4. Turning next to the Epistles to the Corinthians, we must bear in mind that this church was quite as much in danger from practical Antinomianism as from legalism, and from philosophical scepticism as from Jewish superstition. But even here, mingled with widely different tendencies, we may trace Ebionitish principles. Note the following:—

Christ on a level with Paul, Cephas and Apollos (1 Cor. i. 12, iii. 4, etc.).

The questions about circumcision (ch. vii. 18, 19), and about idol sacrifices (ch. viii.).

The supreme importance of charity (ch. xiii.).

The gospel that "Christ died for our sins" (ch. xv. 3, and 2 Cor. v. 14-21).

The contrast of the ministration of the letter with that of the spirit (2 Cor. ch. iii.).

And especially the underlying references, in 2 Cor. chs. x. and xi., to men who boast in another man's line of things made ready to their hand; who preach another Jesus and another gospel, and boast that they are Hebrews.

All these particulars go to show that while the principles of Ebionitism were still in a rudimentary state their essential elements were already in existence among those to whom Paul wrote the Epistles to the Corinthians, and, indeed, the assertion of Jewish prerogatives quite prominent. Twenty years later, when the Epistle to the Hebrews was written, these elements had assumed their full form. And this we might reasonably expect. It was very improbable that a system so closely allied to Judaism should come into existence after the destruction of the temple and the cessation of the Jewish ritual. History also proves that in the age of new ideas and formations the first stages of growth are rapid, and the new systems quickly reach their full development. It is not at all surprising that, though not yet fully developed, this system should from the beginning be apprehended by Paul in all its bearings and potential deviations from the truth. His religious insight was profound, his inspiration of the highest order, and his intellectual power to discern all logical results seldom equalled. In dealing, therefore, with this error, while he grappled with its fundamental principle—righteousness by works of law—we are quite prepared to find him striking at many of its remoter consequences, and demolishing false ideas which became more prominent in after times.

THE EPISTLE TO THE ROMANS WRITTEN IN OPPOSITION TO EBIONITISM.

But admitting that the conflict in which Paul was at this time engaged was a conflict with the essential and germinating principles of Ebionitism, it still remains to be proved that this conflict has entered into the Epistle to the Romans, and has determined both its line of thought and its mode of presentation. We have already mentioned three considerations which would naturally lead to this: Paul's desire that his personal friends at Rome, who could not but hear of the bitter attacks of his opponents, should understand his doctrine as he himself presented it; his wish to visit Rome commanding the full confidence due to an apostle of Christ; and his anticipation of danger from this false doctrine, even at Rome. On this last point Baur asserts roundly that in the second century Ebionitism prevailed at Rome. This we think cannot be sustained, yet the evidence goes to show that in some minds there it had gained a foothold. That it did not earlier establish itself there may have been due to this very Epistle. It certainly was not due to any lack of zeal or enterprise on the part of its advocates. Those who followed Paul from Jerusalem to Antioch, and from Antioch to Corinth and even to remote Galatia, might be expected to precede or follow him to Rome.

If it be objected that the Gentile churches could take no interest in and be in no danger from a Judaizing sect, the reply is that Galatia and Corinth were Gentile churches, and yet they suffered from Ebionite teachings. The churches of the Gentiles were largely planted by Paul among the adherents of the synagogue, the proselytes of righteousness, those who had been already leavened by the monotheistic and ethical teachings of Moses. Paul himself had habitually appealed to Moses and the prophets, so that in all Christian churches they were held in highest honour. At Rome the influences of the elder system may have been still stronger. If the gospel was carried to Rome by the strangers from Rome who listened on the day of Pentecost, then it entered the imperial city as scarcely yet distinguished from Judaism, and the church at Rome may have had a very warm attachment not only to the Old Testament Scriptures but also to the religion which they represented. Nor was it the Jew alone who was in danger from Ebionitism, especially in those more ethical and less ritual forms which we find in the Clementines. It is indeed possible that this work was from Rome. It is also against this form of Ebionitism that the Epistle to the Romans especially bears, as the Epistle to the Hebrews meets its more external and ritual form. The fundamental principles of Ebionitism reproduce themselves in the superficial legalism of every age, even in modern Unitarianism; and as such superficial legalism exists among Gentiles as well as Jews, Ebionitism would attract those thus disposed to itself.

The probabilities in favour of this view are further increased by the fact that Paul was just now full of this subject. The strong language of the Epistles to the Corinthians and Galatians shows how all the intensity of his nature was aroused by it. That he should write at this time without manifesting this influence would be simply unnatural.

Again, every expositor admits at once the controversial style of the first eleven chapters. The antagonist or objector is confessedly a Jew. No one can deny this. Is he an unbelieving Jew? or a professedly Christian Jew? The usual mode of exposition assumes the former alternative. But if Paul were contending with a Jew who did not believe in Christ, then his first point must have been to prove that Jesus was the Christ. But not a word of this is to be found in the Epistle. If unbelieving Jews had been the rivals of the apostle in seeking to influence the mind of the Roman church, then this subject must have come under review. But the question which, as we take it, Paul here discusses is this: What is true Christianity?—a question of most vital interest to all Christians, and the one question of actual conflict at the time. So strongly have the actual facts of the Epistle pressed at this point that many expositors, failing to recognize the relation of the Epistle to the external Ebionitism which opposed Paul, have been forced to regard the Church at Rome as largely composed of believing Jews, to whom the main arguments of the Epistle were addressed in confirmation of their faith.

But the true test of this or any view is, after all, the practical one. You take up the key and inspect it, and it looks as if it would fit the lock. But it is only when you have turned it completely round through all the wards, and find by the trial that it fits and turns back the bolt perfectly, that you are satisfied that you have the right key. We can give but an outline of the trial here—the details must appear in the work of exposition.

1. The fundamental idea of Ebionitism is salvation by works of law. This Epistle maintains the doctrine of salvation by faith without works of law.

2. Ebionitism leads to a denial of the divinity of Christ. The author of this Epistle introduces the fact of his divinity twice side by side with the Ebionite truth of his natural relation to Israel.

3. Ebionitism ignores the mediatorial work of Christ. The writer most clearly presents it as the basis of his doctrine of salvation.

4. Ebionitism presents low views of the guilt of sin. The writer of this Epistle emphasizes this subject in a most profound discussion of sin, both as guilt and as an inward law of death.

5. Ebionitism leads to externalism in ethics. This Epistle enforces the most searching spirituality.

6. Ebionitism clung to a bald literalism in the interpretation of Scripture. St. Paul claims deliverance from the bondage of the law for those who serve "in newness of spirit and not in oldness of the letter."

7. The ambition of the Ebionites was to maintain the claim of the Jews to be the only elect people of God, in virtue of the covenant of circumcision. In chs. ix., x. and xi. Paul proves, in opposition to this exclusive claim, the prerogative, the justice and the wisdom of God in choosing his elect people from all nations upon the basis of a new covenant of grace through faith.

8. Even the practical parts of the Epistle give examples of the same antagonism of truth to this narrow error. The positive precepts are full of the broad, universal spirit of the Pauline gospel, enjoining especially charity toward the narrowness of the weaker brother; the negative guard against the self-conceited, critical spirit so easily awakened by controversy.

We might further show that the objections introduced by Paul's "What thens" are all the objections of the Ebionite, many of them of course also objections of the Jew, but not one of them those which would be urged only by an unbelieving Jew. Many other details will appear in the course of the exposition.

From the foregoing considerations we conclude the following to be the true view of the historical antecedents of this Epistle:—

HISTORICAL PROLEGOMENA.

To Paul as the apostle to the Gentiles was committed the gospel of the uncircumcision. This fact is the key to the life and work of Paul and to his relation to the church. Down to the time of the destruction of Jerusalem, or even to the time of Hadrian, the distinction between the Jewish Christian and the Gentile Christian was somewhat marked. The Jewish Christian received Christ as the Messiah and his Saviour, and rejoiced in the gift of the Holy Ghost received through faith in his name. But he continued none the less zealous for the law, and strict in the observance of its precepts. Many of the Jewish Christians believed that their salvation required that they should be literally included in the Abrahamic covenant by circumcision; and perhaps at first all believed that this was pleasing to God. Thus at first the Pharisees, who were strict observers of the law, were disposed to protect the Christians as against the Sadducees. Stephen seems to have been the first to see clearly that the Jewish dispensation was ended and that Christianity, on a universal and spiritual basis, was to take its place. This was, perhaps, the ground of the accusation that he taught that Christ would "destroy the temple and change the customs which Moses delivered." His fidelity to this universal character of gospel salvation led to his death. But as Stephen cried out, "Lord Jesus, receive my spirit," one stood by on whom his mantle was to descend. He was, like Stephen, a Grecian Jew, cultivated in intellect, and by the wider sympathies of the Hellenist the better fitted for the apostleship to the Gentiles. While this man, Saul of Tarsus, is being fitted for his work, first by converting grace and subsequently by labours among the Hellenists, God is opening the way for his future course. Peter, a rigid Jewish Christian, is chosen to open the door of the church to the Gentiles; and the evident command of God in the case puts to silence not only Peter's scruples but also the murmurs of the *circumcision* Christians. Almost immediately afterward Paul is introduced to his great lifework at Antioch by Barnabas. It would seem that from the beginning he preached the gospel of the uncircumcision, salvation through faith in Christ without works of law. From his language in writing to the Galatians it appears that this gospel was directly taught him by the revealing Spirit, and that he was thus freed from those Jewish prejudices which still entangled some even of the apostles themselves.

But Paul was not permitted to preach this gospel without opposition both within and without the church. First we have the events described in the fifteenth of Acts. Here begins to appear the existence of a distinct party preaching a new gospel—"Except ye be circumcised after the manner of Moses, ye cannot be saved." Moses and Christ were conjoined. Christ was but a lawgiver, teacher or revealer of God's will, as was Moses. This party would appear to have arisen in the church during the rest from persecution which followed the conversion of Saul. The churches multiplied in those days, and doubtless there were gathered in some, perhaps not a few, who drank not deeply into the spirit of the new religion, passed not through deep conviction of sin, and as a consequence apprehended Christ only as a teacher of truth surpassing the rabbis of the age. In such minds there was no new leaven to counteract the old Jewish tendencies to exclusiveness and legality. These were still paramount, and the faith of Christ was but a superficial addition. Here is the great mistake of the system of Baur in failing to recognize that between these men and the teachings of Christ, and between these men and the holy converts of Pentecost, there was as wide a chasm as between them and St. Paul. Paul was one with Jesus in spiritual life and truth, and one with the primitive Christianity of Jerusalem in experience of the renewing power of that truth. He passed beyond them only in discerning that the time had now come to lay off the outward garb of Judaism. This new party was one with the primitive church only in outward forms of faith and ritual. In spirit they were legalists, not Christians. Hence they set to work to make Christianity an instrument for extending their favourite Judaism. And so here in Antioch they came directly into contact with Paul by preaching new conditions of salvation.

Next we have the visit of Peter to Antioch and his vacillation described in the Epistle to the Galatians. We have also evidence, already referred to, of the same Judaizing opposition at Corinth, and especially in Galatia. In fact, there is reason to believe that at the date of the Epistle to the Romans there existed a most determined and widespread conflict between Paul and this party. Shortly afterwards this conflict extended beyond the Christian church into the ranks of old Judaism, and Paul found arrayed against him not only the preaching of Judaizing Christians but also the persecuting zeal of unbelieving Pharisees. His gospel was opposed both to Judaism and Judaizing Christianity. Hence a few months later he is obliged to defend his doctrine before the church and his life before the Sanhedrim.

Thus at the date before us the doctrine of Paul—the gospel of the uncircumcision—had attracted the attention of the whole Jewish and Christian world. A conflict had arisen the issue of which was to decide whether Christianity was to degenerate into a mere Jewish sect or to assert itself as the God-given religion of the whole world. Paul felt the full responsibility of the momentous issue at stake, and under these circumstances he pens this Epistle, in which he enters into the full exposition and defence of the entire system of truth which God had given him to preach.

THE EPISTLE TO THE ROMANS AND THEOLOGY.

Inasmuch as Paul's system of doctrine was the essential doctrine of Christ in its divine unfolding under the inspiration of the Holy Spirit, this full exposition of Paul's preaching becomes at the same time the most perfect exposition of the entire doctrine of Christianity which the church has received from the pen of inspiration. The Epistle to the Romans is thus the foundation of all theology. The writings of John are necessary for the completion of Christian dogma. Later writings of Paul add to our knowledge of the organization and responsibilities, as well as far-reaching aspirations, of the Christian church. The Epistle to the Hebrews perfects our view of the mediatorial work, and the catholic Epistles add many precious promises and holy precepts. But this Epistle to the Romans, appearing just at the time when Christianity had been unfolded to its full and mature form—the form for all nations and all ages—stands alone as the grand full outline of Christian doctrine for the world. No true system of Christian doctrine can be constructed which does not build from this. It is not a substitute for the original Christianity, but it is the original Christianity itself, now first expounded in logical form. The exposition of this Epistle must therefore be chiefly dogmatic. In grammar we shall be especially interested in the logical force of the particles. Occasionally we shall get help from the history of the case. But above all else, a clear grasp of the great dogmatic elements of the Epistle will enable us to understand every argument and every proposition throughout. We shall often get help outside of the Epistle, also from collateral passages in the Pauline Epistles, expanding or illustrating the thoughts presented here.

This leads us to an outline of

THE THEOLOGY OF THE EPISTLE.

The prominent dogmatic elements of this Epistle may be summed up under five heads:—

1. God's revelation.
2. Sin.
3. Christ and his work.
4. Salvation.
5. The saved as an elect people in Christ.

These are followed by ethical teachings, partly growing out of the dogmatic contents of the Epistle, but still more largely out of the historical circumstances under which it was written.

1. The divine revelation is treated of in chs. i.-iv. It is presented as given in nature (ch. i. 19); in the conscience and understanding of men (ch. ii. 15, 16); in the holy scriptures (ch. i. 2), which are oracles of God (ch. iii. 2); and in the gospel of God's Son (ch. iii. 21).

It is the basis of human responsibility (chs. i. 21, 32; ii. 1, 2, 12-16, 20, 21, etc.; iii. 3, 20. See also ch. v. 13).

It reveals salvation through faith (chs. i. 2, 17; iii. 21, etc.).

2. Sin is universal, and, upon the basis of universal revelation of moral law, it everywhere exposes to the present and impending wrath of God (chs. i., ii. and iii.).

Sin entered the world through the offence of one man, and by a law of the unity of the race in moral responsibility it, together with its penalty (death), has descended to all men. This alone accounts for the fact that all have sinned (ch. v. 12, etc.). This sin is in man's nature a law of sin and death, quickened into conscious activity by the incoming of divine revelation, and warring against the conscience in which that revelation is manifested (ch. vii. 7-25.).

3. The Christ is not only the seed of David according to the flesh but the Son of God according to the spirit of holiness (ch. i. 3, 4). The shedding of his blood is a propitiation for sins, *i.e.*, a motive in consideration of which God may justly forgive (chs. iii. 25, 26; iv. 25; v. 5, 8-11). The propitiatory power of his death lies in its being an act of righteousness and obedience parallel to the transgression and disobedience by which sin entered into the world (ch. v. 18, 19). This last point is enlarged in Phil. ii. 6-9.

4. Salvation is righteousness or remission of sin (chs. iii. and iv.); restoration to peace with God (ch. v.); restoration to new life with Christ (ch. vi.), by the spirit of life in Christ (ch. viii.).

Its sole condition is faith (chs. iii. and iv.).

5. The saved in Christ are heirs of God and joint heirs with Christ, and so God's elect people, the peculiar objects of his favour. They constitute the true election according to the divine foreknowledge and predestination (ch. viii. 18, etc.). This Paul defends by showing the sovereignty of God in his election (ch. ix.), his justice (ch. x.), and his wisdom (ch. xi.).

It will be seen from this synopsis that this magnificent thesis of St. Paul covers almost the entire ground of theology. The most complete system of our day can only prefix to it the Old Testament theistic basis of the existence and attributes of God, and the doctrines of creation and providence, and add, chiefly from Paul's other writings, a few words on the mysterious subject of eschatology.

If any should be surprised that so vast a field should be traversed in reply to the mere Ebionite heresy, we have only to call to mind that this heresy was a fundamental error, touching the nature of Christ, of his work, and of his salvation. All distinctively Christian truth is involved in these. It was the office of Paul's logical mind, under divine inspiration, to unfold all the truth involved in these great facts as related to the individual experience of salvation, and to place them in opposition to the shallow theories and false views of his opponents.

This leads us to the consideration of another important topic throwing light upon our work of interpretation.

THE DEVELOPMENT OF THIS DOCTRINAL SYSTEM IN PAUL'S OWN MIND.

This difficult problem the mere expositor might well avoid, were it not necessary to the proper exposition of some parts of the Epistle, and these confessedly the most difficult. Paul himself gives us in one passage a statement which must form the basis of our investigation: "For I make known to you, brethren, as touching the gospel which was preached by me, that it is not after man, neither was I taught it, but it came to me through revelation of Jesus Christ" (Gal. i. 12). This passage has often been understood as relegating the whole question of the origin of Paul's gospel to the region of the supernatural. We cannot so understand it. We must recognize the following facts as lying back of the work of the revealing Spirit:

1. Paul's intimate acquaintance with the Old Testament Scriptures.

2. His contact with the common synoptic gospel of the apostles, as it was traditionally preached in the synagogues and in the temple by Stephen and others, as well as by the apostles, prior to Paul's conversion. From this Paul must have known the main facts of the life of Christ as they are recorded in our three first gospels.

3. The facts of Paul's own spiritual life under the law, into which we get so clear a glance, as through an opened window, in the seventh of Romans.

4. The fact of Paul's early contact with the Greek world, including some knowledge of Greek literature.

Now, we have only to study carefully the writings and doctrinal system of Paul to see how the revealing Spirit took up into his divine work in the mind of God's chosen vessel all these antecedent elements of truth, and wrought them out into the completed system of doctrine, "the gospel," which he was to preach. For instance, that his doctrine of sin has its foundation in the Old Testament is clear from Rom. v. compared with Gen. iii., and Rom. iii. compared with the ethical Psalms there quoted. That his own experience entered into it is evident from Rom. vii. In fact this may be regarded as a main part of the revelation to which he refers.

That even the grand doctrine of justification by faith was not made clear to him apart from the Old Testament is evident from

Rom. iv. and x. Here again the personal experience must have been a part of the revelation; and in fact we cannot mistake the voice of that experience in both the fifth and eighth of Romans. We think, in this connection, of the experience of Luther when, on Pilate's stairs at Rome, he heard the voice from heaven, "the just shall live by faith," he sprang to his feet and immediately the whole Word of God was made plain, and he read the same new truth first revealed to Paul on every page from Genesis to Revelation.

In like manner Paul's doctrine of election is founded on the teaching of Isaiah, supported and illustrated by quotations from the other prophets as well as the Pentateuch. That even the great mystery of the person of Jesus Christ, God's Son, was not revealed apart from an Old Testament basis would seem to be indicated by Rom. i. 2, 3.

That again Paul was dependent for the knowledge of the facts of Christ's life and teaching upon the apostolic tradition as given in our synoptic gospels we conclude from these facts—

1. He mentions only the main points in the history.

2. Whenever he gives detail, except once or twice, the facts and very words are parallel with our synoptic gospels.

3. He never opens up that new field, reserved to St. John, which he could have used so powerfully to his purpose had the whole history of Christ's life been supernaturally placed before him.

4. Luke, his companion and constant hearer, relied upon accurate investigation of the traditions of those "who from the beginning were eye-witnesses and ministers of the Word." What, then, are we to understand when he tells us that the gospel which he preached was taught him by revelation of Jesus Christ? We think this, that these Old Testament teachings, and these facts of the life and work of Christ, were unfolded to him in their *significance as saving truth*, the power of God to his own salvation, and also "to the salvation of every one that believeth," both Jew and Gentile. We may thus confidently recognize that Paul's intimate acquaintance with the Old Testament Scriptures, the deep and bitter experience of his heart in the conflict of sin under the law, his wide knowledge of the spiritual wants of humanity through contact with the Gentile world —all these were in God's providence the preparation, making him meet to be the chosen vessel, needing only the great facts of the

work and life of Jesus, and then a sudden supernatural opening of the inner eye that God's Son might be revealed, not merely to him, for that light was but external, but "*in him*," giving him the conscious *personal* knowledge of the perfect system of Christian truth. At the same time we can yet understand that John's more intimate knowledge of special discourses of the Saviour was further needed to give some parts of the system more complete confirmation and emphasis. In fact, had not John followed Paul it might have been claimed that Paul's was not the true gospel of Jesus Christ; that Christ intended only to purify, deepen and give mystic spirituality to the old Judaism; and that the abrogation of the old sacrifices, the making of Christ's death a universal propitiation, and the consequent exaltation of Christ's person, were but fictions of the self-constituted apostle to the Gentiles. It is true that we can see how perfect is the harmony of Paul's doctrine with the wonderful ethical depth of the teaching of Jesus; how consistent with the idea of propitiation through his death the words of the last supper; how consistent the doctrine of the divinity of Jesus with the facts of his life; how perfectly one the experience of Paul in the revelation of Christ in him with that of Pentecost. But all this would not stand out in the clear, unmistakable light in which we now have it had not John added the topstone to the New Testament revelation in the fourth gospel, the last product of apostolic inspiration.

In these introductory words we have but outlined our conception of how this Epistle and its contained system of doctrine came to be. We have done this as a basis from which we shall endeavour to expound it. As in the course of our work we meet with special points of doctrine, especially that most abstruse doctrine of election, we shall require to expand at length some of the points here briefly summarized.

ARGUMENT OF THE EPISTLE.

As Paul's method of logical connection is without exception from point to point, *i.e.*, each new thought linked directly to that immediately preceding, the grand divisions of the Epistle appear only as culminating points in the progress of the discourse. We shall, therefore, number the topics throughout in consecutive order, marking the grand divisions in Roman numerals,

I. Into his salutation (ch. i. 1-7) Paul weaves reference to every distinctive point of his doctrine.

2. He then presents himself personally to his readers, explaining his motives in writing (vv. 8-15). This leads

3. To the statement of his theme (vv. 17, 18).

IV. This theme has its reason in the wrath of God against man's sin, the justice of which (*a*) against the Gentile, (*b*) against the Jew in spite of his circumcision, Paul proceeds to prove (ch. i. 18-iii. 8), concluding all alike under sin (ch. iii. 9-20).

V. But to meet this universal sin God reveals his righteousness, provided by the propitiation made by Christ (ch. iii. 21-26), excluding boasting, vindicating the impartiality of God, and establishing the law (vv. 27-31).

6. But at once the objection is raised that such a view of God's grace, treating Jew and Gentile alike, is inconsistent with the prerogatives secured to Abraham by the covenant of circumcision. This objection Paul answers by showing that even Abraham himself was saved by faith before the covenant was yet established, and that through this faith he became heir of the covenant promises which were given him, not for his own sake only but for the sake of all that believe (ch. iv. 1-25).

VII. The triumphant vindication of the doctrine against the main objection of the Judaizers is followed by an exulting exhortation to his readers to possess themselves to the full of the peace and joy which this grand doctrine brings—a joy founded on the love and atoning work of Christ (ch. v. 1-11), which atonement he sets forth in glorious contrast to the fall in Adam (vv. 12-21), leading up to the reign of righteousness in life through Jesus Christ our Lord.

VIII. From the religious side of this doctrine Paul next turns to the ethical (ch. vi.), first pointing out the moral obligations involved, and then following them up by hortatory enforcement, especially contrasting death, the wages of sin, with eternal life, God's gift in Christ.

9. The ethical view of his doctrine leads Paul to consider the relation of the Christian to the law. This relation is one of freedom. The law having served its purpose in quickening the consciousness of sin, and so bringing condemnation (a sentence of death), we are by that very death set free from its right to hold us, and so are law-

fully transferred to Christ (ch. vii. 1-6). To this the objection at once appears that this makes the law a mere minister of sin. To this Paul replies by expounding most clearly the real office of the law, and tracing the real source of sin to the law of sin and death within ourselves, which the law can only make evident to consciousness but cannot overcome (vv. 7-25).

X. From this law of sin and death we are set free by the law of the spirit of life in Christ Jesus, which spirit is in us creating new spiritual life, giving promise of new life even to the body, and sealing us the children of God and joint heirs with Christ (ch. viii. 1-17).

11. This leads the apostle to describe the privileges secured to the believer in Christ, running parallel with, but far transcending, the prerogatives of God's ancient *elect* people. In fact, God's elect they are, and from his love nothing can sever them (ch. viii. 18-end).

XII. But this glorious election of the future has its sad counterpart, its dark background, in the seeming reversal of the election of the past This Paul next proceeds to consider, vindicating

(*a*) The prerogative of God to work out his purpose concerning the election according to his own counsel (ch. ix.);

(*b*) The justice of God in the course which in actual fact he has pursued (ch. x.);

(*c*) The merciful wisdom of God in the final results of that course (ch. xi.), concluding with a magnificent doxology to that God "of whom, to whom, and through whom, are all things."

XIII. The covenant "mercies of God" thus established to the elect in Christ become the foundation of all moral obligation (ch. xii.)

(*a*) To the high duties of members of the elect people (vv. 3-8);

(*b*) To the personal duties of the brotherhood of Christ and the brotherhood of humanity (vv. 9-21);

(*c*) To the duties of citizenship (ch. xiii. 1-7);

(*d*) To the duties of civil right (vv. 8-10);

(*e*) Of universal Christian circumspection (vv. 11-14).

14. Finally, Paul considers the special duties arising out of the parties into which the Christian church was just then divided, and which had given the occasion for this Epistle. Those having the broad intelligence and freedom from narrow scruples which the true doctrine bestowed are exhorted—

(*a*) To refrain from a scornful spirit (ch. xiv. 1-13);

(b) To exercise a charitable condescension to the scruples of others (vv. 13-23);

(c) To follow in all things edification and the unity of the church (ch. xv. 1-13).

15. As the letter began so it ends, with personal references to his work and his design in writing the Epistle (ch. xv. 14-33).

16. To the Epistle thus distinctly closed are appended various personal messages, greetings, exhortations, salutations and another concluding doxology (ch. xvi. 1-27).

The variations in position of this concluding doxology have given rise to critical conjectures as to the closing chapters of the Epistle. The text is all but universally admitted to be genuine to the end of ch. xiv. Here, in a number of MSS. and cursives, is inserted the closing doxology. A very few others insert it both here and at the end of chapter xvi. A few omit the doxology altogether. But in ℵ, B, C, D_2, with a large support from other authority of cursives, versions and fathers, the doxology stands at the end of the Epistle.

The mere position of the doxology is a matter of minor importance. The grave question at issue is the genuineness of the chapters xv. and xvi. But all our MSS. in which the entire Epistle is preserved have these chapters. The consistency of the argument is also strongly in favour of chapter xv., while the objections urged against chapter xvi. are altogether insufficient to outweigh the uniform textual evidence. We have therefore accepted the Epistle in its usual form, and have made free use of the important data as to the date and purpose of the Epistle furnished by these chapters.

THE EPISTLE TO THE ROMANS.

CH. I. 1–7. THE SALUTATION.

1. **Paul,**] His Roman name. See Acts xiii. 9.
a servant] "A bondservant." A presentation of himself with unfeigned humility to a people many of whom were bondsmen, as bound with them to the service *of Jesus Christ*, as they with him were the Lord's freemen. (See also Phil. i. 1, Titus i. 1, and 1 Cor. vii. 22.)
of Jesus Christ,] *i.e.*, of Jesus, the Messiah. The headship of Christ over his church, over its ministers, and over its members, is clearly recognized. (See Acts xxvi. 16.)
called to be an apostle,] "An apostle by call." (*Godet.*) The use of the adjective instead of the passive participle is significant. He expands this in Gal. i. 1, and gives minute account of his call in Acts xxii. and xxvi. That he was not an apostle by call of Christ would appear to have been one of the calumnies of his opponents. (See 1 Cor. ix. 1, etc.) On the authority of the apostolic office see also Eph. iv. 11. It would seem to imply the authority, by call of Christ, to lay the foundation of the Christian church by making known to men the mysteries of the gospel of Christ (1 Cor. iv. 1; Gal. i. 15, 16; Eph. i. 9, 10; ii. 20, 21). Evangelists might found churches, and pastors and teachers build them up, but only on the doctrinal foundation of the apostles and prophets, Jesus Christ being the chief corner stone. Paul's apostolic office was therefore matter of the highest importance as authenticating his gospel.
separated unto the gospel of God,] Set apart by special providential preparation, by supernatural divine call and the gifts of the Holy Ghost, for this office. This separation Paul traces back to his birth (Gal. i. 15), recognizing a divine purpose running through his whole life history looking to this end. To such separation is every minister of Christ called (Acts xiii. 2). "Unto the gospel of God"—this preposition everywhere in St. Paul's writings designates purpose or end. This was the gospel of God, not indefinitely, *i.e.*, in any form in which the caprice of men might choose to preach it, but
2. **which he promised afore by his prophets in the holy scriptures,**] This gospel, for which Paul was thus set apart, was the divine complement of the entire Old Testament dispensation. This seems specially to refer to the gospel to the Gentiles (Acts xv. 15, 16),

to whom Paul was specifically commissioned. "Promised afore" is too weak to express the full significance of the original. It is the "blessed announcement which he fore announced;" the contents as well as the preaching of the gospel are intimated in "sacred scriptures, through his prophets," *i.e.*, forth-tellers, or *fore*-tellers, a peculiar play upon the three emphatic words of the clause. Paul, as we shall see, finds the great outlines of his gospel in the scriptures, especially in Isaiah. This was his reply to his opponents, that the very form of the gospel which he preached was foreannounced by the prophets. (See Acts xvii. 3, and xxvii. 22, 23.) The designation Holy Writings had probably even in Paul's time come to be used as a proper noun, hence without the article.

3. concerning his Son,] This may be connected grammatically with either "gospel of God" or "promised afore." The sense is the same, especially bearing in mind the close relationship of the Greek words. The Son of God is not the mere bearer of the gospel; he is its substance, especially in the two supreme facts of his person: **who was born of the seed of David according to the flesh, 4. who was declared to be the Son of God with power, according to the spirit of holiness, by the resurrection of the dead;]** The interpretation of these verses depends mainly on the antithesis. This we take to be threefold: (1) between "was born," or "became," and "was declared," or the public recognition of that which already is; (2) between "the seed of David" and "the Son of God;" (3) between "the flesh" and "the spirit of holiness." The three antecedent terms are comparatively plain. The first signifies a beginning of being, or form of being, which did not before exist. It is thus wider than "was born," and is frequently used of the incarnation (John i. 14; Gal. iv. 4). The second denotes, of course, the offspring or descendant of David, whether in the line of his mother or of his reputed father. This was essential to the Messiahship, which was foretold to be of David's line. The third, "according to the flesh," is used repeatedly by Paul to designate the line of human birth or relationship by blood. (See chs. iv. 1; ix. 3, 5, 8; 1 Cor. x. 18; 2 Cor. xi. 18.) That would seem to be the clear reference here. The second set of antithetic terms must then correspond to these: (1) The word translated "was declared" signifies primarily to draw a boundary line about, hence to separate, and so distinguish from other things of like nature and position. The secondary meaning of declaration or public installation is also common. But in neither meaning is there implied the communication of the attributes or essence so distinguished or declared. The man Christ Jesus was marked out from other men, and before men and angels publicly declared to be the Son of God by the resurrection of the dead. (2) The title Son of God has been interpreted of office, "theocratic king." But this, far from being a contrast to, is almost implied in, the expression "seed of David." It has also been referred to God-likeness, purity of moral nature. But this again presents no antithesis to the designation "seed of David," A little nearer the truth is the interpretation which refers it to the state of divine dignity and glory upon which Christ entered after his resurrection. But a state of dignity and glory is not an antithesis to relationship by birth. Nor was this state declared or marked out so much as conferred in the resurrection. The resurrection, ascension and session at the right hand of the Father, are the three steps of *entrance* upon this glory. There remains, therefore, only the idea of *a divine nature and relationship* in virtue of which Christ assumed this glory. (See John xvii. 5, and Phil. ii. 6-9.) This presents the true antithesis to the seed of David, and harmonizes with the meaning of the verb "was declared," and with the following adjunct, "by the resurrection of the dead." But what is this divine relationship? The answer to this is involved in the third term, "the spirit of holiness." If the term "according to the flesh" expresses the nature of human relationship, then the term "according to the spirit of holiness" should express the nature of the divine relationship. There are but three interpretations: (1) The holy human spirit of Christ. This could only harmonize with the idea that the expression "Son of God" signified the moral perfection of Christ's inner nature which has already been excluded. (2) The Holy Spirit, the third person of the Trinity. This can only fairly harmonize with the idea that the divine relationship lies in the supernatural conception by the power of the Holy Ghost. The interpretations proposed by Moule, that it may mean the operation of the Holy Spirit in the resurrection, or in the prophetic inspiration which announced the Christ, as well as that of Godet, that it signifies the operations of the Holy Spirit upon Christ, in consecrating his entire life, are all outside the simple antithetic line of thought here presented. Besides, the phrase "spirit of holiness" is never elsewhere used to designate the third person. There remains, therefore, this alternative, that this phrase was expressly chosen to designate that essential nature of Deity in the unity of which, with the Father and the Holy Ghost, Christ is the eternal Son of God—not the second person, but the nature in which the three persons subsist. The phrase "according to the spirit of holiness" thus designates the nature of the eternal divine relationship, as the phrase "according to the flesh" designates the nature of the human relationship in time. If it be objected that this too far anticipates the metaphysical doctrine of the Trinity, on this point we must differ. The doctrine of the true Deity of Christ was essentially involved in Paul's system. It was as essentially denied in that of his opponents. It is not too much to believe that Paul understood this; and if so, almost certain that he should embrace it in these sentences in which he contrives to condense almost every great point at issue. (See note following v. 7.) We need now only consider the remaining terms of these two verses and then sum up our interpretation. The phrase "with power" may be connected so as to read "declared with power" or "the Son of God in power." The latter would limit the Sonship of Christ as Paul nowhere else limits it. (See Col. ii. 9.) The act of declaration is rather one of almighty power (compare Eph. i. 19, 20); not mightily or powerfully declared, but declared by an act of power, "by the resurrection from the dead." This designates the act by which the declaration is made. This declaration or public installation became necessary through the humiliation. The resurrection was the first step of the exaltation, and the only one directly visible to men. That it is the attestation and not the constitution of the Son of God is clear from Acts xvii. 31, where the same Greek word (translated "ordained") is also used. The plural of "dead persons" is used as including all resurrection in Christ. (See 1 Cor. xv.) This further confirms the idea of attestation as opposed to constitution in office. We may therefore paraphrase these two verses as follows:—"Who began his existence in the form of man from the Messianic line of the seed of David according to the law of human descent; but was marked out from among men as the Son of God according to the holy, spiritual nature of the godhead, by an act of almighty power in the resurrection of the dead." (Compare for parallel John xvii. 5 and Phil. ii. 6-10.)

even Jesus Christ our Lord,] Paul having thus prepared the way now adds the human name and title of God's Son. Both the fulness of the designation—Jesus, his human name, Christ, the Messiah of Jewish hope, Lord of the Christian church—and the position at the close of this complete designation of the human and divine nature of God's Son, render these words peculiarly emphatic. No mere Ebionite could utter verses 3 and 4 as thus completed (1 Cor. xii. 3).

5. through whom we received grace and apostleship,] Paul having thus completely set forth the relation of his office and gospel message to God the Father proceeds to connect it with the mediatorial kingdom of Christ. The title "our Lord" furnishes exactly the point of attachment for this new thought—" our Lord, through whom "—the preposition governing the genitive exactly expresses mediatorial agency. Paul's specific relation to Christ, as well as the general divine authority of his work, was denied by his enemies (1 Cor. ix. 1). The plural "we" is used as Paul speaks in his official capacity. This renders the interpretation which refers the word "grace" here to his personal salvation somewhat doubtful. (See Eph. iii. 8.) The verb is in the historical past tense, designating a definite fact, occurring at a fixed past time. The bestowment of this double gift took place at the time of his conversion. It was grace as given from Christ, apostleship as an authoritative commission to men.

unto obedience of faith among all the nations,] The preposition here is the usual one to denote purpose—not the result which follows of necessity, but the destination, the result aimed at. This is "the obedience of faith among all the nations." The expression "obedience of faith" seems to be an example of what Winer calls the genitive of apposition. It is not the obedience which faith produces but the obedience which is faith itself. It refers to that moral element in faith by virtue of which faith becomes the test of probation. This obedience of faith is thus the exact opposite of the Ebionite principle of works of law. Paul's commission was to set forth this principle as the test of human probation and destiny among all the nations, an expression designating the whole non-Jewish world.

for his name's sake:] A peculiarly Old Testament or Hebrew expression, such as we often meet in Paul's writings. It denotes that which is the end of all God's dispensations, the manifestation of his nature to his creatures. The wider this manifestation the more perfect the accomplishment of the end. The true end of the manifestation of God in Christ must be not one people, however favoured, but the whole humanity. (See Acts xv. 14, 17.)

6. **among whom are ye also, called to be Jesus Christ's:**] This sentence admits, first of all, two forms of grammatical construction: "ye also, called to be Jesus Christ's" may be taken as subject, "are among whom" as predicate; or "called to be Jesus Christ's" may be made the principal predicate, "among whom" being adjunct. The first seems to follow most naturally from the position of the verb, which is the same in Greek as in our English version. It is also evidently adopted by the Revised Version, as appears from the punctuation. The "also" would thus seem to refer to the other Gentile churches founded by Paul himself. Though this church was not so founded it was among the number of those gathered from among the Gentiles, and hence in a near relationship to Paul's apostolic office. But what are we to understand by the appositive to the subject "called to be Jesus Christ's"? or, as Godet has better paraphrased it, "called ones belonging to Jesus Christ"? (So also Moule, Meyer and Philippi.) The usual interpretation refers this to the gospel invitation to personal salvation. The Calvinistic commentators accordingly find here the effectual call (so Moule and also Riddle, but with a "but"). On the other hand Arminians, like Godet and Beet, refer it to a call obeyed but not irresistible. Notwithstanding the venerable antiquity of this interpretation we feel disposed to question it. First of all, we note that this term "called," and also the verb "calleth" and the noun "calling," as used by Paul designate an abiding state or relationship between God and his people. Hence the verb is sometimes used in the present, as in 1 Thess. ii. 12; v. 14; the adjective is a permanent characteristic of God's people, and the noun is used in the same way. Hence in 2 Peter i. 10, we read, "give the more diligence to make your calling and election sure," *i.e.*, firm, a strong and abiding thing. This can scarcely apply to a temporary act of God by which man is solicited to accept the offer of God's grace. Secondly, the end of this calling is never spoken of as salvation, or pardon, or God's mercy, or acceptance in Christ. It is always saintship, sanctification, holiness, or more

generally the kingdom and glory of God (1 Thess. ii. 12). (2 Thess. ii. 14, in our English version, seems an exception, but it is not so in the Greek, as the antecedent of the relative is certainly not the word salvation.) Thirdly, the calling thus, in 2 Tim. i. 9, is made appropriately to follow salvation. It is not "hath called us and saved us," but "hath saved us and called us." Lastly, the general use of the term is in reference to Christians as a body. They are God's called ones in their united spiritual and holy life. We think we find the key to these peculiarities in the use of these words in the fact that they were borrowed from the old dispensation. The complete catalogue of such terms, which we know were favourite ones among the Jews of the apostolic age, is to be found in 1 Peter ii. 9, 10, where "an elect race," "a royal priesthood," "a holy nation," "a people of whom God has taken possession," are the various designations summed up in the calling, the end of which is the manifestation of God's praises to the world. The term "called ones," in the Old Testament sense, is thus parallel with "election," "God's people," etc., and expresses *their permanent responsibility to God for holiness of life*. Hence in verse 7 we have "called to be saints"; in Titus i. 9, "hath called us with an holy calling"; and in Eph. iv. 1, "I beseech you to walk worthily of the calling wherewith ye were called." There are, of course, passages in the New Testament where the verbs "to call" and "to choose" are not used in this Old Testament sense, especially in the Gospels, where Christ uses them without any reference to this meaning. The call is there the gospel call to repentance. Here, on the other hand, it is something very different—a solemn responsibility as well as glorious privilege which God lays upon his church, in its entire membership, to be his people, exhibiting worthily to the world the light of his grace. (See Col. iii. 12, etc.) So far, therefore, is this calling from having anything to do with Augustinian predestination that, on the other hand, it involves a *continuous probation* and the constant possibility of our proving unworthy of our calling. This term, here applied to the Gentile Christians, at once instates them in the position and privileges claimed by the Jews as their exclusive prerogative. They are already "God's called ones," and hence have no need of Ebionitish circumcision to instate them in any higher or more privileged position. "Of Jesus Christ" is the genitive of possession. The passages already referred to show how the designations "called," "elect," etc., are united with the idea of a people who are God's peculiar possession. Jesus Christ is here the owner and master.

7. **to all that are in Rome, beloved of God, called to be saints:**] The Greek will equally admit of the following order, which is perhaps preferable: "To all the beloved of God, saints by calling, who are in Rome." The emphatic designations are thus brought into the foreground. Here the designations of the chosen people are again repeated. There is a peculiarity in Paul's use of these designations. Here and in 1 Cor. he uses the term "called," together with the

terms "saints" and "sanctified." In the Epistle to the Galatians, written at this time, the term "called" is also used with a statement that they are forsaking their call. In all the other Epistles he uses only the term "saints," or "saints and faithful ones," or else the *Christian* derivative from the same root as the verb "to call," *ecclesia, i.e.*, the assembly or body called out. It would thus appear to be his design to keep emphatically before the churches addressed at this juncture the fact that they were heirs in the fullest sense to all the privileges and responsibilities of the ancient covenant.

Grace to you and peace from God our Father and the Lord Jesus Christ.] The ordinary Greek epistolary salutation was χαιρειν. (See Acts xxiii. 26.) Here we have the Christian substitute, formed on the Old Testament model, where the usual form of address was either *shalom lecha*, "peace be unto thee," or "the Lord be gracious unto thee" (Gen. xliii. 23, 29). We note here the unity of the Lord Jesus Christ with God the Father in the giving of grace and peace. Erasmus endeavoured to avoid the force of this by making "the Lord Jesus Christ" a second genitive after Father —"the Father of us and of the Lord," etc. In that case we think it must have read, "the Father of the Lord Jesus Christ and of us." Compare the variations of this expression in 1 Thess. i. 1; 2 Thess. i. 2; 2 Tim. i. 2; and Titus i. 4. In all these cases the construction is such that there can be no doubt of the ascription to Jesus Christ of the co-ordinate divine authority.

NOTE.—The ordinary Greek epistolary salutation consisted of three simple terms—the name of the writer, the name of the correspondent, and the word of greeting. Paul, evidently of design, expands this into seven verses, five of which are the enlargement of his apostolic office. The character and purpose of the Epistle as we have traced it in the introduction fully accounts for this. It is the overflowing of the great and important matter of which his mind was full. The divine authority of his apostleship; God's design in its special character; the harmony of this with the Old Testament scriptures; the not merely Davidic Messiahship but the divine Sonship of the Lord of the gospel which he preached; the special designation of his apostleship to a gospel of simple faith as the true probational obedience, that so it might reach all the nations, and thus his Lord receive the fullest reward of his work; the relation of his correspondents to this spiritual and universal gospel, and at the same time their claim to all the glorious privileges and responsibilities of the ancient covenant people, even to the same benediction, now coming from Father and Son—all these are crowded into the very opening words of this letter.

CH. I. 8–15. INTRODUCTION.

8. First, I thank my God through Jesus Christ for you all,] Such a thanksgiving stands in the forefront of Paul's Epistles to all the churches with the single exception of that to the Galatians, where a sad rebuke takes its place. Such an act of devotion presented to God as his God through the mediation of Jesus Christ expresses the spirit in which Paul lived. He could not even write a letter without "*first*" presenting his thanksgiving to God (1 Thess. v. 18).

that your faith is proclaimed throughout the whole world.]

Paul's thanksgiving was not a vague generality. In every case it is specifically appropriate. On behalf of the Corinthians, specially gifted with miraculous power, he thanks God for their gifts; and when, in the time of his severest mental troubles, he had received from them a comforting letter, he thanks God for the consolation. Writing to the Ephesians, out of the fulness of an inner life grown exceeding rich with grace during the months of imprisonment, he thanks God for "every spiritual blessing in heavenly places in Christ Jesus." On behalf of the Philippians, who had sent a messenger with their gifts to minister to his wants in prison, he thanks God for their liberality. So here he thanks God for their faith, which, as a beacon light set on the highest eminence, flashes its rays abroad over all the world. Paul well understood the advantage of planting Christianity in the great centres of commercial, political, intellectual and social life. The verb here used cannot properly be translated "is spoken of." Even "proclaimed" scarcely gives the sense. It means rather that from their very position their faith in the gospel becomes a *public announcement* of that gospel to the whole world.

9. For God is my witness, whom I serve in my spirit in the gospel of his Son,] This sentence admits us to the inmost aspect of Paul's life. His spirit, that realm in which there dwells the constant consciousness of the presence of God, in its entire energy is occupied with the service of this God in the gospel of his Son, the service to which Paul was entirely set apart. This service of Paul's spirit was, however, no vague sentiment. It was full of practical ideas, of grand world-wide plans, and of boundless enterprise. Just now it was full of one great thought, *to reach Rome* and thence conquer the world for Christ.

how unceasingly I make mention of you, always in my prayers making request,

10. if by any means now at length I may be prospered by the will of God to come unto you.] It is impossible in any translation to imitate the wonderfully skilful and delicately expressive structure of this sentence. "How unceasing" are his prayers God only knows, and "on every occasion" the "remembrance" of the Christian church at Rome is before him, and the subject of his supplication is this, that "*his way may be opened* to come to them." He prays for this "now" because a crisis has come which leaves him no more room to work in those eastern lands (ch. xv. 23); but yet his ceaseless prayers submit all to "the will of God," both as to time—"at some time," rather than "at length"—and as to manner —"by any means." How little did Paul know then what would be the time and way by which he should reach Rome, and how far it would prove from being "a good way," as men would regard it! It may be that even this unceasing aspiration for Rome was directly connected with "his conflict;" and that, finding that Antioch, the original headquarters of the missionary gospel, and Corinth and Ephesus were all too near Jerusalem, the great centre of Judaizing influence, he hoped from Rome, the very heart of the civilized world, to propagate among all the nations the universal gospel given him.

11. **For I long to see you, that I may impart unto you some spiritual gift, to the end ye may be established;**] Paul's intense earnestness in this matter had reference not solely to his general commission. It contemplated, first of all, the full perfecting of the church at Rome, for only thus could his further designs be effected. (See ch. xv. 23, 24, etc.) The spiritual gift is not mere miraculous endowments, but such an effusion of the Holy Ghost in connection with his ministrations as shall bring to them "the fulness of the blessing of Christ" (ch. xv. 29). Mere miracles could not bring that maturity of Christian grace and character implied in Paul's use of the word "established." This implies that they were already in possession of the true gospel and enjoying its saving power, and needed only to be confirmed or strengthened by more perfect knowledge of the truth, or richer influence of the Holy Spirit. It was more especially the work of the apostolic office to open up the whole field of Christian truth, after evangelists had laid the foundation by preaching the first principles. (See Acts viii. 14, etc.; xi. 22, etc.; and xiv. 22, etc.) But Paul, immediately fearing lest this may be too great a freedom towards a church to whom he was unknown, and which might, in the providence of God, have already attained great maturity in Christian knowledge and character, at once adds—

12. **that is, that I with you may be comforted in you, each of us by the other's faith, both yours and mine.**] This is no mere compliment, but an expression of sincere anticipation of mutual advantage, which any evangelical gospel preacher who goes among a new people, expecting to share with them in the blessedness of a great work of grace, will readily understand. At the same time it wisely forestalls any prejudice which might arise from a seeming assumption of authority. The final expression seems to imply that the faith of the church at Rome was in perfect unison with that of St. Paul. If there had been any leaning on their part toward the legalism of the circumcision party Paul could not have so anticipated that perfect harmony which would be productive of mutual edification. This unity with him in the faith of the simple, universal gospel would be to Paul at this juncture the richest comfort. At the same time they needed that confirmation in this faith which he of all others was best fitted to impart, especially as at any moment they might be exposed to the same subversive teaching which had just invaded Galatia. It was not their mere fervour or strength of religious feeling which needed confirmation. Under the term "faith" we must include the entire religious life, including first of all the truth believed, as well as the influence of that truth in building up the new spiritual life. In both respects the faith of an Ebionite was a very different thing from the faith which Paul preached. When, therefore, he says "both yours and mine" there is clearly implied the fact that they had received the truth in the same form in which

it was preached by Paul. If so, then the foundation of the church at Rome by converts of Paul's ministry is very probable

13. **And I would not have you ignorant, brethren,**] A Pauline phrase (see ch. xi. 25; 1 Cor. x. 1, etc.), expressing earnestness of feeling.

that oftentimes I purposed to come unto you] A purpose easily suggested by his proximity at Corinth, Illyricum, etc., as well as by the importance of the imperial city.

(and was hindered hitherto),] Paul's purposes appear like those of other men—without any claim to infallibility, subject to the variation of providential circumstances (2 Cor. i. 17). The hindrance here was the pressing call of work at hand (ch. xv. 22)

that I might have some fruit in you also, even as in the rest of the Gentiles.] The first fruits had already been gathered, but the field in Rome was sufficiently ample even for Paul. The doubling of the word "also," in "even," might be paraphrased thus: "both among you and likewise among the other Gentiles." This may well be taken as looking forward, the "other Gentiles" being not so much those already gathered as those whom Paul hopes to reach from Rome.

14. **I am debtor**] The obligation of divine command (1 Cor. ix. 16, 17).

both to Greeks and to Barbarians,] The term Greek now included the Romans, and Barbarian was applied only to the outlying members of the empire. This would indicate that Paul hoped from Rome to reach the very extremities of the empire, Spain, and perhaps Gaul and Britain.

both to the wise and to the foolish.] Hitherto not many wise had been called (1 Cor. i. 26). It may be that Paul hoped at Rome to reach even the higher classes. The salutations, perhaps, indicate that this was not an unreasonable expectation. (See ch. xvi. and Phil. iv. 22.)

15. **So, as much as in me is, I am ready to preach the gospel to you also that are in Rome.**] Of the difficult Greek phrase which begins this verse there are three proposed constructions: Meyer construes thus, "The on-my-part inclination is;" Godet thus, "So far as I am concerned there is the liveliest desire;" others thus, virtually, "All in me is ready." The first makes the Greek phrase κατ'εμε an adjective, the second an adverb, the third a substantive and subject of the copulative verb of which the adjective "ready" is the predicate. Meyer condemns this construction as unauthorized by usage. Grotius and others were led to propose it doubtless from feeling the incongruity of the translations proposed for the alternate renderings. They both throw the emphasis on the κατ'εμε—"on my part"—as if the apostle thereby implied the possibility of a lack of readiness on the part of God's providential orderings or of circumstances. We cannot see that any such emphasis attaches to the use of this phrase. As Winer points out, it is used in later Greek in-

stead of the possessive case of the pronoun, though differing from the simple genitive by some shade of meaning involved in the preposition. If such a shade of distinction must be sought for here we might render it thus: "Hence the earnest desire *which presses upon me* to preach the gospel to you also who are in Rome." The meaning thus given is in perfect harmony with what Paul had previously said. From the introduction thus completed Paul turns, as is his wont, by a perfectly natural and logical train of thought, to the announcement of his theme. He cherishes this desire notwithstanding all the opposition and obloquy which he had lately encountered in the proclamation of the *gospel*, the mention of which enables him at once to plunge into its exposition.

CH. I. 16, 17. STATEMENT OF THEME.

16. **For I am not ashamed of the gospel:**] The "not ashamed" has not, we think, so much reference to Rome. The man who had already preached in all the great Greek cities would see nothing in Rome more critical than he had repeatedly encountered elsewhere. But it calls up the tremendous crisis of opposition, the aim of which was to terminate his ministry and destroy his standing as an apostle of Christianity. The gospel is the gospel as he preached it. Notwithstanding all the attacks of his enemies his confidence in it is undiminished. And why?

for it is the power of God unto salvation] Paul's reason is a practical one. He had tested it in its results and proved it to be "a divine power" (the article is wanting in the Greek) "unto salvation." This salvation, which is the aim and result of this divine power working in the gospel, is one of Paul's important terms. He uses it—

1. Of the entire work of Christ on our behalf in virtue of which he is our Saviour and saves us. It is so used some fifteen times.

2. Of that work as now applied to the sinner by grace, through faith. It is thus used some twenty-three times.

3. It is also used of the final redemption of God's ancient people from their present reprobation, though this is by individual salvation.

4. It is also used of the completed work of Christ for his people as it will appear in the resurrection and final judgment perhaps nine or ten times in all.

5. It is also used of the work of those who labour in the gospel for the salvation of men.

In the present case the reference must be primarily to (2), the moral and religious change wrought in the individual man through the gospel. What is implied in this is fully placed before us in the sequel. This term is one which comes from the lips of the Master himself. It was a favourite term in the Old Testament, especially with Isaiah. That it should stand, as we have seen it does, in the forefront of Paul's gospel, is one proof of his unity with the Master.

to every one that believeth;] (the subjective condition of salvation). This word furnishes us with another of the leading terms of St. Paul's theology. The verb "to believe" and the corresponding noun "faith" are used by Paul, the former fifty-four and the latter one hundred and forty times, and almost exclusively of the gospel condition of salvation. Once or twice the noun seems to signify the body of Christian doctrine, once or twice fidelity, and once or twice historical faith. The words are probably derived from the Greek root signifying to persuade or win over by words, and in the passive to be persuaded, and hence to obey. The derivatives from this root include the various ideas of conviction, confidence, trust, submission and obedience as between a leader and a follower, and finally, the corresponding fidelity in which these result. Hence the words express a personal relation between leader and follower, teacher and pupil, God and man, sinner and Saviour. It does not so much express the mental relation to mere abstract truth as to truth coming from a persuading to a persuaded intelligence. Hence it is not a merely intellectual act but a moral state, and a motive power which is never perfect till it obeys. The verb "to believe" is followed first by the accusative of the subject matter, the truth by which we are persuaded; secondly, by the dative of the personal object of faith, *i.e.*, God or Christ. Instead of the dative the prepositions "in," "upon" or "unto" are also used. The accusative of subject matter is used by Paul only ten times, including nearly all the instances in which the word is used in other than the evangelical sense. The personal object follows the verb sixteen times, always God or Christ. The noun shows the preponderance of the personal object of faith over the mere subject matter, being followed by personal object fifteen times, while subject matter is mentioned only five times. Thus in Paul's conception of faith the foremost idea is its personal relation to God and Christ. The moral aspect of faith is referred to in such expressions as "obedience of faith," "work of faith," and "faith working by love." In respect to the relation of faith to salvation as righteousness or justification, Paul's favourite method of connecting them is by the preposition "out of," expressing origin. This he uses twenty times, and its equivalent genitive, "righteousness arising from faith," twice. He uses the preposition expressing instrumentality or agency fourteen times, and the two together once (Rom. iii. 30). He uses the dative of instrument and another equivalent preposition once. These facts, better than mere definitions, will help us to understand this term as used by Paul. The term "every one," in the sentence before us, expresses at once the freeness and universality of the salvation as conditioned by faith.

to the Jew first, and also to the Greek.] A moment before Paul had embraced all men under the terms Greeks and Barbarians. Why does he change his categories here? The answer may be found in the circumstances under which he writes. The Jews are now claiming *the exclusive monopoly of this salvation.* Hence Paul says concessively, "to the Jew, I grant you, first, also to the Greek." He concedes to his opponents their priority in the offer of salvation, but denies their monopoly. Only such underlying thought can account for the mention of the Jew here. (Compare the surprise expressed in Acts xi. 18.) The Greek is mentioned as also claiming a prerogative of his own (ch. ii. 10; iii. 9).

17. For therein is revealed a righteousness of God by faith unto faith:] The apostle here clearly presents the gospel as a *new* divine revelation, thus placing it on an equality with the whole ancient dispensation. The verb here used and the corresponding noun are constantly employed to designate the unfolding of the successive steps of God's redeeming purpose towards man. (See Rom. viii. 18, 19; 1 Cor. i. 7, etc.) It is also used to express special communications by the Holy Spirit to the individual. (Gal. i. 16; 1 Cor. xiv. 30.) It will bear both significations here. That which is revealed in the gospel is a righteousness of God, *i.e.*, a divine or Godgiven righteousness. Here is presented to us the third of Paul's important terms. It denotes not the absolute attribute or idea of righteousness but the character or state of the man who practises righteousness. It is thus distinguished from $\Delta \iota \kappa \eta$, the absolute idea of right, especially as punitive justice, which is used by Paul only once in its strictly classical sense. It is also distinguished from $\Delta \iota \kappa \alpha \iota \omega \mu \alpha$, the objective work or act which satisfies the demands of justice (Rom. viii. 4), or the precept which commands such act (Rom. i. 32). The term $\Delta \iota \kappa \alpha \iota \omicron \sigma \upsilon \nu \eta$ is thus subjective in its meaning, and in Paul's use designates a conscious subjective state, a moral condition sensibly manifesting itself in conscience. Its opposite is "condemnation" (Rom. viii. 1), also manifest in conscience, and distinguished from the objective "judgment" which brings the condemnation (Rom. v. 16). The sense in which Paul uses the word is so peculiarly human that we doubt whether he ever applies it except to men. Even Rom. iii. 5 may be better taken in what seems the otherwise universal sense of the word as employed by Paul thirty-six times in this Epistle and sixty times in all. This subjective sense was familiar to the early rabbis. (See Dr. McCaul's "Old Paths," quoted in the appendix of Moule on Romans: "Every one of the children of men has merits and sins. If his merits exceed his sins he is righteous; if his sins exceed his merits he is wicked.") This inward mystic searching of conscience has been common to men of all ages, and was certainly well known to Paul. This righteousness is God's gift. The genitive here expresses origin. This idea, which emphatically distinguished Paul's teaching from all forms of legality, we find very clearly foreshadowed in Isaiah. There the Hebrew *ts'dukah* corresponds to Paul's term. This is represented as divinely bestowed in such passages as Isaiah xlv. 24, 25; xlvi. 12, 13; xlviii. 1, 18; li. 1, 4, 8; liv. 14, 17; lvi. 1, etc.; lvii. 12; lviii. 1, 2, 8; lix. 9, 14, 15, 16; lx. 21; lxv. 5, 6. See also liii. 11. (See Appendix.) This righteousness is "from faith," growing out of faith as its source. This especially distinguishes it from the righteousness which is "from works." Both are subjective states, involving the right relation of conscience to God; the first springing from the act of faith in God, the second from the act of will in harmony with law. Hence one is called pre-eminently "a righteousness of God," the other "a righteousness of law." The sense of the two adjuncts "by or from faith" and "unto faith" will appear more distinctly if we place a comma between them. They are two distinct adjuncts of the verb, and the sense and construction may both be presented thus: "For in it a righteousness of God is revealed as being from faith, unto the production of faith." The very announcement of this righteousness out of faith tends to produce this faith in our hearts.

as it is written, But the righteous shall live by faith.] This Old Testament quotation (Hab. ii. 4) is intended to illustrate not so much the broad principle of justification by faith, to which it could scarcely be applied without forcing an unhistorical meaning into the words of the prophet, as the special aspect just mentioned by Paul. Just as God's righteous people of old lived in peace in the midst of threatened danger by virtue of faith—confidence in God—so those to whom God grants the righteousness which comes of pardoning grace are called to live by the confidence which that pardoning grace inspires. This same interpretation fits Gal. iii. 11. The apostle having thus stated his theme as the gospel, a divine power unto salvation, revealing God's righteousness by faith, proceeds to the exposition of this gospel, first of all in the reason for it. Man is universally exposed to the wrath of God on account of sin. This he states, (*a*) of the Gentiles as an admitted fact; (*b*) and proves of the Jews that by the same principles they, too, are condemned; (*c*) denying them any favoured exemption from God's justice; and (*d*) summing up the universal situation in words of holy writ.

Ch. I. 18-32. The Conceded Guilt of the Gentiles.

18. **For the wrath of God is revealed from heaven**] "For" here assigns not the mere logical proof but the cause. The revelation of God's righteousness is given because a revelation of wrath already exists. The manner of this revelation is given below, where we shall be able to note the unity of the natural and the supernatural in revelation. The term "wrath," opposed to "righteousness," is chosen to designate our apprehension of the immutable opposition of God's nature to sin. It does not imply either the fickleness or the unreasonableness of human passion; but it does express an awful subjective reality in the divine nature. This wrath is revealed from heaven as God's throne, the seat and centre of his moral government.

against all ungodliness and unrighteousness of men,] The two great classes of sin are here designated—sin against the order of religion and sin against the order of justice. This is not quite synonymous with sins against God and against man. Note that men are spoken of here without the article—not some particular class of men but of men generally.

who hold down the truth in unrighteousness;] This is not a limiting but a descriptive adjunct. It characterizes not a particular class of men but men universally (not the men who hold, etc., but men, who hold, or since they hold). The verb here translated "hold down," and in the margin "hold," includes the two ideas of possession and yet repression. They possess and yet abuse the possession. This repression consists in living in unrighteousness in spite of the truth.

19. **Because that which may be known of God is manifest in them;]** "Because" here introduces the cause as well as the logical proof of the general statement just made. "That which may be known" is literally "the knowable," a direct contradiction to agnosticism. This peculiar Greek form in Plato, etc., signifies not that which is or has been known but what is capable of being known. (See Kühner, p. 291.) Though used by the historical writers of the New Testament for the past participle it is not improbable that Paul uses it in the classical sense. This Paul says is manifest, *i.e.*, *is open to be seen* "in them," or perhaps "by them." Paul does not affirm that they did see it but that God placed it before their eyes.

for God manifested it unto them.] The aorist tense here used expresses either a single historical fact which took place at one particular past time or that which is always a fact. Either sense will apply here. This manifestation is clearly in nature and conscience rather than by supernatural revelation. And yet this is part of God's apocalypse, *i.e.*, progressive opening up to man of the knowledge of himself. In fact, this universal divine manifestation is the basis of the entire *apocalypsis*.

20. **For the invisible things of him since the creation of the world are clearly seen,]** The invisible things are defined at the close of the sentence. Their manifestation began "from the creation." They (the invisible) "are seen," a play upon the words such as is frequent in Isaiah, one of Paul's favourite authors. How is expressed by the participial clause,

being perceived through the things that are made,] The participle is from the root which expresses man's higher reason, the *nous*. The eye which sees is thus the eye of faith. But the instrumental cause of this vision of the invisible is that which is itself visible, viz., "the things that are made." Godet notes that this Pauline doctrine of a universal revelation in nature, laying the foundation of universal human responsibility, appears in Acts xiv. 17; xvii. 27, 28; 1 Cor. i. 21; and Rom. iii. 29, and, we may also add, ii. 14, 15.

even his everlasting power and divinity;] These specify the invisible things more particularly. The power of God stands most prominently revealed in his works. The term "divinity" expresses not so much the absolute essence as the sum total of divine attributes. It is especially the attributes which are revealed in the works of God. The term "everlasting," belonging to both these nouns, denotes that which is "ever-divine." It is rarely used in the New Testament.

that they may be without excuse:] The end aimed at by God in this manifestation of himself in nature is to lay the basis of universal responsibility. Responsibility is not a mere result, but it is God's intended result. Paul presents here the darker side of human responsibility, in which we see men tried and found wanting, because this was the actual state of the case. It does not imply that God revealed himself in nature to condemn the world, but it does imply that God revealed himself to make the world morally responsible, and so, where they failed to meet that responsibility, to leave them "without excuse." This last term implies the full sufficiency of this divine manifestation for its intended purpose as the basis of moral responsibility.

21. **because that, knowing God,**] We have here in the Greek a striking repetition of the formulary of verse 19. The ordinary connection which makes this verse assign the reason or cause of what immediately precedes, "They are without excuse, because that, knowing God," etc., loses sight of the merely hypothetical character of the last clause of verse 20. It is not "they are without excuse" but "to the end that they may be without excuse." We are therefore inclined to make verse 21 co-ordinate with verse 19. The parallelism of form is thus fully brought out. They possessed the truth, proven by verse 19, "*because the knowable* things of God," etc.; yet repressed this truth, proven by verse 21, "because thus knowing God," etc.

they glorified him not as God, neither gave thanks;] The adjunct "as God" belongs equally to both verbs and may be rendered thus: "They rendered him not, as God, either glory or gratitude." The aorists here express historical facts, hence co-ordinate with the facts stated in verses 19 and 20. This does not imply that they ceased from worship, but that they ceased from the only worship proper to God—a holy and spiritual service. This Paul indicates by the sentence next following.

but became vain in their reasonings,] This word, used by the LXX. to render the Hebrew *machshabah*, may well be rendered "imaginations," their fancies, their current of thought. We think the apostle here refers to the mythological fancies of the heathen. It was by the emptiness of these of all moral truth and earnestness that they were led away from the true idea and worship of God; and, giving their poetical fancy full play, they drifted only the farther from the truth which God had made manifest.

and their senseless heart was darkened.] The three terms of this clause are also so peculiarly Hebrew that we must look to that language rather than to classic Greek for their interpretation. The heart was to the Hebrews the seat of moral discernment, that sensitiveness of the moral nature which keenly distinguishes right from wrong, good from evil. The senseless heart is therefore the blunted moral discrimination, which is still further emphasized by the verb "was darkened." The best commentary on these verses is the historical study of both the poetry and the philosophy of the Greeks. The process of moral decline and of intellectual darkening through the influence of both myth-forming fancy and philosophical speculation may be clearly traced. The original heritage of truth was still very rich in the days of Æschylus and of Socrates, but from that time it was rapidly "repressed."

22. **Professing themselves to be wise, they became fools,**] We cannot in our own day judge of the vast body of Greek culture from what remains to us. The stream of time is a wonderful purifier, and only the noblest and purest products of art and philosophy now remain. The dining halls, baths and dormitories of the Roman cities, buried ten years after the date of this letter, and so sealed up and preserved to our time, show us how *culture* was prostituted. The accusation of Paul is not against philosophy merely, though the popular epicureanism justifies his strongest language, but against poetry, painting, sculpture and music as well. In the glory and pride of their intellectual culture they became, morally speaking, "fools."

23. **and changed the glory of the incorruptible God**] How fully this glory had been revealed to them appears clearly from the finest passages of the great Greek tragedians, and from both Greek and Roman philosophy. Of the opposition of mythology to these conceptions they were fully conscious, as testify the following lines of Euripides:—

> "I deem not of the gods as having formed
> Connubial ties to which no law assents;
> Nor as oppressed with chains. Disgraceful this,
> I hold; nor ever will believe that one
> Lords it o'er others. Of no foreign aid
> The god who is a god indeed hath need.
> These are the idle fables of your bards."

for the likeness of an image of corruptible man, and of birds, and fourfooted beasts, and creeping things.] This charge lies against the whole course of heathen culture, from the first beginning of myth formation down to the latest development of their art. It was a debasement, a vilifying, an abominable defilement of the idea of God. Paul here is clearly committed to the view that the religious history of the heathen world is not an advance from fetichism, but a degradation from an original theism. But while this represents the course of downward religious development, there is a collateral downward moral development parallel to and resulting from this to which Paul now turns.

24. **Wherefore God gave them up in the lusts of their hearts**

unto uncleanness,] Paul here expresses the divinely ordained relation of religion to morality, and, conversely, of irreligion to immorality. The root of immorality is in the lusts of the human heart. The authority to rule and restrain these is the consciousness of the omnipresence of a holy God. The men who exchange the idea of a holy (incorruptible) God for that of a lascivious (corruptible) man are, by the very moral law of their being, "given up." God hath appointed no other moral influence by which man can be saved from the tendencies of his fallen nature. We cannot find in this expression "gave them up" anything more positive than that God held them responsible to all the moral and physical sequences of their own actions, both in their own moral nature and in their moral environment. Even the withdrawal of the Holy Spirit proceeds according to this law. To affirm anything more positive than this would be to make God the author of sin.

that their bodies should be dishonoured among themselves:] The genitive of definition, pointing out the special form of moral impurity to which idolatry in all ages leads. The dishonouring of God leads to the deepest dishonouring of man. The very body to the likeness of which he had dishonoured God is itself dishonoured below the level of the beasts.

25. for that they exchanged the truth of God for a lie,] The name of God was retained, but the conception was so changed as to become an utter falsehood. Paul recalls and once more enlarges this thought to impress the heinousness of this sin of idolatry.

and worshipped and served the creature rather than the Creator, who is blessed for ever. Amen.] The various forms of energy in nature, and especially the productive powers of nature, were made the objects both of reverence (fear and trust) and also of sacrificial and other liturgical worship. But all these, in Paul's view, are but God's creatures, the wonderful mechanism which he has constructed. The charge of creature worship thus lies not merely against the outward and grosser forms but also against the most refined forms of heathenism. It is the supreme personal Creator, and not the mysterious processes through which he works, who is the object of the eternal benediction of his creatures.

26. For this cause God gave them up unto vile passions:] We have here, with the change of the relative conjunction into the demonstrative emphasizing the cause as restated in verse 25, a repetition of the introductory words of verse 24; and the whole paragraph is a more minute specification of what was referred to there in general terms. These sins are called "passions of dishonour," disgraceful passions. For a picture of the life of wealthy Romans of Paul's time see Farrar's "Early Days of Christianity."

for their women changed the natural use into that which is against nature:] Paul uses not the noble term "woman" but the merely sexual designation. All womanliness disappeared in these vices.

27. and likewise also the men, leaving the natural use of the woman, burned in their lust one toward another, men with men working unseemliness,] The same terms are used throughout this verse, men and women alike falling below the level of the brute.

and receiving in themselves that recompense of their error which was due.] This may refer to these vices as the punishment of their idolatry, or it may look further, to the fearful penal diseases which followed such vices.

28. And even as they refused to have God in their knowledge,] Paul here turns to another aspect of the sin of the Gentile world. Their heathenism was not only a degradation of the idea of God but a rejection from their minds of the thought of God as a holy God. The moral element lies back of heathenism as well as atheism. Men do not like the restraint which the thought of the divine holiness puts upon their sin.

God gave them up unto a reprobate mind,] There is a play on the words "refused" and "reprobate." "Reprobate" signifies that which is refused or rejected as bad. But there is another and deeper meaning in both words. The first signifies "to examine or explore." The sentence could thus be paraphrased: "They did not use the power of examination to keep God before their minds." "The second term would thus signify a mind devoid of this power to explore or discern the divine." (Godet.) This seems to fit in well with the next thought.

to do those things which are not fitting;] Having lost the power to discern moral propriety or right they could easily give themselves up to the most "unfit," or even disgraceful, acts. A rightly constituted mind would revolt from such enormities. But the loss of the moral conception of God has undermined all the moral sense of their reason. The terrible phrase "God gave them up" is repeated in this verse the third time.

29. being filled with all] The result of this complete ruin of moral nature is the outburst of all immoralities. These Paul enumerates under various classes.

First, four elements of immoral character—"full of all"

unrighteousness, wickedness, covetousness, maliciousness;] These are cardinal vices: "injustice," disregard of right; "wickedness," delight in stirring up evil; "covetousness," the grasping spirit; and "maliciousness," thorough badness, moral rottenness. Then follow five forms of active sin—

full of envy, murder, strife, deceit, malignity;] The adjective "full" denotes the complete occupation of these men with these actions. Then follow seven epithets or names of reproach, designating habitual characteristics of the Gentiles—

30. whisperers, backbiters, hateful to God, insolent, haughty, boastful, inventors of evil things,] Each member of this terrible catalogue is represented in the Greek by a single word, except the last. The first three, if we take the term "godhated" in the classical sense of spies or informers, designate as a group the sneaking sinners of the age—"whisperers, backbiters, informers." The second three form a very different group, the lofty sinners, "insolent, haughty, boastful." The final term, "inventors of evil things," may be applied to all, but especially to the wild young spirits referred to in the second group. Next follow five terms each beginning with the Greek privative *a*, designating the absence or extinction of as many cardinal virtues—

31. disobedient to parents, without understanding, covenant-breakers, without natural affection, unmerciful:] Something of the peculiar rhythm, both of sound and thought, found in the original may be expressed as follows: "Without reverence to parents, without sense of right, without sense of honour, without natural affection, without pity." The "understanding" here referred to is the moral understanding, the discernment of right. "Covenant-breakers" signifies men who cannot be held by their covenants, "without sense of honour." We have in these terrible "withouts" the death-knell of all that is good and noble in man.

32. who, knowing the ordinance of God,] We have here not the ordinary relative but the indefinite "whoever," which may be paraphrased thus: "Being such as." The term "knowing" is also strengthened—"clearly recognizing." "The ordinance," *i.e.*, the requirement of justice, that which justice demands either to be done as fulfilment of right or to be suffered as penalty of wrong; in this case the latter.

that they which practise such things are worthy of death,] The word rightly translated "practise" refers to habitual act.

not only do the same, but also consent with them that practise them.] The term "consent" is scarcely strong enough to express the original, which implies a mutual enjoyment of each other's wicked doings. In this closing verse Paul sums up the proof of the charge in verse 18: They possess, "knowing," the truth; they repress it, "doing and delighting in such iniquity."

CH. II. 1-16. THE TRANSITION: RESPONSIBILITY FOR KNOWLEDGE.

1. Wherefore thou art without excuse, O man, whosoever thou art that judgest:] "The point of difficulty among commentators of all ages, here, has been, who is the man here addressed? and what, accordingly, is the force of 'wherefore'? Gentile magistrates, say the old Greek commentators; the best of the Gentiles, say the Reformers; the Jews, say most of the moderns." (Godet.) The state of the case we take to be this: If our view of the object of this Epistle is correct, then Paul is not aiming at the special condemnation of the Gentile world but at the proof of a universal necessity for a salvation by grace, through faith, and not by works of law or by prerogative of covenant right. This necessity lies in *man's universal guilt*. He begins with a case which all will admit, but basing their responsibility upon unmistakable evidence of two fundamental facts—(*a*) they knew the right, (*b*) they did it not. Therefore are they "*without excuse*," i.e., without possibility of escape from condemnation. They are condemned, not as Gentiles, nor as uncircumcised, but as sinners against light and knowledge. Having thus established the true principles of human responsibility he proceeds to apply them to all who sin against light and knowledge, even though they may outwardly acknowledge and make loud professions of respect for the right (ch. ii. 1-16). In this category he expressly includes both Jews and Greeks. And finally he shows (vv. 17-29) that from this just judgment of God no national prerogative such as that boasted of by the Jews can save them, proceeding in chapter iii. to meet objections to this purely ethical view. The parties addressed in the text, therefore, are all, Jew or Greek, who *say* but *do* not. The conjunction "wherefore" builds upon the two fundamental principles reasserted in verse 32, knowledge and sin against knowledge. This view is confirmed by the fact that Paul repeats here the term "without excuse," already used in verse 20; that in chapter i. he does not mention the Gentiles as such (because he is laying down general principles which will apply to Jew and Gentile alike); and that in chapter ii. he first mentions Jew and *Greek*, not Gentile, because next to the Jews the Greeks were most likely to set themselves up as the moral censors of the world. We take Paul's aim to be, not by an induction of two or three great classes (Heathen, Moralist and Jew, or Gentile and Jew) to prove the fact of universal guilt, but to establish a principle which will of itself prove the universal guilt. This principle, that guilt depends solely upon two factors, knowledge of right and sin against knowledge, he first establishes in a case about which there will be no controversy, next in the case before us, and lastly, against all claims to special exemption on the part of the Jew. "Whosoever thou art that judgest"—Moralist, Satirist or proselyting Jew; for all these classes set themselves up as censors of the age.

for wherein thou judgest another, thou condemnest thyself;] giving in this very judgment evidence of the first factor of responsibility—knowledge of the right.

for thou that judgest dost practise the same things.] This is the second factor. Paul states this as a fact. Probably his readers needed no proof of it.

2. And we know that the judgment of God is according to truth against them that practise such things.] In this verse Paul asserts the general principle already referred to. This constitutes the major premise, of which the minor premise and the conclusion are put rhetorically in the question of verse 3. These two verses thus constitute the expanded proof of the assertion made in the close of verse 1, "thou condemnest thyself." Hence in some ancient MSS. we find the conjunction "for." We may very well, with Godet, translate the present text by "now we know,' etc. The

"we know" does not refer to Jews or to Christians, but is a general assertion by the author in this common form. The word "truth" here, like the Old Testament *mishpat*, designates the essential principles of justice.

3. And reckonest thou this, O man, who judgest them that practise such things, and doest the same, that thou shalt escape the judgment of God?] The minor premise is, "Thou doest such things;" the conclusion, "God will judge thee according to the truth." But Paul throws the conclusion into the form of an unanswerable dilemma. By his judgment of others the man addressed admits the major premise. He cannot deny the minor premise. Therefore he is either reckoning on some impossible way of escape or he is presuming on, and hence despising, the goodness of God (v. 4). In either case the argument points against the Jew, whose case Paul has especially in mind as the opponent of the gospel which he is vindicating.

4. Or despisest thou the riches of his goodness and forbearance and longsuffering,] If the man is not trusting in that which God's justice renders impossible then he is wilfully and knowingly sinning against the goodness which has endowed him with the knowledge of the right, and the forbearance and longsuffering which continue his probation in spite of his sin. All these terms would have special force as applied to the Jew, though the principle which they announce applies universally.

not knowing that the goodness of God leadeth thee to repentance?] Literally, "ignoring that the gentle dealing of God leadeth thee unto repentance;" "unto" designating, as usual, the aim or intention.

5. but after thy hardness and impenitent heart] The interrogative form of the dilemma is here laid aside and the direct assertion of the real state of affairs resumed. The preposition denotes the rule of action, which is here the moral obduracy resulting from sin against light.

treasurest up for thyself wrath] Treasures of wrath, opposed to the despised riches of God's goodness.

in the day of wrath and revelation of the righteous judgment of God;] This may refer either specifically to the rapidly approaching day of divine judgment against the Jewish nation, or more generally to the final and universal judgment of the human race. Such a final judgment of all men, according to principles of absolute justice, was the very foundation stone of Paul's doctrine. Compare with the present passage 2 Cor. v. 10; 1 Thess. iv. 17–v. 11; 2 Tim. iv. 1. See Acts xxiv. 25 as to the use Paul made of this doctrine. This doctrine, of which the present passage is Paul's fullest exposition, implies—

1. That the moral character of each life determines its eternal destiny.
2. That this destiny is finally fixed by God.

3. That this act of divine judgment proceeds upon principles of absolute justice.

4. That any arbitrary preference of any one man or of any class of men over others is absolutely excluded.

As we shall hereafter see, Paul's entire doctrinal system is built upon this foundation and in harmony with it. This doctrine he has in the next six verses thrown into the Hebrew poetic or proverbial form, indicating its importance and the frequency with which he made use of it.

6. Who will render to every man according to his works:

7. To them that by patience in welldoing
Seek for glory and honour and incorruption,
Eternal life:

8. But unto them that are factious,
And obey not the truth, but obey unrighteousness,
Shall be wrath and indignation,

9. Tribulation and anguish,
Upon every soul of man that worketh evil,
Of the Jew first, and also of the Greek;

10. But glory and honour and peace
To every man that worketh good,
To the Jew first, and also to the Greek:

11. For there is no respect of persons with God.

Note (*a*) the parallelism of the first line with the last; (*b*) the introverted parallelism of the first triplet with the last; and (*c*) of the middle stanza in its two triplets. This can scarcely be accidental, and may indicate that Paul was quoting either a recognized formula of the ethical teaching of the time, or a formula which he himself had constructed for use in his own teaching. The expression in verse 16 would suggest the latter. If so Paul depends upon the conscience of his readers to recognize its truth, as he makes no attempt to establish it by argument other than to guard against an objection. A few words of these verses, in their general tenor so perfectly clear, are worthy of special note. The "patience" of verse 7 is clearly a probational patience, *i.e.*, perseverance. The term "good work," to denote the right life, is not to be opposed to Paul's doctrine of salvation by faith. He is now laying down the universal and fundamental principles of moral probation, without reference to the gracious means by which the probation of fallen humanity may reach a successful issue. When he comes to that question, and propounds his doctrine of salvation by faith, it is a "faith which worketh by love." Eternal life is not mere endless existence on the one hand nor the life of an æon on the other, but the fulness of the life of that world which the final judgment will usher in. The three phrases, "factious," "obey not the truth" and "obey unrighteousness," describe the character of those who reject the gospel. The phrase "respect of persons" is the Hebrew expression for personal favouritism. (See 2 Chron. xix. 7 and Deut. x. 17.)

12. For as many as have sinned without law] Paul here anticipates a possible objection to the important doctrine laid down. How can those be fairly judged according to principles of strict justice who have not enjoyed the light of God's law?

shall also perish without law:] Paul's reply is that their final destiny will correspond to their probation. As one was without law, *i.e.*, the revealed and written law, so will the other be. This he explains more fully in verse 14 when he has completed the antithesis of the two great classes of human probation.

and as many as have sinned under law shall be judged by law;] The distinction between "shall perish" and "shall be judged" may indicate the more detailed and definite character of the higher probation. Paul, in this and the next following sentence, strikes at the very root of Jewish assumption. They held that the possession of the law, as a mark of God's special favour, assured them of salvation. Paul asserts that it merely involves greater responsibility.

13. for not the hearers of a law are just before God,] The mere possession of greater probational advantages does not secure salvation.

but the doers of a law shall be justified:] Jewish privilege avails nothing except the terms of probation are met. (See v. 25.) Paul is thus surely and clearly approaching the great point required by the scope of his argument. The circumcision party built upon the privileges of a special election: already Paul's doctrine overturns from the very foundation such assumption by showing that final justification must be according to works. This justification is clearly from the context the justification of the final judgment; this alone completes human probation. But the objection again arises, if *only* doers of law can be justified how can there be a just probation of those who have no law? To constitute probation there must be knowledge of right. To this difficulty, which emerges in verse 12 and is continued in verse 13, Paul next replies.

14. for when Gentiles which have no law do by nature the things of the law,] Paul here evidently means by "law" written law. "The things of the law" are the actions prescribed as right by the written law. These are said to be done "by nature," not as opposed to grace, or a universal inner working of God's Spirit in human conscience, but as opposed to acts performed in view of the express command of a written law.

these, having no law, are a law unto themselves;] Thus they are not absolutely without law. They have a law sufficient for the purposes of responsibility and of probation. The nature of this law Paul proceeds immediately to explain. In the meantime it should be noted that verse 14 describes not an impossible hypothesis but a possible case. The Greek construction which is here used clearly implies the actual historical possibility of the condition, and hence he draws his conclusion in the present indicative, "these *are* a law unto themselves." He finds in this possibility of their doing right full proof of the universal presence of a law sufficient to establish probational responsibility; and the expression "without law," in verse 12, must be limited by the presence of this inner law of nature. This connection of verse 14 directly with verse 13, and indirectly with verse 12, combining Meyer and Calvin, does not imply a possibility of salvation or justification of the Gentile beyond what is absolutely essential to a true probation. It may be as Calvin would have it, that all the Gentiles perish. But if so they perish justly. The last clause of verse 13 is really negative, and might be paraphrased "the doers of law *alone* shall be justified." Paul is not here discussing the question of how either Jews or Gentiles actually are saved or can be saved. He is proving that final justification can only depend upon the moral character of life, and that this principle is of universal application—to the Jew notwithstanding his peculiar privileges as possessor of the law, and to the Gentile notwithstanding the absence of those privileges. Presently he will show us that, but for grace, the issue of human probation must be universal condemnation.

15. **in that they show the work of the law written in their hearts,**] The work of the law may be either that discrimination of right from wrong which a written law produces (see Moule) or, as we think simpler and better, the course of conduct which the law prescribes. This is written in their hearts in this sense, that their understanding or moral judgment points out the right act. With the Hebrews the heart was the seat of moral government. That this moral judgment is in harmony with the precepts of God's law is shown by their actions, not to themselves but to the world at large.

their conscience bearing witness therewith,] *i.e.*, with the moral judgment of the understanding. The conscience thus appears to signify the feeling of obligation to do the right, as distinguished from the understanding which judges that this particular work is right. The conscience attests the truth of the judgment by its response, perhaps especially by the *after-feeling* of approval or remorse. The classical use of the word "conscience," as the witness which a man has within himself and against himself, seems especially to point to this after-feeling.

and their thoughts one with another accusing or else excusing them;] These "thoughts" are the after-thoughts which either aggravate or endeavour to extenuate the reproaches of conscience. "One with another" thus refers, not to persons with each other, but to the thoughts within the person.

16. **In the day when God shall judge the secrets of men, according to my gospel, by Jesus Christ.**] The first difficulty in

this verse is the connection of the clause "in the day." Most of those who interpret it as referring to the day of final judgment find it necessary to propose a remote connection with verses 5 or 6, or with verses 11, 12 or 13. Against this is the fact that Paul's grammatical connection is usually from clause to clause directly. But it may be doubted whether Paul's reference is to the final day of judgment. The verb used here may with equal propriety be construed in the present tense. The phrase "judge the secrets of men" is not elsewhere used by Paul for the judgment of the final day. On the other hand, comparing 1 Cor. xiv. 24, 25, we find it used of the judgment which takes place in the conscience of the sinner under the preaching of the gospel. The process described in verses 14 and 15, although occasionally realized in the commission of flagrant offences, becomes a general experience only under the preaching of the gospel, which by the power of the Holy Spirit brings all men immediately before the bar of God in the presence of their own conscience. (See Lange.) If this is the meaning of the phrase here then it can only be connected directly with verse 15.

CH. II. 17-29. APPLICATION OF THE TRUE PRINCIPLES OF PROBATION TO THE JEWS.

We arrive now at the third part and the real culmination of Paul's argument. Beginning with a statement, readily granted by his opponent, that the wrath of God is revealed from heaven against all ungodliness and unrighteousness of men, he has shown that it is so revealed, not against the Gentiles as Gentiles, but against those who have the truth but sinned against it, and that the very enormity of Gentile sin is the divine penalty for the perversion of their privileges. From this position, thus established, he turns unexpectedly upon all who speak of the Gentiles as "sinners," and affirms that this very principle condemns them, asking how they hope to escape the just judgment of God, which he asserts must take place according to principles of strict equity, rewarding every man according to his work, without respect of persons, justifying, not the mere hearers, but the doers of law. Now, in the third part, having thus completely prepared his ground by expounding the true principles of probation, Paul proceeds to attack that main citadel of assumption of privilege which he had from the very outset in view. It is the Jew alone who claims exemption from these rigid principles of justice on the ground of his covenant privileges. The Judaizer or Ebionite built upon this Jewish foundation when he taught, "Except ye be circumcised after the manner of Moses, ye cannot be saved;" for the whole value of circumcision lay in the fact that it admitted into the charmed circle or covenant of Jewish national life. If these indisputable principles of divine justice in the final judgment of men are to be applied even within this circle, then the foundations of both Jew and Judaizer are destroyed. This Paul now proceeds to do.

17. **But if thou bearest the name of a Jew,**] Godet proposes to translate the conjunction "now" instead of "but," for there is no real antithesis—only an addition by way of culmination. Paul here catalogues at length the favourite titles by which the Jew distinguished himself from sinners of the Gentiles. He begins with the title Jew. "Salvation is of the Jews" was an aphorism, used in its true sense by Christ, but taken in a very different sense by the Pharisees.

and restest upon the law,] Compare John vii. 49: "This rabble which knoweth not the law are accursed."

and gloriest in God,] as being his favourite people.

18. **and knowest his will,**] Probably this, like the other phrases, had passed into the Jewish cant of the time.

and approvest the things that are excellent,] This is one of the blessings solicited by Paul for the Philippians. But it involves a responsibility as well as a privilege. This gift in Paul's time degenerated into the most ridiculous casuistry. (See Godet.)

being instructed out of the law,] a formal term denoting careful religious training, literally catechized. (See Luke i. 4.) This completes the first catalogue of prerogatives, the special advantages enjoyed by the Jews.

19. **and art confident that thou thyself art a guide of the blind, a light of them that are in darkness,**

20. **a corrector of the foolish, a teacher of babes,**] These were all familiar terms used by Christ and his apostles, doubtless from the current language of the time. Christ calls the scribes and Pharisees "fools" and "blind," and speaks of men as "walking in darkness;" and Paul calls the Corinthians "babes." They form the second part of the catalogue of prerogatives, indicating the moral and religious authority assumed.

having in the law the form of knowledge and of the truth;] The "form" is not the mere outward form as contrasted with the substance, but the exact pattern, the perfect representation. This was the foundation of all their prerogatives. They supposed that this law was incapable of change or improvement, and were scandalized when told that it was to pass away, and be "changed" and replaced by that which was more perfect. The protasis we take to end here and not (as Godet) to extend to verse 24. The conjunction "therefore" repeats this protasis in the various adjectives and participial clauses, "that teachest another," etc.

21. **thou therefore that teachest another, teachest thou not thyself?**] This question is the sum total of the whole apodosis. It is followed by the particulars which are at the same time the proof. These particulars are three:

thou that preachest a man should not steal, dost thou steal?] The avarice of the Jews made this a common sin.

22. **Thou that sayest a man should not commit adultery, dost thou commit adultery?**] This charge was laid against some very

eminent rabbis. See also our Lord's teaching on the subject of divorce.

thou that abhorrest idols, dost thou rob temples?] On this, a charge against the Jews, see Acts xix. 37. If our view of the scope of Paul's argument is correct then we have a perfect demonstration. If a single Jew could be cited as a thief, an adulterer, etc., then either the doctrine of God's justice must be abandoned or the assumption that a Jew is infallibly saved because he is a Jew is false. The prerogative title "Jew" became responsible for every form of sin committed by any one who held by birth or proselytism the right to wear it; and the fact that such men were publicly well known to commit such sins was a death-blow to the assumption that the mere fact of being God's elect people would or could save them from God's just wrath. On the other hand, the argument is exceedingly weak as an inductive proof that all men, both Jews and Gentiles, are sinners. We shall see presently how Paul does prove that important fact when, by establishing and applying alike to Gentile and Jew the true doctrine of probation, he has first swept away all the refuges of lies. This argument, already so perfect for its purpose, is completed by a general charge substantiated by scripture itself:

23. thou who gloriest in the law, through thy transgression of the law dishonourest thou God?] This general charge Paul immediately proves by an apposite quotation from Ezek. xxxvi. 20–23.

24. For the name of God is blasphemed among the Gentiles because of you, even as it is written.] Paul in this quotes not the words of a single verse, but in part the words and in full the idea repeated in each of the four verses of the passage referred to. Such a charge, proven against the Jews of Ezekiel's time, was just as apposite to Paul's argument as if it were a fact of the present. The logical force of these burning rhetorical questions Paul now asserts as a general principle, affirming or proving the idea conveyed in the interrogative form. This general principle is not "All have sinned, even the Jews;" but "Your assumption of special prerogative is of no avail."

25. For circumcision indeed profiteth, if thou be a doer of the law:] This thought hinges directly on the conclusion to be drawn from the argument just advanced. That conclusion was, as we have just seen, "assumption of privileges through the covenant of circumcision is of no avail if God be just." Paul puts it, however, in a more concessive form: "I grant you that the covenant of circumcision is a great blessing if you are faithful to the terms and responsibilities of that covenant."

but if thou be a transgressor of the law, thy circumcision is become uncircumcision.] If the terms of the covenant be broken then there is no claim to its privileges. Paul thus advances the true doctrine of the ancient covenant. It was in perfect harmony with the justice of God, and provided for the true probation of man by conditioning the blessings on the keeping of the law. The doctrine which Paul is overthrowing is the false assumption that the blessings of the ancient covenant were infallibly secure to the Jews as Jews. The true doctrine of the ancient covenant was quite as much opposed to this as was Paul's argument from the absolute justice of God, and hence is adduced to substantiate that argument. We find in the Rabbis such expressions as these, in perfect keeping with the doctrine which Paul is opposing: "All the circumcised have part in the world to come." "Circumcision is equivalent to all the commandments that are in the law." (See Moule, App.)

26. If therefore the uncircumcision keep the ordinances of the law, shall not his uncircumcision be reckoned for circumcision?] This is the converse of the true doctrine of the old covenant which Paul had just announced. It follows logically that if the circumcised may lose the blessings of the covenant by disobedience the uncircumcised may gain them by obedience. We have here a repetition of the thought of verses 14 and 15. In both cases the construction used recognizes the perfect possibility of the hypothesis, and presents it as a thing to be actually expected, though it does not assert that it has actually occurred. Godet's objection that the salvation of the Gentiles would thus be of works proceeds upon the false hypothesis that Paul regards the whole Old Testament dispensation as a covenant of works. The very term which he here uses, "reckoned," points to grace. For proof that Paul held that the principle of grace lay back of the Abrahamic covenant see chapter iv.; also Gal. iii. 15–18. For the extension of this principle still further see Heb. xi. In fact, the very idea of a covenant is founded on grace. Verse 26 is, however, but a stepping-stone to something beyond. Paul is not yet dealing with the question of how the Gentiles may be saved; he is merely demolishing the false assumption of the Jew. Hence he applies the truth thus gained.

27. and shall not the uncircumcision which is by nature, if it fulfil the law, judge thee, who with the letter and circumcision art a transgressor of the law?] This is the application to the Jew, placing the worthlessness of his assumptions in the strongest possible light. The very Gentile whom he calls "a sinner" will be his judge, that is, by comparison of conduct in the great day, will place his disobedience under the strongest possible condemnation. The uncircumcision was the Jewish term to designate the whole Gentile world. They are such by nature, *i.e.*, by birth, only. By moral conduct they are worthy to be reckoned as circumcision. On the other hand, his very confidence in the mere physical act of circumcision—a merely literal fulfilment of the law—is the means of leading the Jew to more flagrant transgressions of the law. This mention of the contrast between the mere accident of birth, or of an outward literal act, and the true spirit of God's holy covenant, Paul next expands more fully.

28. For he is not a Jew, which is one outwardly;] That is, a true Jew in the highest sense,

neither is that circumcision, which is outward in the flesh:]
In these two sentences the whole ground is taken from the Jew. He
is neither a Jew nor circumcised in the true sense;

29. but he is a Jew, which is one inwardly; and circumcision
is that of the heart,] This was no new thought, and should have
been familiar to the Jews. (See Lev. xxvi. 41; Deut. x. 16; Jer.
iv. 14; Ezek. xliv. 9, etc.) Paul has thus in this thoroughly prophetic declaration arrived at the culmination of his thesis. This
principle includes all that he set out to prove.

in the spirit, not in the letter; whose praise is not of men,
but of God.] This addition thrusts the argument home. The
whole prophetic order insisted on the moral spirit of the law; the
Pharisee, *i.e.*, the formalist, and the legalist, of every age, is satisfied
with the letter. The latter especially in Paul's time sought to make
a grand display of the vast number of proselytes gained by their
Judaistic Christianity. (See Gal. vi. 12, 13.) But Paul holds that
for such work there is no credit before God.

CH. III. 1–8. ANSWER TO OBJECTIONS.

NOTE.—In studying this short section, acknowledged by all commentators to be
the most difficult in the entire Epistle, it is essential to begin with a correct conception of its general purport. It is a reply to obvious objections to the conclusion just stated. These objections are such as would naturally suggest themselves
to the minds of Paul's readers, and occur to Paul himself, and probably had at
times been actually advanced by his opponents. Still we are not to suppose that
Paul here adopts the form of a dialogue in which the objector asks the questions
and the apostle answers. He does indeed propound the objections in the interrogative form, but he also to some extent uses the same form in propounding the answer.
This is especially the case where he uses the form of argument known as *reductio
ad absurdum*. We must therefore clearly distinguish the questions which are used
to present the objections. All are agreed that in the first verse the double question presents a main objection which is directly answered in verse 2. To this answer a subordinate objection seems to be presented in the first part of verse 3,
and answered by *reductio ad absurdum* in the second question of the same verse,
the answer being confirmed by the quotations in verse 4. The commentators generally suppose that verse 5 starts an objection arising out of these quotations, and
hence in some sense subordinate to the preceding. But it is by no means after
Paul's manner, nor would it for a moment occur to any Jew, to raise an objection
to any direct statement of scripture or to anything plainly implied therein. Besides,
verse 4 does not at all speak of the commendation but only of the vindication of the
divine equity, or rather faithfulness. To make the connection proposed we have
to leap over this logical hiatus, and further, to find introduced two entirely new
terms—instead of unfaithfulness, unrighteousness; and instead of faithfulness the
word which in every other case is used to express God's gift of righteousness to
man through the gospel. Further, the conjunction here used connects co-ordinate
clauses, sentences or paragraphs. With what is verse 5 co-ordinate? Either with
verse 3 or with verse 1. If with verse 3 then it should supply a second substantia-
tion of verse 2 as against a new objection. But the thought presented will not
admit of this. We are therefore obliged to co-ordinate it with verse 1, *i.e.*, to regard
verse 5 as presenting a new and independent form of objection to Paul's main argument, or to some conclusion which can already be drawn from it. What the nature
of this objection is we shall consider under the verse itself. To this we think Paul
makes a twofold reply, each in interrogative form, with a *reductio ad absurdum*—
"Surely not God is unjust," and "Surely not 'Let us do evil, that good may
come'" (vv. 5, 6 and 8). But how, in that case, shall we dispose of the latter clause

of verse 6 and verse 7? The latter clause of verse 6 is usually taken as supporting the argument which is involved in the last question of verse 5, and directly asserted in the "God forbid" which immediately precedes. Verse 7 we take to be a second and personal argument sustaining Paul's emphatic "God forbid." The extreme difficulty of this passage must justify the length of this introductory note.

1. What advantage then hath the Jew? or what is the profit of circumcision?] The two terms "Jew" and "circumcision" were the terms which Paul had used above as expressive of the special prerogative claimed by his opponents. Paul's argument sweeps away the unfounded assumption of prerogative, and at first sight might seem to sweep away everything which the Jew was supposed to enjoy more than the Gentile, and to deny that any benefit or moral help accrued to those who were embraced in God's covenant of circumcision, which would be to deny altogether the divine authority of the Old Testament dispensation. To this Paul replies:—

2. Much every way: first of all, that they were entrusted with the oracles of God.] This first advantage may also be regarded as the root out of which, as branches, all other advantages spring. The oracles of God included, first, God's law, and secondly, God's promises. The whole revelation is embraced in these. These the Jews held not as a possession for their own sole benefit but as a trust to be used as the ancient promises and prophetic declarations all intimate, for the benefit of all nations. To be put in charge of such a trust was indeed a proud privilege as well as an awful responsibility. And the keeping of these oracles was not only a privilege but also a moral help, as every member of the covenant had not only all the light of the law but also all the blessed assurance of the promises.

3. For what if some were without faith? shall their want of faith make of none effect the faithfulness of God?] The words translated "faith" and "without faith" here correspond to "entrusted" of the preceding verse. We think, therefore (Meyer to the contrary), that they should be taken as signifying fidelity and lack of fidelity to trust. The question is also asked in that form which anticipates the strongest negative answer, the very form of asking the question implying the absurdity of anything but a negative answer. We may therefore paraphrase the verse thus: "For what if some proved unfaithful to the trust (dishonouring God by breaking his covenant)? surely you cannot pretend to say that their unfaithfulness renders God's fidelity of none effect?" The true view and the false view of the covenant privileges are thus placed in striking contrast. The falsely-assumed privileges are completely swept away by the infidelity of even a few. But God's faithfulness maintains all the advantage of the true privileges even to "a very small remnant" who alone represent his faithful people.

4. God forbid: yea, let God be found true, but every man a liar;] If, instead of some, or even the great body of the nation, being unfaithful, the whole people, every man, had proved so, still God's truth, his fidelity to his covenant promises, would not be impeached.

as it is written, **That thou mightest be justified in thy words, and mightest prevail when thou comest into judgment.**] This quotation has been interpreted as if it implied that David's sin was committed for the purpose of justifying God, etc., or, more mildly, overruled to the glory of God. Neither the former idea nor yet the latter (however true it may be in some cases) is contained here. Paul quotes verbatim from the LXX. Psalm li. 4. For the interpretation of the entire passage we must look to the original psalm. Here the strophical structure of the psalm is strongly in favour of the interpretation which connects our quotation directly with verse 3, making 4 a parenthetical expression, thus:—

"For I acknowledge my transgressions,
And my sin is ever before me;
(Against thee, thee only, have I sinned,
And done this evil in thy sight;)
That thou mightest be justified," etc.

As Paul quotes only the last couplet of the strophe we have nothing to indicate that his view of the connection differed from this. In fact, this view is most apposite to his purpose. David, in making a public confession of his sin that God's justice may be publicly vindicated in having punished him, directly attests the principle here laid down by Paul. God's fidelity to his covenant promises is not impeachable from the fact that he is sometimes obliged to punish for their sins even the greatest of those to whom those promises have been given. Having thus completed the answer to this the only plausible objection to his great argument, which he really commenced chapter i. 18, the apostle would now seem to be ready to make a formal statement of his conclusion, and to apply it to the final purpose which he has in view, as he does presently in verse 9. But that conclusion is so obvious that it is already before his own mind and before that of his readers. Why has he thus swept away the legal righteousness of the Jew? For no other purpose than to "establish the righteousness" which is of God and revealed in the gospel. This suggests a new line of objection, which Paul first states and answers.

5. But if our unrighteousness commendeth the righteousness of God, what shall we say?] Unrighteousness would here be used in the sense of lack of righteousness, as Paul had by his argument swept away the righteousness in which they trusted. This lack of righteousness forms the dark background out of which God's righteousness stands forth in striking relief. (On this contrast compare ch. x. 3.) Man's universal lack of a righteousness of his own is the necessary presupposition of God's righteousness, and thus demonstrates it as the only possible righteousness. It is to this fact, or to the conclusions which might be drawn from it, that the objection is taken. The fact itself Paul states in its strongest form in chapter xi. 32. This objection—the antinomian abuse to which Paul's doctrine was exposed—is one to which he reverts again and again in the course of the Epistle. "What shall we say?" *i.e.*, what conclusion shall we draw? The conclusions are not stated in the question, they are supposed to be apparent, but are presented in the emphatic interrogative denials (vv. 5, 6 and 8).

Is God unrighteous who visiteth with wrath?] The form of the question is equivalent to the most emphatic negation, and thus carries refutation on the face of it. God cannot be unjust. It is only by laying aside all the unquestionable postulates of the divine nature and speaking by the same rule which we apply to men that such a thing could even be uttered.

6. **(I speak after the manner of men.)**] The expression "who visiteth with wrath" has usually been referred to the day of judgment. The evident reference, however, back to chapter i., verses 17 and 18, etc., as well as the employment of the present tense, seem to favour the reference to the wrath of God as manifest in his providence and in human conscience. The expression may, however, be taken generally of all manifestations of God's wrath against sin.

God forbid:] God's justice cannot be impeached.

for then how shall God judge the world?] The conjunction "how then" implies a suppressed protasis. It is equal to "for in that case." But in what case? "In case God were unjust," say a large number of expositors. We prefer to follow those who read, "in case God cannot justly judge any whose sin may be overruled for good." The expression "judge the world" may thus be taken in its widest sense as including the whole course of divine justice both here and hereafter. This would be impossible in case all were exempted whose sin was overruled for good. In fact, one great end of the divine judgment is this very result.

7. **But if the truth of God through my lie abounded unto his glory, why am I also still judged as a sinner?**] There are two general lines of interpretation of this very difficult verse. A large number of expositors take verse 7 as a repetition, in another form, of the main objection presented in verse 5. This is in harmony with the view that the apostle there speaks of God's righteousness (justice) as demonstrated by our unrighteousness. The reading of the revised text is against this in some of the forms presented. Still more is the fact that it is separated from that which it is intended to explain by the whole extent of verse 6 and verse 5*b*. These certainly are not parenthetical. This explanation supposes the "I also" to personate the sinner, upon whom God's wrath rests. The second line of interpretation takes the same view of the phrase "I also," but makes the whole verse an explanation of verse 6, showing how in the final judgment almost any sinner might plead for excuse. But if the apostle had intended to express this thought we cannot understand why he should use the aorist indicative in the conditional and the present indicative in the apodosis. The idea to be expressed would be this: In every possible case of God's glory through man's sin why

should such man also be judged as a sinner? which would be expressed in the strongest way admissible by the combination of the subjunctive with the indicative. The present construction of the Greek states two acknowledged facts—one in the past, historical, the other in the present. It may be paraphrased thus: "If (as you affirm) the truth of God has abounded through my lie unto his glory, why am I any longer judged a sinner (as is actually the case)? This can scarcely refer to a mere hypothetical case taken from the final day of judgment, nor even to such a case taken from the judgments of Providence in human history. We are therefore disposed to suggest the following: The pronoun in the first person singular, wherever used by the apostle thus far, refers to himself personally or to himself as opposed to the Judaizing teachers. (See ch. i. 8–17 and ch. ii. 16.) We have but to take it in the same natural sense here and we have a most perfect and apposite *argumentum ad hominem*, leaving his opponents without possibility of answer. The connection then runs as follows: *Objector*—"If our lack of righteousness establish the righteousness of God what conclusion follows?" *Paul* —"Certainly not the conclusion that the anger of God against sin is unjust, for in that case how will God's judgment of the world be carried on? and further, why, on that principle, do you judge me also to be a sinner if, as you say, God's truth has abounded through what you may call my lie to his glory? This is in perfect harmony with the interpretation we have offered of verse 5, and will also form a fitting transition to verse 8. Only a few notes need be added. This explanation is the only one which gives its full emphasis to the expression "I also." The adverb "still" we have paraphrased as equal to "in that case," and co-ordinating the question in verse 7 with the question closing verse 6, and taking the place of the adverbial conjunction "for then." The *argumentum ad hominem* implies that his adversaries acknowledged the utility of his labours in opening the way for themselves, although they called his gospel a lie. They certainly could not but admit that the great principles of monotheism were widely extended among the heathen through his preaching. This we take to be the meaning of the expression "truth of God." (See ch. i. 18, 25.) On the use of the term "sinner" in this connection see Gal. ii. 15–18.

8. And why not] The word "why" is not found here in the Greek. The revisers, departing from their usual rule, have interpreted as well as translated by connecting directly with the preceding sentence and supplying "why" from that. If, as we propose, this sentence is co-ordinate with v. 5*b*, then "why" must be omitted and this made a direct question. The force of the Greek particle translated "not" will then be interrogative, implying a strong negative answer.

(as we be slanderously reported, and as some affirm that we say),] "Slanderously reported" is literally "blasphemed." This parenthesis evidently refers to misrepresentations of Paul's doctrine ("we say") by his opponents. This is in perfect harmony with our line of exposition which supposes that in verse 7 his thought is directed to such misrepresentations.

Let us do evil, that good may come?] This is at once a statement of the misrepresentation and a statement of answer to the objection; "And certainly not, Let us do evil that good may come." Paul's reasoning would stand thus: "No man can draw this conclusion, so immoral in itself that every person will justly condemn it, although some are slanderous enough to charge us falsely with teaching this." We should therefore translate the entire verse thus: "And shall we (as we be slanderously reported, and as some affirm that we say) do evil that good may come? whose condemnation is just." This is a strictly literal translation.

whose condemnation is just.] That is, the condemnation of all who hold such a principle. It is to be noted that Paul does not here reply to either of the objections raised. He merely dismisses them for the time being, to return to a full reply hereafter. The objector had said, "If our unrighteousness demonstrates the righteousness of God may we not draw from that some terrible conclusions." Paul says, "No. You cannot conclude that God's wrath against those whose sin is overruled for good is unjust, for this would put an end to all God's judgment of the world, and, moreover, would excuse me in my so-called sinful course in preaching what you call a false gospel; and you cannot conclude that we may do evil that good may come—a doctrine justly condemned by every right mind, although slanderously attributed to us." A direct answer to the objection in full would require Paul to prove at length, (a) the consistency of the divine justice in punishing the Jews with the fact that makes their sin the occasion of establishing a wider gospel of grace for all the nations, which he does at length in chapters ix.-xi.; and (b) that the righteousness of God, which requires as its basis the demonstration of the unrighteousness of man, is not antinomian in its tendency. This he does in chapter vi. To have introduced these lengthened arguments here would have unduly postponed the great conclusion to which he is now hastening.

CH. III. 9–20. THE GREAT CONCLUSION.

9. What then?] This formula is used repeatedly by Paul, not only to introduce objections but to call attention to the point reached in the argument. Some suppose that here it introduces a new objection. This interpretation, which has set the American and the English revisers at cross purposes in their translation, spoils both Paul's rhetoric and logic, and makes him feebly repeat himself from verse 1. We take it here as calling specific attention to the great conclusion which he now announces.

are we in worse case than they?] The American revisers translate, "are we in better case than they?" Both are interpretations rather than translations. The margin, "do we excuse ourselves?" is more nearly correct, though still paraphrastic. The single Greek word translated by the entire phrase above is found in the New Testament only here. Meyer says the only meaning warranted by linguistic usage is "to hold before" or "put forward" something for one's defence as a shield. This meaning fits our line of argument perfectly. The verb in the revised text is present indicative, either middle or passive. Two important MSS., A. and L., read the subjunctive. We can use either form and translate, "do we hold forth" or "can we hold forth" any shield? *i.e.*, *any moral covert from God's wrath*, such as the Jews claimed in their *covenant of circumcision* or the Greeks in their *culture (wisdom)*. This is the question *of the entire preceding argument*, to which Paul now replies *in final conclusion:*

No, in no wise:] *i.e.*, in no possible way. This is the conclusion. Any such moral covert in any form is inconsistent with the justice of God. But this is not all. The very sweeping away of all covert leaves all exposed to the wrath of God against sin. This Paul hastens to add, because it is the part of the conclusion which he intends to use. The long train of argument from chapter ii. 1, sweeping away the "refuges of lies," was only to make this more clear.

for we before laid to the charge both of Jews and Greeks, that they are all under sin;] The word translated "before laid to the charge" is the exact counterpart of the word "hold forth a shield." If, then, we are not to lose the beautiful force of Paul's form of expression and resolve it into a mere senseless play of sounds, we must render the particle *pro* in the same way as above, not as expressing time but position. We thus translate: "We have held forth a charge against both Jews and Greeks, that they are all under sin." The temporal sense of the particle *pro* would have required a specific mention of the charge in the preceding context. This moral charge has been held forth against Jew and Greek, not by express mention, nor yet by formal proof, but by the very fact of the demolition of their coverts. If the Jew cannot shield himself behind his national prerogative, nor the Greek behind his superior knowledge, then there is no escape from the conclusion that, like the rest of mankind, they are under the guilt of their sins. The existence of these sins is too obvious to need proof. Paul assumes it; and they entirely mistake the unanswerable force of his argument against all moral coverts who suppose that he is in the preceding chapters engaged in an inductive proof of actual sins, first of Gentiles and then of Jews. The fact that all have sinned is assumed. The question is, is there any escape from the penal consequences of this sin? Can the Jew shield himself behind his national covenant? or the Greek behind his philosophy? Paul says, "No, for we have held forth over every head the *aitia*, the *blame*, of their sins." And to this conclusion the words of scripture correspond.

10. as it is written,] If we have not mistaken the line of Paul's

argument, the quotations here adduced are not made to prove the fact of universal sin so much as the universal *chargeableness* of that sin. This they prove perfectly; the other they would prove only by methods in logic or else in exegesis which we do not think Paul used, and which, not unjustly, have been called *rabbinical*. The passages are taken from various parts of the Old Testament, especially the Book of Psalms, and they unite in charging home against all classes of men the *guilt* of their sins—exactly the conclusion which Paul draws from them in verses 19 and 20. The first quotation is taken from Psalm xiv. 1-3.

There is none righteous, no, not one;
11. There is none that understandeth,
There is none that seeketh after God;
12. They have all turned aside, they are together become unprofitable;
There is none that doeth good, no, not so much as one:

This quotation is found also in Psalm liii., where it is unmistakably applied to the Gentile world as the persecutors of the chosen people. The reference also to Gen. vi. 5 and 12 is almost beyond doubt. If so then Paul, in the order of his quotations, follows the same order as in his argument, beginning with the wide extent of the Gentile world. Evil-doing charged as sin was universal at the time of the deluge, and equally so at the time of the psalmist. Out of the entire psalm the apostle selects such parts as serve his purpose, setting forth the fact of universal unrighteousness, lack of moral discernment, alienation from God (compare ch. i.), and hence a giving up to iniquity to the utter extinction of all good. A better summary of chapter i. 18-32 could scarcely be constructed than we thus have in this quotation. The next group is taken from three psalms (v. 9; cxl. 3; and x. 7). In the original they all refer to personal wrongs between man and man, in the use of the tongue, and are hence of universal application. They fit in very well as parallel with chapter ii. 1-16, where the responsibility of those who say and do not, and who are given to passing harsh judgments upon their neighbours, is described.

13. Their throat is an open sepulchre;
With their tongues they have used deceit:
The poison of asps is under their lips:
14. Whose mouth is full of cursing and bitterness:

Psalm v., from which the first two sentences are taken, treats of universal ethical principles. God "hath no pleasure in wickedness," and "an evil man cannot dwell with him." The descriptions thus apply to human nature universally. Psalm cxl., from which the next sentence is taken, refers to David's enemies, probably within the theocracy, as does also Psalm x., though in this last case the enemies may be foreign foes. The final quotations have originally unmistakable application to the sins of Israel.

15. Their feet are swift to shed blood;

16. Destruction and misery are in their ways;
17. And the way of peace have they not known:
18. There is no fear of God before their eyes.

The first three verses are taken from Isaiah lix. 7, 8—an address to the chosen people charging home their sins. This quotation thus corresponds to the latter part of chapter ii., which brings home the guilt of sin to the Jew. Verse 18, taken from Psalm xxxvi. 1, applies to the wicked man as such, describing his wickedness as essentially lying in the throwing off of all sense of moral responsibility, and fitting well with Paul's argument, the main aim of which is to assert the universality of man's responsibility, and to prove the guilt of those who, in word or deed, presume upon exemption from such responsibility.

19. **Now we know that what things soever the law saith, it speaketh to them that are under the law;**] This introduces the application of the quotations to the purpose of his argument. We have therefore the advantage of the author's direct statement on that point. He begins by appealing to their "common sense" (Godet): "We know" that these words, being found in the written law (scriptures) of the chosen people, were all uttered for their benefit, *i.e.*, to place before them the sin of such things, with the direct intent of holding them, as well as the Gentile world, responsible in the event of committing such things. Paul, however, draws not this specific conclusion but the universal one—

that every mouth may be stopped, and all the world may be brought under the judgment of God:] This universal conclusion Paul was entitled to draw from the fact that his quotations described the sins of Jews as well as Gentiles, and also from the fact that his Jewish opponent would at once admit that if he, a Jew, could not foreshield himself the Gentile certainly could not. As Bengel and Morison say, "it is the Jews chiefly who are referred to." The condemnation of the Gentiles he takes for granted, and thus the particular conclusion is made universal. This universal enforcing of responsibility against Jew as well as Gentile Paul represents as the divine intention in the teachings or utterances of the law. This is in harmony with Paul's fundamental doctrine of the great purpose served by the law in God's economy of salvation. "Through the law cometh the knowledge of sin (v. 20). (Compare chs. iv. 15; vii. 5, etc.; Gal. iii. 19-24.) There can therefore be no valid objection to the idea of design in the conjunction here used—"That every mouth may be stopped," *i.e.*, be silent before the judge through consciousness of guilt, and so "all the world," Jew as well as Gentile, "may be brought under the judgment of God." The word here used expresses the state of the criminal who has been found guilty and awaits sentence for his crime. In these two sentences, by a very striking metaphor, Paul presents to us the most profound consciousness of guilt as being the intent of the law. This consciousness of guilt he applies both individually, "every mouth," and universally, "all the world." This is the final conclusion of the argument by which he had applied the principles of moral responsibility, first to the Gentile and then to the Jewish world, and so swept away all false coverts behind which men foreshielded themselves from the convictions of their own conscience. The full force of Paul's argument will not be apparent to any one who loses sight of the postulates which conscience is constantly supposed to supply to the minds of his hearers. But to the destruction of the false covert Paul once more refers in a way that opens up to view the next great theme of his discourse.

20. **because by the works of the law shall no flesh be justified in his sight:**] "Because" may refer to the divine intention, "It speaketh . . . in order that," or to "we know." Either makes excellent sense. We know that God's intention in giving these moral precepts of written law was to produce universal deep conviction of sin, "because" the other alternative, justification by works of law, is an impossibility. This would be the second line of thought. The first, however, we consider preferable, as follows: The law saith these things for the purpose of producing universal deep conviction of sin, because justification by works of law is impossible to man, and the foundation must be laid in the conscious knowledge of sin for a new method of justification. This line of thought leads out more perfectly to Paul's next point. The reason thus assigned for the divine intent of the law in God's economy is announced in one of Paul's grandest postulates, a postulate which he proves only by appeal to universal experience and conscience. The postulate is, "By works of law shall no flesh be justified in his sight." The law immediately in the apostle's mind is without doubt the Mosaic law (Old Testament), from which he had just quoted. But he puts the principle in the broadest form, avoiding all specifying articles, and announces a principle equally applicable to any form of moral law apart from grace. If there had been any other form of law by which righteousness were possible to man it doubtless would have been given. On this fundamental position of St. Paul see verse 28; chapters iv. 2, 4, 6; ix. 11; x. 4, etc.; xi. 6, etc.; and especially Gal. ii. 16.

for through the law cometh the knowledge of sin.] This is the proof which Paul offers to his great fundamental postulate, an appeal to the conscious experience of his hearers. He made a similar appeal to Peter (Gal. ii. 16). The force of this appeal Peter had publicly acknowledged (Acts xv. 10, 11). How deep was Paul's own experience of this consciousness of the effects of law we see in chapter vii. 5, 7, etc. The universally experienced result of revealed law is conscious guilt, "the knowledge of sin."

CH. III. 21-31. GOD'S RIGHTEOUSNESS.

21. **But now apart from the law**] Paul sometimes emphasizes the failure of law to bring forth righteousness (ch. viii. 3), so here

this clause occupies the emphatic place. It corresponds to, and is the opposite of, "out of works of law." It should be noted that it is not "a righteousness apart from law." The Greek text will not permit such a grammatical construction, and the idea would be too antinomian for St. Paul. This righteousness does not make void but establishes the law. It fulfils in us the righteousness of the law (ch. viii. 4).

a righteousness of God hath been manifested,] We have already (ch. i. 17) defined this term "righteousness of God." There is, however, a difference between that passage, to which we are in thought carried back, and the present. There the righteousness of God is said to be revealed in the gospel, referring to the opening up of a new dispensation of God's dealing with man. Here it is said to be "made manifest apart from works of law," pointing to the exhibition of this righteousness to the individual conscience. On the distinction between these two terms see Cremer's Lexicon. The one is the opening up, by divine outward acts or providence, of some new phase or fact of God's great plan of grace. The other is the placing of such revealed fact before man's mind as an object of his conscious apprehension. This divine righteousness can be manifested to us only by personal possession or experience, which manifestation takes place apart from works of the law, and yet

being witnessed by the law and the prophets;] The law attests this righteousness by awakening a consciousness of our need of it; the prophets, by the hopes which are inspired by the promises. But this twofold subjective attestation projects itself far into the past. Men have ever felt the pressure of this moral want, and have longed for this hope. And in both law and prophets God had met these necessities of man by the service of "shadows of the good things to come," as well as by prophetic predictions. Hence the attestation is objective as well as subjective. The unity of Paul with Peter and with Christ in this regard appears from Acts xxviii. 23; x. 43; and Luke xxiv. 27, etc.

22. even the righteousness of God through faith in Jesus Christ] An explanatory addition by means of the conjunction here rendered "even," and occasionally used in Greek for this purpose. The definition is, "through faith in Jesus Christ," or literally, "of Jesus Christ," (see margin). For the definition of the term "faith" and its use with the genitive of the object see chapter i. 17.

unto all them that believe;] The margin reads, "unto all and upon all them that believe." This is a case of conflict between the four oldest MSS. and four versions who read as in the revised text and the great majority of MSS., versions and fathers. The revisers, following the rule of preferring the oldest MSS., have placed the added words in the margin. They were, however, in the text of Theodoret, in the fifth century, when he makes special comment on them, and in the Syriac version, which dates back to the second century. They are therefore retained by many of our best critics and commentators. If retained, then, with Meyer, we must construe the first "unto all" absolutely as expressing the intent or purpose of God in manifesting his righteousness. It is "for all." The second adjunct, "upon all that believe," represents the actual result of God's manifestation. "Upon all who believe" it actually rests. "To all who believe" it is applied. (See Morison for a full elucidation of this view. It is worthy of note that in the Greek "who believe" is expressed by the present participle, denoting not a momentary act but an abiding activity. The faith by which this righteousness is enjoyed is not a momentary act once for all. It is a confidence held fast to the end.

NOTE.—If "unto all them that believe" is the true reading of this passage it becomes almost a repetition of chapter i. 17. "Out of faith" or "by faith" there corresponds to "through faith" here, and "unto faith" there corresponding to "unto all them that believe" here. It is in its very nature a "righteousness," or "conscious state of rightness with God," arising out of faith, and granted "to faith" or "unto all them that believe." This analogy of the two passages would favour the shorter reading.

for there is no distinction;] *i.e.*, between Jew and Greek. (Compare Acts xv. 9 and 11.) This emphasizes the word "all" in the preceding clause.

23. for all have sinned,] The reason for this abolition of moral distinction. God treats all alike in the bestowal because all stand on the same level as to moral desert—"all have sinned." Paul here for the first time puts in this direct form this corollary of his entire argument from chapter i. 18 to chapter iii. 20. He states it here as an undeniable fact, given upon the testimony of conscience, as cleared of confused notions by the preceding argument. We shall find him returning to the elucidation of this great fact again in chapter v. The universal fact is here expressed by the Greek aorist, rendered by our perfect.

and fall short of the glory of God;] The popular apprehension of the meaning of this expression is doubtless correct; but to learned men it gives some difficulty. Perhaps the simplest explanation is that which presents man's probational life as a race, the successful end of which yields to God a tribute of glory, and is rewarded by a crown of glory. Paul at Corinth was familiar with the racers who brought glory to their native city, and were rewarded by their crown of glory in return. (See 1 Cor. ix. 24, etc.) The righteousness which glorifies God and is glorified by him men, in their moral probation, fall short of.

24. being justified freely by his grace] The present participle in Greek has here a peculiar significance. It may be represented in English thus: "Being justified when they are justified," or, as Alford renders, "needing to be justified." Beza translates, "being such as are justified freely," etc. (See Winer, xlv. 6, *b.*) We must remember that the subject of discourse is carried through by direct grammatical as well as logical connection from verse 22, "upon" or "unto all them that believe," among which "all" there is no difference, for *they* "all" have sinned, "being all (as believers) justified *freely*," etc. The emphasis thus falls on the adjuncts "freely" and "by his grace," etc. We meet the verb "to justify" here for the first time in the evangelical sense. In verse 20 it was used in the legal sense. Its primary meaning is to make righteous or just. It is also found in the forensic sense of acquitting of accusation or pronouncing righteous, and very frequently in the general sense of proving or establishing one's righteousness. This is generally supposed to be the basis of the evangelical use of the term. This would be, however, to empty the term of all the positive elements of its significance. Forensic justification is purely negative. It removes the charge of crime. The righteousness of which Paul speaks is positive. It meets and satisfies to the full the equitable demands in conscience of our moral responsibility toward God. It is a moral state or relation in which a man stands *consciously* right before God in respect to the claims of moral probation or responsibility. A babe would be forensically just, *i.e.*, free from any imputation of crime. But he could not be said to be righteous in this positive sense of being consciously right in respect to his moral responsibility. This positive righteousness can only be attained in one of two ways: by a perfect fulfilment of all moral obligation as it arises, in which case a man is justified, attains to righteousness, by works; or by God's gracious gift of righteousness in Christ. To be justified, then, is to attain, either by works or by grace, that conscious relation to God which satisfies all claims of moral responsibility. It is to be remarked that the verb is used in this sense only in the passive voice when applied to justification by works. God is not said to justify by works except in the final judgment, where the sense is very different and more properly forensic. But when applied to evangelical justification it is used in both active and passive form, the active voice signifying the bestowal of this state as a gracious gift of God. So far as there is any forensic element in this evangelical use of the verb "to justify" it is purely subjective. The bar of judgment is the conscience (see note on ch. ii. 15, 16), and there the justification is pronounced. This justification is more fully defined and distinguished from legal justification by three adjuncts: (*a*) "freely," *i.e.*, as a matter of gift, as opposed to legal justification claimed or attained as a matter of right or merit; (*b*) "by his grace," *i.e.*, the compassionate love of God which bestows this gift, and which provided the means for its bestowal in the work of Christ; and (*c*),

through the redemption that is in Christ Jesus:] This verse defines the relation of our justification to the work of Christ which Paul next proceeds to set before us. We must therefore study every term used with the most exact care. The preposition here used governing the genitive case signifies the medium or channel through which one acts, something that comes in between the actor and the acted upon as essential to the act, without which the act could not be. It differs thus from the same preposition governing the accusative, "on account of," "for the sake of," which represents an accessory motive to act rather than the channel or medium through which the act is performed. This same preposition governing the genitive is also applied to faith, which is thus likewise made the medium or channel of justification. The work of Christ is the channel from the Godward side, faith from our side. The work of Christ is, so to speak, the hand in which God extends his gift; faith is the hand which we reach forth to receive. When the two hands meet the communication between God and man is complete. The work of Christ which is the medium of justification is called a "redemption." This term may be applied to Christ's work either in reference to its results, deliverance from a bondage or captivity, or in reference to the manner of reaching the result, the payment of a ransom price. In the former sense it sometimes refers, as here, to the moral deliverance from sin as a bondage of guilt and depravity bestowed on man through Christ in the present life (1 Cor. i. 30; Eph. i. 7; Col. i. 14; Titus ii. 14). It is also used of the final deliverance at the resurrection (ch. viii. 23; Eph. i. 14; iv. 30). In all these passages the emphasis would seem to be on the deliverance from the state of captivity or slavery. But that alongside of this there is reference to the method of deliverance, the payment of a ransom price, appears from 1 Tim. ii. 6, and from the use of another similar form of expression in Gal. iii. 13. There seems also a clear reference to the ransom price in Eph. i. 7. A comparison of this passage with our text would suggest the view that here the nature of the ransom price is set forth in verse 25, "a propitiation, through faith, by his blood." As we thus seem justified in taking Paul to use the term "redemption" here in its full import of deliverance from a state of bondage, obtained by payment of a ransom price, it may be useful to distinguish this from our modern commercial idea of payment of a debt too often substituted for it.

1. Payment of a debt is fixed as to amount by the nature of the obligation. The ransom price is fixed by the captor.
2. Payment of a debt cannot be legally refused. Acceptance of a ransom is optional.
3. Payment of a debt grants unconditional discharge. A ransom price may be accompanied by conditions, according to the will of the captor.
4. There is no grace in the release of a debtor when his debt is paid. There may be the richest grace in granting release to a captive upon generous and righteous terms of redemption.

If in our exposition we look at the ransom price we shall retain the full force of the preposition "in" Christ Jesus; Christ was himself the "ransom price" (1 Tim. ii. 6). If we look rather at the deliverance then the preposition takes the force of "by," a usage not uncommon in Greek.

25. whom God set forth to be a propitiation,] If in the preceding verse the apostle refers to Christ as a ransom price then this verse sets forth the valency or value of that ransom price. If we confine ourselves to the idea of deliverance then that deliverance comes through Christ as our propitiation. We are thus from any point of view introduced to the very heart of the great doctrine of the atonement as an essential part of Paul's doctrinal system. The first term here to be considered is the verb. The corresponding noun is everywhere used by Paul of God's purpose or plan for the redemption of the world in Christ (chs. viii. 28; ix. 11; Eph. i. 11; iii. 11; 2 Tim. i. 9; iii. 10). The verb occurs in but three passages of St. Paul, viz.: chapter i. 13, of Paul's purpose to visit Rome; Eph. i. 9, of God's purpose or plan of redemption; and the text. The Pauline usage is thus without exception in favour of the marginal rendering instead of the text; so Godet, "established beforehand." The other sense, adopted in the text of the revisers, and by Meyer, Morison, etc., is "to set forth openly" or "publicly." This is sanctioned by various passages in the New Testament outside of the Pauline Epistles, and by perhaps the predominance of classical usage. We, on the whole, prefer the first sense, for the following reasons: It is the otherwise uniform sense of the word in Paul's writings. It represents a conception of Christ's work as an eternal purpose of God familiar to Paul; this we cannot say of the idea of the crucifixion as a public exhibition of propitiation. It is in harmony with Paul's thought as viewing the virtue of Christ's work as pertaining not to the present or future alone, but as projected back into the past (v. 26). This naturally leads him to speak of God's purpose of propitiation through the blood of Christ as antedating the entire application of that propitiation in the divine mercy to men in the past. The word "purpose" is, however, scarcely strong enough to express the full thought, which is "something fixed, set down, determined beforehand." It is an act, or series of acts, fully settled upon. It is usual for Paul thus to speak of the work of Christ. (See especially Eph. i. and Col. i.) The aorist is not against this, as the same tense is used (Eph. i. 9) where there is no room for doubt as to the meaning. The aorist expresses that which is always fact as well as individual historical facts. God's purpose was that Christ should be a "propitiation." The word in Greek is an adjective, and expresses that which serves for "propitiation." It may refer (1) to the mercy-seat where propitiation was made (Heb. ix. 3); or (2) to the sacrifice by which propitiation was made; or (3) be taken as an abstract noun, a means of propitiation, or as a predicate adjective referring to "whom." The difference in result between these various constructions, each of which has its advocates, is very slight. In any case the word cannot be severed from its reference to the sacrifice of the great day of atonement, which was said to "make propitiation for . . . all the congregation of Israel," a reference further manifest in the phrase "in his blood." We have therefore to deal with the meaning of the word "propitiate," or "propitiation." The mere etymological discussion of this term in its Hebrew, Greek or Latin form gives us very uncertain results. But the usage leaves no doubt that the word expresses that in sacrificial offering which moves God to forgiveness. That we should understand *wherein* that power consists is not practically necessary. The word simply asserts *a power in the sacrificial offering to move God to forgiveness*. Such a power no Jew would be disposed to deny. Their faith here was implicit. The sacrifices appointed by God must possess power to secure forgiveness. Paul, therefore, in dealing with his Jewish opponent, has no need either to prove or explain the valency of atoning sacrifice. He simply asserts that Christ is the primally appointed propitiatory sacrifice or propitiation, thus transferring to Christ the confidence which the Jew unhesitatingly placed in the valency of expiatory sacrifice appointed by God. The simple fact of such valency is here asserted. The nature of the valency we prefer to consider when Paul himself hereafter touches the question. We shall find more light there than can possibly be gained from the study of the nature and power of Jewish sacrifices or the etymology of sacrificial terms here.

through faith, by his blood,] Christ is a propitiation, or propitiatory, only through faith. Here we have the same preposition which in verse 24 was applied to Christ's redemptive work. God's gift of righteousness comes to us only through the channel of the redemptive work of Christ, who is by divine appointment propitiatory, *i.e.*, invested with power to secure the forgiveness of sins. But this propitiatory efficacy reaches its object only through the human channel of faith. Faith and Christ's redemptive work are not thus co-ordinate channels of God's grace. But God's grace flows to us through Christ: we reach to Christ, and so receive that grace, "through faith." The adjunct "by his blood" is by most of the older commentators joined to faith and rendered literally "through faith in his blood." This makes the blood, *i.e.*, the life given as an expiatory sacrifice, the direct object of justifying faith. It should, however, be remembered that this is the only passage in the New Testament in which the term "faith," either as noun or verb, is found with such an adjunct. The usual form is an adjunct of the *personal object*, believe in, on or upon, or faith of, in or towards, "*God*," or more frequently "*Christ*." This has led the revisers to separate the adjunct "by" or "in his blood" from faith and refer it directly to the preceding term, "propitiation." We have thus two adjuncts of propitiation, "through faith" and "in his blood." The first designates the subjective means by which the propitiation is applied, the other the objective means by which the propitiatory power exists, *i.e.*, the shedding of his blood, or giving his life an expiatory sacrifice. So Godet. Or else we have, with Meyer and Riddle, the adjunct "in his blood" joined with "set forth," *i.e.*, God publicly set forth in the shedding of his blood Christ as a propitiatory sacrifice. This last construction seems, however, extremely artificial; and even Godet's, which is better, seems to make it unaccountable that the phrase "in his blood" should not be joined directly with "propitiation." We are therefore disposed to retain the old connection, "through faith in his blood," *i.e.*, in his expiatory offering of his life. (Compare ch. v. 9; Eph. i. 7; and Col. i. 20, for Paul's use of the expression "his blood.") The fact that saving faith is thus limited but this once should put us on our guard against fixing faith on *theories* of atonement. Paul never goes beyond the point of attaching faith to the propitiatory efficacy of Christ's blood. If an apprehension of an absolutely correct theory of that efficacy were needful, who could be saved? Faith in a personal Saviour saves.

to shew his righteousness,] the object or design of God in his foreappointment of Christ as a propitiation, expressed by the preposition commonly used by Paul to express aim, purpose or intention. But what is the meaning of the noun "shewing"? and of the phrase "his righteousness"? The term "his righteousness" is the expression elsewhere used by Paul of that gift of righteousness which God bestows upon man. The word translated "shew" signifies a "setting forth in open light," a "pointing out," an "exhibiting." This would be parallel with the "manifestation" of verse 21, and with the "revelation" of chapter i. 17. The meaning would thus be: God thus foreappointed Christ a propitiation for the purpose of revealing, or bringing forth to view, his gift of righteousness. This interpretation, which we think the right one, is as old as Chrysostom, and is supported by many able names. The alternative interpretation is given in Godet's translation, "for the demonstration of his justice." To this the objection lies that it requires us to take one if not both words in a forced meaning. Certainly Paul does not ordinarily use the word translated "righteousness" in this sense, and we may fairly question whether it is ever so used. The word translated "demonstration" can only bear that meaning as a proof by example, an exhibition in act. However well this might harmonize with one theory of the atonement we fail to find it in this form in Paul's writings, and cannot thrust it in here in the face of his common use of the words employed. The first interpretation gives us a plain sense in harmony with Paul's use of the words and with his line of thought.

because of the passing over of the sins done aforetime,] This clause we take to be an adjunct of the verb "set forth," or as we should render it, "foreappointed." The preposition here used designates the *occasion*, the circumstantial cause, of an act, that which renders it necessary. The cause or occasion which made necessary the *fore*appointment of Christ a propitiation, for the purpose of bringing forth to view a divine righteousness, was "the passing over of the sins done aforetime." The fixed "purpose" of a propitiation must exist from the time sin existed, otherwise there could be no forgiveness, or as Paul here calls it, passing over of sins that were done aforetime, *i.e.*, prior to Christ's coming. The word "pretermission"—passing over—a term less strong than "remission," which

Paul elsewhere applies to the Christian justification (Eph. i. 7), is used to distinguish the old time exhibition of God's mercy from the full exhibition of God's "righteousness" now bestowed upon the world. Yet that old time "passing over" was based upon God's fixed purpose of the propitiation which was designed to bring to view the perfect righteousness.

in the forbearance of God;] God's grace to men while he is awaiting the full accomplishment of his purpose of propitiation is called forbearance.

26. for the shewing, I say, of his righteousness at this present season:] The apostle here repeats the design of God's foreappointment. But he does so with a change of preposition which expresses that design as no longer *a mere design or intention* but *an accomplished result*. This change of preposition is lost in our English versions. We have therefore not a mere repetition but an advance of the thought which may be paraphrased thus: "Looking to the exhibition of the divine gift of righteousness, because of the passing over, etc., and *now resulting in* the exhibition of his righteousness." The phrase "in this present season" is parallel with Paul's "fulness of time" (Gal. iv. 4) and with his "now" in verse 21.

that he might himself be just, and the justifier of him that hath faith in Jesus.] We have here the Greek preposition expressing intention followed by an infinitive clause with subject accusative. The whole sentence thus becomes an adjunct expressing intent, aim or purpose. To what does this adjunct belong? Not to "set forth," for the purpose of that had been already expressed by the very same preposition, and repeated as a present accomplished result. We cannot suppose it to be here repeated as a future puprose for the third time. We must therefore, with Godet, attach it to the clause immediately preceding. But if so then clearly his interpretation of the meaning of that clause is, as we have already seen on other grounds, astray. How could a "demonstration of the justice of God" be made in order "that God might *be* just"? We therefore take the connection to be as follows: God sets forth his gift of righteousness to men (a gift founded on the propitiation, etc.) that thus he himself may be just, *i.e.*, continue to be a just God while he is the justifier, etc. This is what we consider to be Paul's method of stating the truth which our expositors have been searching for in the preceding phrases. We must therefore carefully analyze his statement and endeavour to find its exact bearing on the nature of the atonement.

We note at once that it says nothing about the demonstration, or public vindication of the divine justice. It does not conceive that justice to have been under a cloud during all the ages before Christ. It touches the *reality*, not the mere appearance, of the divine justice. God sees to it that he *is* just, and leaves appearances to care for themselves. And in Paul's view he provides for the maintenance of his justice side by side with justifying grace, not by making a public spectacle, or exhibition, or proof, of justice, but by setting before men a way of attaining to righteousness founded on Christ's propitiation, in which way (of faith) he can be just and yet the dispenser of pardon. The real doctrine of Paul, then, is, that the atonement really maintains (not merely exhibits or proves) the justice, or rather rectitude, of God. The word here used is much wider than the idea of mere penal justice. It affirms the perfect *rectitude* of God in relation to all that bears on man's probation, *i.e.*, in his entire dealings with man.

It would almost seem that in this magnificent exposition of "the righteousness of God" Paul had lost sight of his opponents. Such, however, is not the case. If our view of his meaning is correct, then every point from verse 21 to verse 26 has been skilfully constructed with a view to commend or defend his doctrine in the presence of the rival gospel.

The law as a means of righteousness had failed, hence God brings to light "his righteousness apart from law," yet not in opposition to but in harmony with "the law and the prophets." This righteousness of God through faith in Jesus Christ, "unto all them that believe," does away with all the assumed distinctions. The Gentiles are not the only sinners, for "all have sinned." The Jews cannot claim the glory as theirs alone (see ch ix. 4), for all have fallen short of it. Thus righteousness is no longer a matter of merit, or of covenant right, but the free gift of God's grace, bestowed not through the covenant of redemption from Egypt (Heb. viii. 9) but through the new covenant of redemption that is in Christ Jesus, whom God, not now but from the beginning of the world, purposed and promised (Titus i. 3; see also 1 Peter i. 20) as the true propitiation through faith in his blood—not the blood of bulls and goats—looking to this bringing to light of the true righteousness all the while that he was passing over the sins committed under the legal dispensation (see Gal. iii. 23, 24), and now bringing forth to light this righteousness (Eph. iii. 4-7), that God may justify all that believe on Jesus and yet be true to all moral right as he could not be true under any arbitrary and exclusive dispensation of his mercy such as the Jews claimed, which claim God's justice sweeps away (ch. ii. 25-29). Well may Paul, having brought his opponent to this point by the contrasted exhibition of the true righteousness, exclaim,

27. **Where then is the glorying?**] *i.e.*, the national boasted claim of the Jews to exclusive privilege; and reply,

It is excluded.] as by a door closed and barred.

By what manner of law?] Not "by which law?" but as in the revised version. Law may here be taken as the rule or test of probation by which righteousness is attained.

of works? Nay: but by a law of faith.] The Greek reads, "of the works," pointing to those works upon which the Jew relied for the attainment of his covenant privileges, *e.g.*, circumcision. "Law of faith," on the other hand, is without the article, as presenting something which has not been previously spoken of as a law or rule by which a man may be judged "righteous."

28. We reckon therefore that a man is justified by faith apart from the works of the law.] Instead of the conjunction "therefore," which makes this verse the formal conclusion of an argument, Tischendorf and Westcott and Hort read, with ℵ, A, D, etc., "for," as in the margin. The critical authorities are about equally divided. The commentators therefore largely prefer the reading which maintains the continuity of the argument. The reading "for" does so perfectly. Justification is the goal of moral probation. "Law" is the rule by which the issues of probation are determined. This mention of faith as a rule or law of probation is explained by the restatement of the great truth now *settled in mind* ("we reckon"), "that a man is justified by faith apart from the works of the law."

29. Or is God the God of Jews only?] The revised version rightly translates the Greek particle as a conjunction. If it were an interrogative it would require the affirmative answer. But if a disjunctive where is the other term, the alternative? We think, with Morison, it is to be found in the next interrogative. If Paul had carried through his construction as he begins he would have read, "Whether is God the God of Jews only? or of Gentiles also?" But before he arrives at the alternative the strength of his convictions leads him to take up a new form of interrogative implying in the strongest possible way the affirmative answer, which he immediately subjoins. This question, as well as the preceding, shows how completely Paul has all through kept his opponents in mind.

is he not the God of Gentiles also?] This negative form of question in Greek, as in English, implies an affirmative answer, and is thus a very strong rhetorical assertion. The answer to the logical alternative with which Paul opened the verse is thus anticipated, and the second member of the disjunctive alternative converted into this direct rhetorical interrogation followed by words of direct assertion.

Yea, of Gentiles also:] or, as we might render it, "surely" or "verily" "of the Gentiles also."

30. if so be that God is one, and he shall justify the circumcision by faith, and the uncircumcision through faith.] Of the two readings of the first word of this verse both make excellent sense, and each is supported by high critical authority. The only difference is in logical form as between the direct and the conditional syllogism. No truth was more fundamental in Judaism than this, "God is one." To say "Yea, of the Gentiles also, if God is truly one," was to signify the utter absurdity of any other position. To say "Yea, of the Gentiles also, since God is one," was to bring to the proof of his thesis the most indubitable of all truths. The relative clause which closes the verse is well rendered in the revised version, "and he shall," etc. This is not, however, to be taken as an additional reason, depending on the initial conjunction, but as an *ndependent proposition*, announcing *the final conclusion of the entire argument*. This explains the use of the future indicative. It states the economy of God's grace for all time to come. "He will (not shall) justify," etc. (On this use of the relative see Winer, Pt. III. lx. 7, *a, a.*)

The distinction between the two prepositions here used seems to be this: The circumcision under covenant of law will, "out of faith" as a root of obedience, find the principle which fulfils law (Rom. viii. 4), and so justifies. The uncircumcision, outside of law, will find in faith the means through which they will reach justification outside of law. Such is Paul's grand conclusion of the exposition of his universal gospel. He now turns to answer one principal Jewish objection.

CH. III. 31–IV. 25. HARMONY OF THE RIGHTEOUSNESS OF FAITH WITH THE DISPENSATION OF THE LAW.

31. Do we then make the law of none effect through faith? God forbid: nay, we establish the law.] In this passage the term "law" is used in the Greek without the article. It has accordingly been taken as signifying moral law in general, and regarded as an anticipation of the antinomian objection considered in chapter vi. The connection of thought, however, forbids this. The law which has been rejected as a means of attaining righteousness is the Old Testament dispensation, beginning from Abraham in the covenant of circumcision, but fully introduced by Moses. We must therefore so understand it here. The question will then represent an objected inference from the preceding argument. "Does not this represent the whole Old Testament dispensation as of no account, valueless?" Paul answers, "Nay, we establish the law." The real force of the question lies in the meaning of the two verbs, "make of none effect" and "establish." The question is not one of the *repeal*, or cessation, of the Old Testament dispensation, but of its *success* in the accomplishment of its intended result. This success is not hindered but *promoted* by the faith. This he now proceeds to prove.

1. What then shall we say that Abraham, our forefather according to the flesh, hath found?] Of this difficult verse we accept the revisers' text as on the whole the best attested. Two general constructions are possible: (1) To make it a new and independent objection co-ordinate with verse 31. This construction gives us no link by which the objection raised in verse 31 and that supposed to be presented in verse 1 are connected. We shall also find that it presents insuperable difficulty as to the connection of the following verses. We therefore prefer (2) To make this verse depend immediately on the preceding one. The logical formula here used introduces an argument in the form of an objection, disproving something either directly stated or implied, and to which the word "then" directly points. What this is is the difficulty. It is generally supposed to be Paul's general line of reasoning by which he has overthrown the Jewish claim to special prerogative. This makes verse 1 voice the objection of Paul's opponent. But this again gives us no link of thought by which we can pass from verse 31 to verse 1. We should find the point of our logical "then" in the clause "we establish the law." But this gives no valid ground for the objection supposed to be raised in verse 1. The only alternative is to make verse 1 voice Paul's own thought—a refutation of the position implied in the question of verse 31. The objector says, "You then make the law of none effect through faith." Paul replies, first directly, "God forbid," etc.; then logically, If we do, "What then shall we say that Abraham, our forefather according to the flesh, hath found?" We shall see presently how perfectly this connection harmonizes both with the sense of verse 31, as we have taken it, and also with the true meaning of verse 1. The question itself may be interpreted in two ways. The great body of expositors connect it immediately with what follows, and refer it to Abraham's personal attainment of righteousness, *i.e.*, to a fact occurring during Abraham's life. We think neither the grammatical structure nor the peculiar verb employed warrant this. The verb is in the perfect tense, pointing to something *reaching down to the present*, and not in the aorist, as would be required for the statement of a fact occurring during Abraham's life. Then the verb "to find" strikes us as incongruous with the idea of justification, which is never spoken of by Paul as something lighted on by chance, or even by good providence. We have therefore to look for something reaching down to the present, and something which came to Abraham in the providence of God as his great good fortune. And this we have exactly supplied in the heritage which God promised to him. This high, pre-eminent gift of God to Abraham was that "in him should all nations be blessed." Paul's question, unanswerable by his antagonist, is this, "What becomes of Abraham's heritage?" What heritage of blessing for all nations has he ever found, unless the new dispensation of righteousness by faith "establishes" or "fulfils" those promises of the old? The subject thus introduced, a favourite one with Paul, occupies the remainder of this chapter. The answer to the question of verse 1 is practically found in verse 13, etc.; and a very instructive parallel to the whole line of thought is found in Gal. iii. 7, etc. The argument of these two introductory verses, then, runs as follows: "Is the whole aim and hope of the ancient dispensation disappointed and cast aside by the introduction of this new dispensation of faith? God forbid. It is only in this way carried into effect; for in no other way can we say that Abraham has ever obtained the heritage of blessing which God promised him in the original covenant.

2. For if Abraham were justified by works, he hath whereof to glory;] We take the conjunction here as introductory. The two preceding verses are closely compacted together as the statement of the new thesis *that the dispensation of faith alone carries out* *the old dispensation of the law.* They end in a rhetorical question equivalent to a strong assertion. It is to this assertion that the proof now following attaches itself. "Abraham has found the fulfilment of his promised heritage only through faith," "for" from the very beginning Abraham's relation to God was based upon faith. This point, however, Paul approaches very skilfully, first conceding to his opponents their claim so far as it exists—"If Abraham were justified by works." The "if" is merely concessive, but does not imply a negative which would require a stronger particle. We may express the meaning thus: "In so far as Abraham may have been justified by works." The force of the subjunctive is thus given. Paul does not grant that he was so justified, nor does he deny it. He supposes it possible, and grants the conclusion, "he has a ground of boasting;" but immediately proceeds to show that such conclusion is limited by the declaration of scripture. His personal justification is here referred to as the first-fruits of Abraham's blessing for all nations, as in Paul's view that blessing is the gift of righteousness to all through faith.

but not toward God.

3. For what saith the scripture?] The preposition here used is the one used John i. 1, "with God." It expresses immediate or direct contact or relationship. Abraham's ground or subject of boasting does not reach up to God. It may exist as compared with man, but his final relationship to God stands on a different basis, the scripture being witness.

And Abraham believed God, and it was reckoned unto him for righteousness.] This passage (Gen. xv. 6) was probably a familiar quotation among the Rabbis of the time. (See Lightfoot on Gal. iii. 8.) The passage becomes thus one of very great importance as the proof-text upon which Paul grounds his doctrine of "righteousness by faith." We note (1) That Paul here, like the writer in Heb. xi., presents the general principle of faith as securing justification before God. (2) That this faith (not the righteousness of Christ; see verse 5) is "accounted for righteousness." The word "accounted," says Cremer, signifies "to reckon anything to a person, to put to his account, either in his favour or as what he must be answerable for." The preposition "for" does not signify "in the place of" or "a substitute," but "unto," that to which faith *leads*, as God graciously "puts it to our account." The "righteousness" is not, however, "holiness," "a right course of action," or of life, but "a right *relation* to God" in reference to probational responsibility, and hence directly apprehended in conscience. This is Paul's universal use of the word. The idea then is, that God so graciously accepts faith as to place us in right relation to himself. In these passages note that this important word "count," or "reckon," is used first indefinitely, then of faith, then of any reward of moral conduct, then of righteousness as one form of such reward, and finally of sin. In every one of these cases it refers to the settling, or reckoning, or decision of the account of man's probational responsibility; and only that is so reckoned which *belongs to man's probation.* "Faith" is so reckoned as the gracious condition of probation. "Righteousness," or the right state of our probational account, is so reckoned. The "reward," or merit in probation, of good works is so reckoned. "Sin," as ill desert in probation, is so reckoned. Beyond this application of the term Paul gives us no right to go. The *ground* or *basis* upon which God makes faith the condition of our gracious probation, and so accounts us righteous, lies outside of our "*personal probation,*" and so does not come into this "reckoning."

This great principle of gracious probation through faith, or evangelical righteousness, Paul now proceeds to further illustrate by contrasting it in general with righteousness of works.

4. **Now to him that worketh, the reward is not reckoned as of grace, but as of debt.**] This is not so much an analogy from a hired labourer as a general statement of the principle of equity which governs all probation. Man's sense of right teaches him that responsibility for duties discharged earns the right to the reward of those duties. Paul is not afraid to recognize probational *rights* as well as obligations.

5. **But to him that worketh not,**] *i.e.,* has failed to fulfil the obligations or duties of his probation. This is not an innuendo against good works. It does not imply that there is anything commendable in this "not working."

but believeth on him that justifieth the ungodly,] His not working, so far from being meritorious, has classed him with the "ungodly." His probation of works ends in failure. But the gracious probation of faith is still open. He can still believe on him that "justifieth," *i.e.,* giveth or accounteth righteousness to even the ungodly, and

his faith is reckoned for righteousness.] (See note on verse 3.) Through God's grace the probation is fulfilled by faith. And lest the application of this New Testament probation to the old dispensation should seem strange Paul summons further witness.

6. **Even as David also**] "Even as" introduces an example of the general principle just stated, from Psalm xxxii. 1, 2.

pronounceth blessing upon the man,] Literally, congratulates, pronounces happy.

unto whom God reckoneth righteousness apart from works,] As the term "righteousness" is here not the Greek signifying the acts or works which fulfil law, as in Rom. v. 18, but the word expressing the right relation to God in respect to our probation, Riddle is not justified in identifying the word used here with that used in chapter v. 18, and referring both to Christ's righteousness. While that is the basis of God's gracious act it is never in scripture said to be imputed to us. On the contrary, all objective works of righteousness are just here out of view. *The only objective works that could be put to account are our own,* and these are wanting. But God rights the account without them, not by bringing in some other works, but by forgiveness, cancelling the contra account of sin. On this balancing of man's probational accounts see McCaul (quoted in Moule's Appendix), where it is shown to be a favourite form of Jewish moral teaching.

saying,
7. **Blessed are they whose iniquities are forgiven,
And whose sins are covered.**
8. **Blessed is the man to whom the Lord will not reckon sin.**
This peculiar view of God's account with man on probation thus extends back to the time of the Septuagint version. The three synonymous terms here used are worthy of note, as they appear in the original Hebrew—"borne away," referring to the great atonement; "covered," put out of sight; and "put out of God's thoughts." The affirmative of which this last is the negative is used in Gen. xv. 6, "God thought it to him" (or "esteemed it to him") "for righteousness." This Hebrew word was by the LXX. translated by the Greek which we render "reckon" or "impute," though impute is rather a translation of the original Hebrew. It is only in the LXX. that this idea of a written account of the merits and demerits of man's probation first appears.

9. **Is this blessing then pronounced upon the circumcision, or upon the uncircumcision also?**] Paul by the conjunction "then" returns to the points at which he left his main argument in verse 3. He had there asserted that Abraham's "boasting," *i.e.*, ground of confidence as based on works (*i.e.*, covenant of circumcision), did not reach up to his ultimate relation to God. This he had proven by a passage of scripture in which Abraham's justification or righteousness was referred to faith; and he had pointed out the fundamental difference between this and a righteousness of works, illustrating it by a further conspicuous Old Testament example. He now proceeds to prove that this righteousness of faith on Abraham's part was *by faith only*. We will find the force of Paul's argument as against his opponents by bearing in mind that to their minds "circumcision" and "works of law" were identical. The Jew was not contending for righteousness on the basis of the merit of abstract morality, but of the fulfilment of the Mosaic law, of which circumcision was with them the first precept, or as the Rabbis said, "Circumcision is equal to all the commandments." When therefore Paul proves that this righteousness or blessedness comes upon the "uncircumcision" he proves that it is entirely independent of works of law in the Jewish sense of the term. The form of his question implies the answer, "Upon the uncircumcision also." And to this implied answer the next clause is linked as proof.

for we say, To Abraham his faith was reckoned for righteousness.] This carries us back to verse 3, where the case of Abraham was under consideration. From the history of that case Paul establishes his new point that Abraham's righteousness was purely of faith, *i.e.*, apart from circumcision, and hence from works of law.

10. **How then was it reckoned? when he was in circumcision, or in uncircumcision?**] This question refers us to the comparative dates of Gen. xv. 6 and xvii. 25. The circumcision was a year before the birth of Isaac, and when Ishmael was thirteen years of age. Gen. xv. 6 dates before the birth of Ishmael. Hence Paul concludes,

Not in circumcision, but in uncircumcision:] This conclusion completely sweeps away the fundamental doctrine of the "circumcision" party. (For a similar line of argument see Gal. iii. 16, 17, etc.) Paul draws this conclusion here, however, not so much to contradict his opponent as to establish his main thesis, that the righteousness of faith gives its true effect to the old dispensation by accomplishing to Abraham the promises. To this he now leads us.

11. **and he received the sign of circumcision, a seal of the righteousness of the faith which he had while he was in uncircumcision:**] Paul here places circumcision in its true place. It was not the cause or condition of righteousness but a seal, *i.e.*, an attesting symbol of a righteousness already independently existing. (See Eph. i. 13 for the seal of the new dispensation; and on the relation of this to baptism, Titus iii. 5. We have thus the true doctrine of a sacrament: it does not save, but is a seal of salvation.)

that he might be the father of all them that believe, though they be in uncircumcision,] This expresses God's purpose. God first fully revealed the righteousness of faith to Abraham. Though Abel, Enoch and Noah (see Heb. xi.) preceded there was not to any of them the explicit revelation of Gen. xv. 6. Abraham thus becomes the "father of the faithful." The universal doctrine of "righteousness out of faith" finds its prototype in him. The preposition "through" here governing the genitive expresses, not means or agency, but extent: "through the whole extent of uncircumcision."

that righteousness might be reckoned unto them;] A second expression, or an enlargement of the divine intention. This completely annihilates the doctrine of those who said, "Except ye be circumcised after the manner of Moses, ye cannot be saved." The purpose of God's grace as traced back by Paul has no such narrow limits.

12. **and the father of circumcision to them who not only are of the circumcision, but who also walk in the steps of that faith of our father Abraham which he had in uncircumcision.**] The dispensation of circumcision had its place, but even then only in harmony with the principle of faith. Even the covenant of circumcision availed only to those who walked in the steps of Abraham's faith. God's purpose was to make Abraham first the father of all those who believe in every age and dispensation (this was the fundamental and universal divine idea); then the father of a covenant people who till the fulness of time was come should exhibit to the world the example of this faith. But this special covenant was sub-

ordinate to the original universal idea, and its whole end was the final bringing in of the everlasting and universal righteousness of faith. For this application of his thesis Paul is now ready. On the peculiar grammatical difficulties of this verse see Meyer.

13. **For not through the law was the promise to Abraham or to his seed, that he should be heir of the world,**] This is the negative side of the fundamental thesis announced in the opening verses of this section (verses 31, 1). In the Greek the verb is wanting, and so commentators supply verb and tense according to their conception of the sense. Moule supplies the verb "came;" Godet (in sense the same), "was made;" Meyer supplies "procured." Riddle and Lange substantially agree with this. But is Paul here speaking of the *first giving* of the promise or of *its present fulfilment?* Evidently the latter. Only the common misapprehension of verse 1, which we have already pointed out, could lead to a similar misapprehension here. The next clause makes this evident.

but through the righteousness of faith.] How can it be said that the promise was given through the righteousness of faith, as all these commentators make Paul say, when he has just proved or stated at full length that the righteousness of faith *was attained by believing this very promise already given?* We cannot take Paul's summary of the Abrahamic promises ("heir of the world") to refer, as Riddle takes it, merely to the possession of the promised land. That has no particular connection with Paul's line of thought. It refers rather to the promise that he should become "a great nation," that "in him should all families of the earth be blessed," and that his seed should be as "the stars of heaven." These are the promises which Paul evidently has in mind in harmony with his line of thought. (See verse 17.) Now, Paul does not assert that these promises *were* given "through the righteousness of faith," but that they *are to be* fulfilled through the righteousness of faith. The promise was of "an heir" (Gen. xv. 4). Paul immediately speaks of this heirship, not in the past tense but in the present perfect (verse 14), showing that he is not speaking of the *past* act of God in giving, but of the work of God in fulfilling the promise up to the *present*. This, Paul says, has taken place through the righteousness of faith. All who through faith attain this righteousness are Abraham's seed, and heirs according to the promise (Gal. iii. 7, 9, 14, 29). In this way alone, Paul claims, has the object of the law been attained and Abraham secured ("found") the promised inheritance. This he proceeds further to substantiate.

14. **For if they which are of the law be heirs, faith is made void, and the promise is made of none effect:**] The hope of the Jews was that the promised heirship, which was to reach all nations with its blessing, was to come through the legal covenant of circumcision. Hitherto this covenant had embraced few beyond the natural descendants of Abraham. In their very willingness to accept the help of Paul, by building on his foundation and perverting to their

purpose his converts, Paul's enemies had confessed their despair of the old methods of extending the Abrahamic covenant so as to make it embrace all the world. Paul here asserts that if the legal covenant of circumcision is to be the basis of the heirship, then (1) "faith has been made void," *i.e.*, made an "empty," useless, superfluous thing. The real basis of the heritage being the law, faith "counts for nothing," and the introduction of the principle of faith has been a useless superfluity. And if that be the case (2) "the promise has become of none effect," *i.e.*, has failed of fulfilment. The reason of this lies in the fact that even those who have been brought under the covenant of the law, whether by birth or by proselytism, instead of finding or inheriting a "blessing" have found only a "curse" (Gal. iii. 9, 10), or as Paul puts it here,

15. **for the law worketh wrath;**] Instead of finding the blessing promised to Abraham, and described by David as an inward, conscious righteousness, or rightness with God, the law has only brought the conscious condemnation. In fact, so far as peace of mind was concerned, they would be more blessed without the law, for (read "but" as equivalent to "*on the contrary*")

but where there is no law, neither is there transgression.] The law, instead of bringing the desired blessing, had, on the contrary, multiplied the misery by multiplying the occasions of sin. (See for Paul's reiteration of this thought chs. v. 13; vii. 9, 10; also Gal. iii. 10 and Acts xv. 10, 11.)

Paul, having thus pointed out both the fact and the cause of the failure of the law to bring the promised inheritance, next proceeds to show why the principle of faith has been introduced.

16. **For this cause it is of faith, that it may be according to grace;**] The connecting phrase "for this cause" is usually taken as referring back to the statements just made, and is accordingly sometimes translated "therefore." We think it rather points forward to the sentence beginning with (ἵνα) "that." The negative statement of hypothetical failure is not so much or so properly the cause as the positive opposite of the completion of God's purpose which immediately follows. (The Greek ἵνα thus becomes appositive to τοῦτο, giving the most intense emphasis to the clause thus pointed out.) The pronoun "it" supplied in the translation is referred by some to "righteousness," by others to the "promised heritage." But the "promised heritage" is nothing else but "the righteousness of faith." (See verses 22-24; compare Gal. iii. 6-9.) They are therefore identical in Paul's mind; and doubtless the promised blessing was in Paul's thought both as a heritage and as a gift of righteousness when he wrote the words "of faith." The conjunction "that" denotes design. It includes result of cause where intention follows a line of cause and effect, as here. "Of faith" is Paul's usual expression to designate faith as the condition of "righteousness." *This*, then, is God's intention (Paul would say) in making the promised heritage of righteousness conditional on faith, that it may be accord-

ing to grace. The preposition "according to" seems here to designate the rule or measure. This is God's grace, *i.e.*, his merciful goodwill. To the measure of *grace* the condition of faith gives full scope, hence God's intention to make his loving grace the measure of the fulfilment of the promise includes a further design,

to the end that the promise may be sure to all the seed;] The promise here referred to (Gen. xii. 3) is one of blessing to all nations. The bringing of all nations to share in the promised blessings of the covenant people is called inheriting all nations, This seems to have been a common phrase in Paul's day. (So Tacitus, "They should go forth from Judea who should possess the world.") The Jewish view of this possession or heritage was external and legal; Paul's, spiritual. And God's design in making the principle of heirship thus spiritual (by faith) was to give the intended extent to the blessing. "All the seed" are evidently all nations; or as Paul puts it,

not to that only which is of the law,] About these there was no doubt in the minds of Paul's opponents. Paul, however, says the promise becomes sure even to *them* through *faith*.

but to that also which is of the faith of Abraham,] This designates the true universal paternity which embraces "all the seed." They become Abraham's children through the same faith which secures to them the promised blessing. The two lines of paternity are thus contrasted and brought into unity. One is natural, "of the law," or of circumcision (verse 12); the other spiritual, "of faith." Both inherit the promise through faith. Only when both are included has the promise its true fulfilment.

NOTE.—The clear contrast of the two classes of paternity in verse 16 increases the doubt raised in our minds by the construction of verse 12. We have only there to read ουκ τοις instead of τοις ουκ and the phrase is the exact parallel of verse 16. The meaning of verse 12 will then become entirely different, and may be paraphrased thus: "A father of covenant relation not to those only who are naturally or legally in the covenant, but also to those who walk in the steps of the faith which Abraham had even before the covenant was sealed to him." In verse 12 Paul would assert (if the conjectural reading be adopted) the divine intention to bring the believing Gentiles into covenant relation to himself through faith. The abstract noun "circumcision" would then be taken, not for "circumcised people," but for the relation to God of which circumcision was the sign and seal. Abraham himself was taken into the covenant relation of circumcision that as the father of the faithful he might gather them all into covenant relation to God. This interpretation would advance Paul's argument much further than the current reading and explanation, and harmonizes with his line of thought.

who is the father of us all] *i.e.*, of both the legal and the spiritual seed.

17. (as it is written, A father of many nations have I made thee)] Paul here quotes (Gen. xvii. 5) another form of the promise, still making prominent the universal extent of God's design in his covenant promises to Abraham.

before him whom he believed,] *i.e.*, "the father of us all in his sight," as he views Abraham and his spiritual seed.

even God, who quickeneth the dead,] (Compare verse 9, and also Heb. xi. 12.) The reference is clearly to the miraculous character of the birth of Isaac.

and calleth the things that are not, as though they were,] (Compare Isa. xlvi. 10; xlviii. 13.) It is literally "calling the nonexistent as existent." The reference is clearly to that almighty power of God which creates, and which in the whole course of his dispensations brings into existence all that is needful for the accomplishment of his purposes. No doctrine of Paul is more continuously presented than this of God's purpose of the ages, and his continuous working for its accomplishment (Eph. i. 11).

18. **Who in hope believed against hope,**] A second descriptive sentence attached to Abraham, an example of Paul's method of coordinating a number of clauses in similar grammatical and logical connection. Note the play upon the word "hope." This generally implies a distinction in meaning. "In hope," literally "upon hope," probably refers to the basis of hope given in the promise. "Against hope," literally "aside from" or "beyond hope," may refer either to the human standard of hope or to the natural feelings of hopefulness or expectancy in such a case.

to the end that he might become a father of many nations,] The preposition which expresses aim, the result to which a thing moves, is here used. Subjectively it is not intention but hope that is here in question. The meaning is not that he believed or hoped for the purpose of becoming, but that the object or end upon which his faith and hope were fixed, to which they looked, was "the becoming a father of many nations."

according to that which had been spoken, So shall thy seed be.] This promise was the foundation or ground, and hence also the measure or rule, of Abraham's faith and hope. The preposition is not a mere symbol of quotation; hence Paul does not say "as it is written" but "it had been spoken." It calls attention to the promise as spoken to Abraham, and hence the basis of his believing hope. The record of this promise is found in Gen. xv. 5. To suppose, with Riddle, that Paul in this verse is describing, not the nature of Abraham's faith—surpassing all human hope, and fixing itself upon the object set before it in God's promise, and measuring its expectation by that promise alone—but is setting forth "God's purpose" in the existence of Abraham's faith, is to introduce an idea without special relevancy here, and is to deprive Abraham of the merit of the very quality which fitted him for his distinguished position as the example of faith for all ages, making that faith a thing imposed by the divine predestination. There is, indeed, a divine predestination here (verse 16), not imposing faith upon Abraham but rewarding a faith the pre-eminent character of which this and the following verses describe.

19. **And without being weakened in faith**] The two following verses are connected by the copulative conjunction with verse 18, and are thus a part of, or expansion of, the relative clause there in-

troduced. The emphasis of this verse lies on the participial clause "without being weakened in faith," which thus stands in the forefront of the sentence. The *textus receptus*, by introducing a negative between this and the principal verb following, in part removes this emphasis, and so changes, not the sense, but the mode of expressing it, very materially weakening Paul's bold rhetoric.

he considered his own body now as good as dead (he being about a hundred years old),] "Considered," *i.e.*, clearly recognized the fact. The verb expresses, not a process of reflecting, but a full, perfect act of understanding. The Greek predicate is simply "already dead." The mention of his age establishes both the natural fact and also the knowledge of that fact on the part of Abraham.

and the deadness of Sarah's womb:] This addition brings out to the full the grandeur of Abraham's faith. It stood firm in the face of all natural impossibilities. We see thus most clearly that the main thought of Paul in verse 18, of which this is the expression, is, as interpreted above, the greatness of Abraham's faith.

20. yea, looking unto the promise of God, he wavered not through unbelief,] The increasing fervour of the apostle's mind as he approaches the climax of his argument leads to a rich rhetorical amplitude and force already apparent in verses 18 and 19. In the clause before us these two verses are recapitulated with intense energy of expression impossible to reproduce in any translation. "Looking unto the promise of God" recapitulates verse 18. (There the very same preposition occurs, and might be rendered there as here, "Looking unto his becoming a father of many nations, according," etc.) "He wavered not through unbelief" recapitulates verse 19, and thus fully prepares the way for the final clause in which Paul's thought is completely expressed.

but waxed strong through faith,] More literally, we think, "in faith," the preposition being compounded with the verb. This is the grand thought in Paul's mind throughout, and he has most perfectly expressed it both by rhetorical preparation and by its final utterance; but the theme so entrances Paul that he still cannot leave it, but must linger round it in participial clauses for other varying views.

giving glory to God,] Such faith honours God. Therein lies its moral value as the test of the new probation. Hodge very properly adds, "The sinner honours God in trusting his grace as much as Abraham did in trusting his power." By sin we "came short of the glory of God." By faith we "give God glory." In scarcely any of his grand ideas does Paul present a profounder thought than this. It presents to us the supreme moral value of faith as standing over against the supreme demerit of sin.

21. and being fully assured that, what he had promised, he was able also to perform.] The emphasis of this verse lies on the words "fully assured." As Moule well observes in one of his finest notes, this verse sets before us the true "nature of faith as essentially trust." It has as its object *something to be done;* it comes to a *person who is able to perform;* it looks to his *promise;* it is fully conscious of the *magnitude* of the work to be wrought and of the natural impossibilities which intervene; but it glorifies God by *full assurance.*

22. Wherefore also it was reckoned unto him for righteousness.] The apostle here most definitely states that it is this moral value of faith, so grandly illustrated in the example of Abraham, which is the ground of its being made the probational condition of justification or righteousness. And mark, it is this faith which Paul says is "reckoned for righteousness." By this we do not understand Paul to say that this faith is a substitute for good works, or that it dispenses with good works. The word translated "for" here is not $ἀντί$, "in the stead of," but $εἰς$, "leading to." Again, the righteousness here spoken of is not $δικαίωμα$, "the right works required by the law," but $δικαιοσύνη$, "the right state or relation toward God," the sense in which we think Paul everywhere uses this word. What, then, Paul here affirms is that faith is graciously counted in man's probation to instate him in the right moral relation to God, both absolutely or objectively and subjectively or in his own conscience. And he states that the reason for this divine order, by which faith is thus reckoned in moral probation, lies in its supreme moral worth as honoring God, and so being the root from which spring all right works before God. (See Heb. xi. 6 and Gal. v. 6.) The perfect harmony of this doctrine with Jas. ii. 14–26 is apparent.

23. Now it was not written for his sake alone, that it was reckoned unto him;

24. but for our sake also,] Paul sees in the history of Abraham, as recorded in Genesis, not a mere glorification of Abraham, nor even a personal declaration of his acceptance with God, but the primitive revelation of the order of divine grace to prevail in all ages; hence "for our sake also."

unto whom it shall be reckoned,] We must here supply, from the preceding context, the antecedent of it, or rather in Greek, where there is no pronoun used, the subject of the verb, *i.e.,* "faith," and also the complement of "reckon," *i.e.,* "for righteousness." It is also noteworthy that Paul uses here, not the future indicative, but the present infinitive, "to be reckoned," with the present indicative of a verb signifying the introduction of a new order or state of things, or of a new course of action. The gospel was the then present beginning of a new dispensation of faith. This new dispensation, however, does not rest upon the temporal promises of the old. Hence Paul must define the basis of the new as distinguished from the old, which he does in the three concluding sentences. The unity of the new with the old, which has been throughout the theme of this section, thus leads up to the fundamental distinction between the new and the old. This distinction lies in the fact that our faith rests in God, not as revealed in temporal promises, or in acts of supernatural creative power, but in the supreme act by which *God attests the atoning work of Jesus Christ.*

who believe on him that raised Jesus our Lord from the dead,] We cannot, with Riddle, look upon the raising of Christ from the dead as a mere example of divine power surpassing that to which Abraham's faith looked. The doctrine of the resurrection has everywhere in St. Paul a far higher significance. It is the seal of Christ's mediatorial work and authority. (See Acts xvii. 31; Rom. i. 4; 1 Cor. xv. 14; Eph. i. 20.) To believe in God who raised up Jesus our Lord from the dead is to believe in God as, in this act of power, setting his seal upon the office and work of Jesus our Lord. That office Paul has already designated by the supreme title "Son of God"; here he designates it by the equally divine title "our Lord." On the significance of this title in reference to the atoning work of Christ see chapter xiv. 9 and note there. It is applied to Christ by Paul some two hundred and fifty times, and is preferred by him over all other titles to designate the relation of Christ to us as our Saviour. It is not a mere title of honour or majesty, but enters into the very essence of our faith. As our Lord he hath purchased us to be his own people (Acts xx. 28, where, as in Titus ii. 13, the divinity of the Lordship appears). But (as in ch. xiv. 9) Christ becomes our Lord by what he has done for us, which Paul now adds as entering into the essential groundwork of our faith.

25. who was delivered up for our trespasses,] This is a variation of Paul's formulary of faith. (See 1 Cor. xv.; 1 Tim. i. 15.) The same term used here "delivered up" is used again (ch. viii. 32) to designate that act of God the Father in which, from his love to man, he surrenders his Son to death. This surrender is said here to take place "on account of our trespasses," *i.e.*, our trespasses are the reason or necessitating cause of the surrender of God's Son to death. The apostle elsewhere employs another preposition for "the sake of" (1 Cor. xv. 3). Here lies another element of Paul's doctrine of the work of Christ, which we must collate with such passages as chapter iii. 25, 26 in seeking for a complete view of the atonement as presented by Paul.

and was raised for our justification.] The same preposition used in the preceding clause is used here, "on account of our justification." Our justification made necessary the raising of Christ. The word "*justification*" must not, however, be confused with "*righteousness*." Justification, δικαίωσις, is God's act; righteousness, δικαιοσύνη, is the gift which we receive. It is not the *gift* which rendered the resurrection necessary, but the process of God's *act of justification*. The foundation of every individual act of justification is laid in that supreme act of the Father in which he set his seal upon the office and work of his Son. It is not merely indirectly, as the basis of our faith for justification, that the resurrection is necessary. The

resurrection is the first and foundation of a series of acts in which God publicly declares his acceptance of sinners in Christ. These acts are—
1. The resurrection, followed by the ascension and mediatorial glory. This is the justification to the whole universe of the collective body of God's elect in Christ (Rom. viii. 34).
2. The gift of the witnessing Spirit to those who believe (Acts xv. 8). This is the individual justification. That the apostles held in common that this was based on the preceding, and could not take place apart from it, appears from such passages as John vii. 39; Acts ii. 32, 33, etc.
3. The final act, both individual and collective, of the day of judgment. The resurrection is therefore the necessary basis of our justification. No sentences in the Epistle sum up to us a more weighty body of doctrine than is to be found in these two concluding verses, which thus posit the foundations of the Christian faith as distinguished from the yet imperfect faith of all previous dispensations. The announcement of these foundations leads the apostle next to break forth into

Ch. V. 1-21. An Exhortation Founded upon the Doctrine of Righteousness by Faith.

Part I. The Exhortation, vv. 1-11. Part II. The Grounds, vv. 12-21.

PART I. THE EXHORTATION.

1. **Being therefore justified by faith,**] The conjunction here used introduces the apostle's practical conclusion from the entire preceding argument, or rather from its great fundamental thesis, to which Paul had once more returned in verses 24, 25. This thesis he sums up in the participial clause "being justified by faith." The revised version, following the order of the Greek, conveys the impression that the participial clause is itself the conclusion—"We are therefore justified by faith." But this conjunction introduces, not so much the statement of that which has been proven by reasoning, as the statement of that which follows by natural or necessary consequence. Paul has indeed proved that we are justified by faith, and hence in the participial clause he assumes this as no longer capable of question. But *the necessary consequence* of this proven thesis is the exhortation which follows with the principal verb. "Therefore"
let us have peace with God through our Lord Jesus Christ;] This is the exhortation. The verb might fairly be translated "let us hold." It denotes that active effort by which we do not let slip that which we have received. The aorist participle "being justified" designates a definite single historical fact, the act of God by which we are placed in right relation to himself. "Peace with God" designates the abiding state into which this act has introduced us.

The preposition used is the same used in chapter iv. 2 and John i. 1 and 2 to denote ultimate and immediate relationship to God. This "peace with God" is "through our Lord Jesus Christ." He is the mediator, not only in the act of justification, but also in the abiding state of peace which we are exhorted to hold fast; or, as Paul puts it in the next verse, not only of the abiding state but also of the door of entrance.

2. through whom also we have had our access by faith into this grace wherein we stand;] "*The* access" (translated in the revised version "our access") points to the fact that to the Gentiles this relationship to God, this state of "grace," was opened by Christ. The aorist (a definite historical fact) may refer either to the opening of the door of faith to the Gentiles at large or to these individual believers in particular. So far as the Roman church was concerned the two facts were one.

and let us rejoice in hope of the glory of God.] Throughout we have treated this section as an exhortation expressed by the Greek subjunctive mood. Moule, while admitting that the weight of critical authority is in favour of the subjunctive, thinks that the indicative "'we have' exactly fits into the context," while the subjunctive "'let us have' is foreign to it." On the other hand, we think the hortatory form perfectly natural here. In favor of this is especially the fact that all the assertions thrown into participial and other subordinate clauses are such as would naturally be used to strengthen an exhortation. See especially verses 3-10 and 12-21. "Let us rejoice" is literally "let us make our boast." This, in contrast to the Jewish glorying in their Abrahamic ancestry, is fixed upon the hope of the glory of God in the bringing in of a universal kingdom of righteousness. (Compare Isa. xl 5.) The establishment of the kingdom of right is in Paul's esteem the true manifestation of the divine glory. All the Old Testament scriptures, which his countrymen and his age interpreted in a natural or temporal sense, Paul interprets as ethical, spiritual and eternal.

3. And not only so, but let us also rejoice in our tribulations:] There is here a change of preposition from $\epsilon\pi\iota$, "upon," to $\epsilon\nu$, "in." This would seem to indicate that Paul does not present the tribulations as the subject-matter of boasting, or the ground of boasting, but as the environment or condition in the midst of which we may still continue our boasting, inasmuch as these tribulations do not hinder but rather promote the establishment of God's kingdom and glory in our hearts.

knowing that tribulation worketh patience;] "patience," that is, persevering endurance, is wrought out, *i.e*, not merely exhibited but strengthened and perfected under circumstances of tribulation.

4. and patience, probation;] This is probably not probation in the wide sense of God's moral proof of men, but our proof in our own experience of the power of God's grace in tribulations.

and probation, hope:] Our testing experience not only justifies our hope in the past but strengthens our present hope for the future. We have only to bear in mind that the object of this hope is the accomplishment of God's kingdom in our own hearts and in the world, to see how each proof of the power of that kingdom works out enlarged hope.

5. and hope putteth not to shame;] "Putting to shame" is the opposite of boasting, and refers to the confusion experienced by a boaster whose boastings were not made good. The Christian's boasting fails not of verification,

because the love of God hath been shed abroad in our hearts] As we take the theme of the entire passage to be subjective experience of saving grace, so we must take it here. The manifestation of God's love in our hearts is represented as the pouring of a stream, referring, perhaps, to the pouring of the anointing oil. The heart, the seat of conscience or the moral understanding, is also the seat of religious affections. The love of God denotes, primarily, God's love to us; but this is at once answered by our love to God (1 John iv. 19). The perfect tense indicates that this is not an occasional or isolated experience but continuous up to the present, and yet perfect in itself at each moment. This constant experience of God's love verifies the hope of God's glorious kingdom being fully revealed within us, on which we boast. The agent of this experience is next set before us.

through the Holy Ghost which was given unto us.] Here for the first time Paul introduces the Holy Spirit as the agent by whom is wrought the work of the inward experience of the Christian. The gift of the Holy Ghost refers us to the promise of Christ recorded in John xiv. and xv. and Acts i. The aorist participle refers to a definite fact in the history of the Roman Christians, as the fulfilment of Christ's promise. Paul's doctrine of the work of the Spirit is most fully expanded in chapter viii., where we may more fully consider the question of the personality of the Holy Spirit.

6. For while we were yet weak, in due time Christ died for the ungodly.] God's love to us is the grand preceding thought to which this verse attaches itself. "For," $\gamma a \rho$, may here be taken as explicatory. (Godet proposes to translate it "in fact." The object of the writer is to show how God's love assures our hope, and he brings out the full force of his argument only in verses 9 and 10, "Much more then." The first adverb "yet" attaches itself to the participial clause "we being yet weak." The second "yet" (omitted in the English version) attaches itself to the principal clause and has the force of "nevertheless"—"Christ none the less in due season died for the ungodly." The "due season" was the time which God had prepared for the accomplishment of the atonement. (Compare Gal. iv. 4.) The characteristic of those for whom Christ died as "ungodly" gives greater emphasis to the argument already implied in the expression "weak," and which expanding in the apostle's mind immediately leads to the enlarged comparative statement of verses 7 and 8. It is not safe to press the preposition "for" here as if it meant "in the place of"; its simple force is "for the sake of" or "for the benefit of."

7. For scarcely for a righteous man will one die:] The conjunction is here again the γαρ, explicatory, enlarging by a comparison the idea of the previous verse. The term "righteous" is here compared on the one hand with the "ungodly" for whom Christ died. Christ died for the "ungodly," man will scarcely die for the "righteous." On the other hand it is compared with the "good man" of the following clause.

for peradventure for the good man some one would even dare to die.] This clause, which is somewhat parenthetical, Paul introduces as stating the utmost limit to which human self-sacrifice can reach. Righteousness is scarcely sufficient to call out this supreme sacrifice; "*scarcely*," "for by chance," *i.e.*, on some rare occasion, its highest form, goodness, may call it out. In the article there may be the force of the Hebrew superlative, of which it may be an imitation equal to "the best of men."

8. But God commendeth his own love toward us, in that, while we were yet sinners, Christ died for us.] The verb "commendeth," which occupies the emphatic place in the sentence, may be translated "demonstrates" or "proves." The reflexive pronoun "his own" need not be taken as the antithesis to another, but as expressing the divine peculiarity of this redeeming love. It is a love found in God alone; this is the point of the enlargement and comparison contained in these two verses. This peculiar divine love is embodied in the fact which Paul now repeats from verse 6, "that while we were yet sinners, Christ died for us." This completes the thesis of the argument introduced by "for" (γαρ, explicatory) at the beginning of verse 6—so far the enlargement of the idea of God's love; next follows the conclusion—the enlargement of the idea of assured hope.

9. Much more then, being now justified by his blood, shall we be saved from the wrath of God through him.] The conjunction "then" or "therefore" (ουν) draws a conclusion; "much more" vindicates the apostle's assurance of hope. The love that sent Christ to die for the *ungodly* can surely be trusted to save from 'the wrath" (the adjunct "of God" is not in the original) those who are justified by his blood. This sets forth the negative side of the Christian's assured hope. The apostle hastens forward to add the positive.

10. For if, while we were enemies, we were reconciled to God through the death of his Son, much more, being reconciled, shall we be saved by his life;] This presents in the hypothetical form the argument stated in direct form in verses 8 and 9. But besides the variation in mere logical form there is an advance in the thought. "Enemies" is parallel to, but stronger than, the term "sinners." It designates, not the mere subjective feeling of the sinner toward God (hater), but rather a state or relationship the exact opposite of friend; hence it includes the idea of that separation from God which is the consequence of sin, and which is expressed positively as being under God's "wrath." And yet it is not equivalent to "hated of God," for he loves us even in this condition. The term "reconciled" is parallel to the term "justified," perhaps not a stronger term, but corresponding to the new designation of our state—the "enemies" are "reconciled," the "sinners" are "justified." The term "reconciled" is therefore as full in its meaning as the term "enemies." It is not a mere subjective change in our feelings toward God; it is a change in our relation to God. In fact, in the two verses the apostle presents the same idea under two analogies—that of the judge and the criminal, and that of the king and his rebellious subjects. The conclusion varies in but a single expression, "in" or "by" his life. This is contrasted with the expressions "Christ died for us," "by his blood," and "by the death of his Son," which are stated as the means of our justification or reconciliation. Godet's explanation of the expression "saved by his life" transfers us from the standpoint of justification or reconciliation to that of renewal or regeneration. As there is nothing in the context to suggest such a change in the writer's line of thought, it is perhaps better to explain the present clause by the parallel to be found in chapter viii. 34, "Who is he that shall condemn? It is Christ Jesus that died, yea rather, that was raised from the dead," etc. Here it is evident that Christ's living as our intercessor is intimately related to his death as the means of our justification. In studying Paul's idea of the valency of Christ's 'work this must not be forgotten.

11. **and not only so, but we also rejoice in God through our Lord Jesus Christ,**] In the Greek the verb "rejoice" stands, not in the present indicative, but as a present participle. It is therefore co-ordinate, not with "shall be saved," but with the preceding participle "being reconciled." This participle is therefore, as Meyer has shown, the ellipsis to be supplied after "not only," and which has been indefinitely supplied by "so" in our English versions. We may therefore render thus: "And not only being reconciled, but also making our boast in God through our Lord Jesus Christ." But why does the apostle, after he has seemingly completed his construction and the full sense, append in this way an idea already fully expressed in verses 2 and 3? The ordinary interpretation, which brings the paragraph to a complete close at the end of verse 11, gives no answer to this question. We think, however, that Paul calls up again this idea of boasting in God through our Lord Jesus Christ that he may give us the magnificent exposition of the grounds of this boasting which follows (verses 12-21). Meantime the attachment of this participial clause to the participle "being reconciled" suggests a relative adjunct.

through whom we have now received the reconciliation.] that is, the reconciliation already expressed in the participle "being reconciled." The full idea is thus: "Not only reconciled but also boasting in God through the same Lord Jesus Christ through whom we have been reconciled." It is no longer proper to translate the word used here as "atonement." "Atonement" once signified "at-onement" or "reconciliation." It is now a theological term denoting the work of Christ by which the reconciliation is effected.

12. Therefore,] The Greek phrase thus rendered is not a conjunction but a prepositional adjunct, διὰ τοῦτο, "on account of this." Two grammatical questions must be answered preliminary to the interpretation—first, to what does the demonstrative pronoun τοῦτο, "this," point? on account of what? Secondly, to what predicate does the adjunct διὰ τοῦτο, "on account of this," belong? What is or is done on account of this? In answer to the first question it is admitted by all that the demonstrative points to some statement or thought contained in the context. That context is supposed to be the preceding argument. Some find the thought to which τοῦτο points in verse 11; others, in the entire preceding argument, extending even as far back as chapter i. 18. But in verse 11 there is *no one definite thought* to which the demonstrative naturally points and which gives a good point of connection for the grand discourse which follows. The idea of "reconciliation" is supposed to satisfy the requirements of the case. But if this were sufficient then verse 11 is superfluous, as verse 12 could be quite as well, if not better, attached to verse 10. On the other hand, the singular demonstrative τοῦτο is altogether too definite to point back to a long train of argument extending over several chapters. We know of no example in the New Testament to justify such an explanation of διὰ τοῦτο as a connective. The ordinary answer to our second question is equally unsatisfactory. It is at once admitted that there is no verb or predicate following to which διὰ, "on account of," naturally links itself. The attempt, therefore, to make διὰ τοῦτο *link* to a predicate following and *point* to a logical connection preceding fails at both ends. Giving it the most favourable construction possible it would read thus: "Through one act of righteousness the free gift came unto all men to justification of life on account of the reconciliation." This might pass as good logical connection at first sight, but it will not bear minute examination; and in whatever Paul may fail as to perfection of style he never fails in perfectly accurate definiteness of logical connection. We must turn, therefore, to examine the use of διὰ τοῦτο as a logical connective.

First, does this connecting phrase invariably introduce a conclusion from *antecedent* premises to which premises τοῦτο points? While it is true that τοῦτο usually refers to what precedes, it is not unfrequently used in classical Greek to point to what follows. (See Kühner, 303, 1 Rem. 1.) May it not then be sometimes used to assign the basis or ground of an antecedent statement, to which basis or ground τοῦτο points forward? The following are examples of Paul's use of the phrase:—

Rom. iv. 16.—"It is of faith on this account, that it may be according to grace." Here evidently τουτο points forward to a ground or reason for the statement made in the antecedent clause to which τουτο belongs.

Rom. xiii. 6.—"For on this account ye also pay tribute, because they are God's ministers," etc. Here again τουτο points forward to the reason following for the statement made in the antecedent clause.

1 Cor. iv. 17.—"On this account I have sent unto you Timotheus, etc., who shall remind you," equivalent to "that he may remind you." Here again the τουτο points forward to a reason.

1 Thess. ii. 13.—"On this account also we give thanks . . . because having received the word . . . ye received it not as the word of man," etc. Here again the τουτο points forward to the following statement of the ground or reason of the apostolic thanksgiving.

In all these cases the following clause may be construed as a substantive in apposition with τουτο. These passages, however, differ from the one before us in two respects: first, δια τουτο stands at the beginning of the clause to which it belongs; secondly, the substantive clause to which τουτο points has a specific introductory particle, as ἱνα, ὁτι or γαρ. These two differences, however, have a natural explanation in the peculiarities of the individual passages. The following are still nearer our present construction:—

John vii. 21, 22.—"I have wrought one work, (and ye all wonder) on this account:—Moses gave you circumcision," etc. Here we have a perfect logical connection if we make δια τουτο, not introductory, but pointing to our Lord's defence, which follows without any introductory particle.

Matt. xviii. 22, 23.—"I say not unto thee, Until seven times; but, Until seventy times seven, on this account." Then follows the parable to which the τουτο points, and which assigns here again, without any introductory particle, the ground or reason on which our Lord bases his teaching. On this use of the demonstrative in reference to a following clause see Winer, pp. 200, 201; also, for the classical use, Kühner, § 304, 2. The demonstrative so used always gives special prominence or emphasis to the clause, sentence or paragraph so pointed out.

We have but to accept this use of δια τουτο here and then the connection with verse 11 is perfectly plain, and the writer's object in introducing that verse in its participial form becomes clear. We then render "And not only being reconciled, but also making our boast in God through Jesus Christ, etc., on this account." We believe this to be the true construction—

1. Because it explains the otherwise superfluous introduction of verse 11.
2. Because it makes a perfect and close connection from clause to clause, as is St. Paul's wont.
3. It throws, by means of the demonstrative, the entire paragraph following, as the ground of Christian boasting, into that *distinctive prominence* which its supreme importance requires.

PART II.—THE GROUNDS.

as through one man sin entered into the world,] The particle of comparison here used is the strongest, equal to "just as." Paul proceeds, however, but a little way with the statement of the first term of the comparison before the points of unlikeness begin to appear, and he is forced to suspend the second member until these have been cleared away. It is not, therefore, till verse 18 that the comparison is completed, and then with a weaker particle. The parallel is between Adam and Christ. By this parallel the apostle aims to bring to view the fulness of the ground of our boasting. This presentation by contrast, requiring first a statement of our relation to Adam, gives us thus incidentally the most complete exposition of the doctrine of original sin to be found in Sacred Writ. The "one man" is evidently Adam. Paul touches the same thought in 1 Cor. xv. 21. Sin is here used with the article as a generic term; not a sin, but sin as a moral fact, henceforth continuous in human history. (Compare ch. vii. for a similar use of the article before the word sin.) The "world" is here, not the planet, but the world *of moral order.*

and death through sin;] Death, like sin, is generalized by the article. Death entered the world by means of sin. That it did so as a penalty is evident, not only from the history of the case, but also from Paul's own words (ch. vi. 23). But this penalty, in Paul's conception, is attached, not to the sin of each individual independently, but to the whole race in virtue of the common sin which was introduced by Adam. Death here must be taken in the Pauline sense of (*a*) conscious separation from God (ch. vii. 9, etc.), and (*b*) the death of the body (1 Cor. xv. 21, 22). This death has not merely a natural but a moral connection with sin, *i.e.*, a connection ordained by moral law.

and so death passed unto all men,] That is, by means of the generic sin introduced by the first man. The adverb "so," referring to the fact stated in the previous clause, fixes the ground of the universal extension of death, not in universal individual sin, but in the generic sin introduced by the one man. If we call this the imputation of Adam's sin to all the race, such a term must be carefully guarded. Paul neither asserts nor implies the universal extension of Adam's guilt to the race. He simply asserts the universal extension of the penalty without touching the underlying question of the principle under which this extension takes place.

for that all sinned:—] According to our revised version this assigns a second explanation of the universal extension of death, the first explanation being contained in the adverb "so." If our versions are correct then these two explanations must be harmonized, *i.e.*, it must be shown how the universal doom of death is at once the result of the introduction of generic death through Adam's generic sin, and at the same time the result of universal individual sin as a fact of history. The aorist tense in the clause before us expresses a historical fact. The tense refuses to accommodate itself to the rendering, "all have been treated as sinners" (Hodge, and most Arminians), or "all are sinful" (Calvin, Watson, etc.). "All sinned in Adam" (Bengel, Olshausen, Philippi and Meyer) involves an unjustifiable addition. The definite historical character of the expression is clearly recognized by Tholuck, Stuart and Lange, and also by Whedon as a generalization of a historical fact. But how can universal death be founded on universal individual sin in harmony with the statement that it is founded on the original generic sin. Only on the theory that generic sin produces universal individual sin, and this individual sin, death. But if this were Paul's thought he could hardly fail to have stated it directly, thus: "By one man sin entered into the world, and so all have sinned, and so all die." Further, such a statement would be true as fact only by some such explanation of the words "all sinned" as we have found above adopted by Calvin and Watson, but excluded by grammatical principles. Infants who die in infancy cannot be said to have sinned, though they may be said to be sinful. Even Whedon's generalization of the expression "all sinned" as a universal fact does not obviate the difficulty, since, if generic sin brings penalty only through individual transgression, it matters not whether that generic sin belongs to the first man or to the race at large, it can, on the theory, touch the individual only through his individual sin. Both the grammatical structure and the logical connection, therefore, compel us to abandon the interpretation which makes this clause assign the ground or reason of the universal extension of death. We are therefore driven back to re-examine the connective particle ἐφ ᾧ. It occurs as a connective in the New Testament four times, all in the writings of St. Paul, viz., here, again in 2 Cor. v: 4, and in Phil. iii. 12 and iv. 10. In the second passage we have in the *textus receptus* ἐπειδή, and the translation is without doubt "because" or "for that." In the remaining passages, where the reading is uniform, it evidently means "on account of which," *i.e.*, the relative pronoun is used in *its simple relative* sense, and not as an abbreviation for a demonstrative antecedent, pointing to the following sentence, followed by a relative conjunctive—"on account of this that." Schleusner adduces classical passages in which this simple relative use obtains. In this case the antecedent of the relative is to be found in some idea contained in the preceding context. Here the relative ᾧ would be taken as neuter, and refers, not to death, but to the entire fact stated in the two preceding clauses. We may render thus: "By one man sin entered into the world, and death by sin, and so death passed through unto all men; upon which antecedent state of things "all have sinned" (as already stated). If we accept this translation the relative clause before us introduces, not a mere reason of a statement just made, but a collateral idea which here breaks in upon him, and which he follows up to the end of verse 14, when he returns to advance his line of thought, not by completing the comparison begun in regular form, but by a new and more indefinite mode of expression. The collateral idea thus introduced Paul had previously repeatedly asserted (ch. iii. 10, 19), and he introduces it anew here to place it in its true connection, since in the facts of the preceding context we have assigned the reason of the well-known fact of universal sin. Paul's full protasis or first member of comparison thus consists of four elements—the sin of one man, death by sin, universal death, universal sin. These same four elements we shall find in the protasis when in verses 18 and 19 he repeats his comparison in perfect form. But this protasis, especially in its fourth element, requires an explanation which will at the same time be a strong proof of the entire thesis. This Paul pauses to insert, thus breaking in on the completion of his comparison.

13. **for until the law sin was in the world:**] Paul, having in the preceding verse completed his protasis or first term of comparison, proceeds in verses 13 and 14 to apply it to the solution of one of the most difficult problems of human probation. What the exact case before his mind was is not to us so obvious, and has given rise to not a little diversity of interpretation. Some suppose that the problem which Paul seeks to explain by this interjected paragraph arises from the case of infants, who could not be held to have committed sin as historical fact. It is quite possible that the category which he has in mind may very properly include infants. But he himself defines it as those "from Adam to Moses . . . who had not sinned after the similitude of Adam's transgression." Again, the peculiarity under which Paul views this category is, that they were not under a law by virtue of which sin could be imputed. Both these characteristics may apply to infants. They have not sinned after the similitude of Adam's transgression, and they are not as yet under a law by which sin could be imputed. But that they were not specially before the mind of the apostle seems evident from the protasis "all sinned," which asserts a fact which could not be asserted in this form of infants. We conclude, therefore, that Paul's illustration of his main thesis was made, not with reference to the case of infants (though it may in part apply them, and also to the Gentiles outside the law), but with reference to the case of the entire world before the giving of the law. That "all sinned" none of his readers would be disposed to deny. That death was the penalty of sin they would also admit. That specific penalty can be inflicted, *i.e.*, that a moral agent can be held amenable to specific penalty only where there is specific law, was also an obvious axiom of morals. But in the case of those who lived before the giving of the law, it is impossible to apply and harmonize these acknowledged principles except on the basis of that doctrine of the *transmission* of sin and penalty which is involved in Paul's fourfold protasis. The fact that God did so apply these principles to these very men (in harmony, as it must be, with his justice) is therefore proof positive, as well as illustration,

of the truth of the doctrine of the protasis. We may therefore tabulate Paul's line of thought as follows:—
1. Protasis or first term of comparison.
   (*a*) By one man *the sin* entered into the world,
   (*b*) and *the death* by *the sin;*
   (*c*) and so *the death passed through* unto *all men.*
   (*d*) Upon which antecedent moral basis *all sinned.*
2. Illustration and proof of protasis.
For (taking the most difficult of all instances of human probation—those who are without specific revelation of moral law)
   (*a*) before the Mosaic law sin clearly existed in the world.
   (*b*) Yet sin is not held for specific penalty where there is not specific law.
   (*c*) But this sin was held for specific penalty inasmuch as death reigned universally; and inasmuch as it was not introduced by specific transgression, as in the case of Adam's sin, it must (both sin and penalty) *have passed through unto all men from the first transgressor.*
3. Apodosis, or second term of comparison, but in irregular form.
"Who is the figure of him that was to come."

Verses 13 and 14 become thus at once the illustration and proof of the apostle's doctrine of *the "passing through" of sin and its penalty of death unto all men.* In the light of this illustration we are now in a position to define this doctrine. It must be carefully discriminated from what we regard as the Augustinian exaggeration of *imputation* on the one hand, and from the Pelagian doctrine of mere example on the other. The Pelagian doctrine is at once excluded by Paul's statement that in the absence of specific law sin cannot originate, or be charged with specific penalty. From Adam to Moses men did not sin after the likeness (nor example) of Adam's transgression. Godet thinks that if this were the thought before the apostle's mind he would have introduced the "law written on the heart" as the basis of responsibility. But the apostle is not here discussing the case of ordinary responsibility for sin. He doubtless would have admitted that these men were individually responsible for their sins according to the light which they possessed. That is an entirely separate question from the one now before the apostle's mind, and to confuse the two will lead to serious error. Ordinary individual responsibility may exist either under general principles of moral law in the heart or conscience, or under a specific positive law. It may exist in an estate of innocency or under a fallen estate. But if we read Paul's axiom aright specific sin, involving specific penalty, can only *originate* under specific law. However, therefore, the men from Adam to Moses might be amenable to the general law of conscience, they could not, like Adam, originate sin against a specific law involving specific penalty, and hence death could not be considered the personal penalty of their individual transgressions The law written on the heart does not therefore apply here. Th

Pelagian theory, that sin passes through by the force of example, etc., is thus excluded by Paul's statement that at least to this part of mankind individual sin could not be charged for specific penalty. Paul's doctrine, therefore, clearly implies some link between the first sinner and all men *by which probational responsibility "passes through."* From Augustine downward the Christian world has recognized this as Paul's teaching in this passage; and to Augustine belongs the great merit of having first clearly understood the inspired teacher on this point. But we must be very careful not to make Paul say more than he fairly implies. This link may be easily magnified into a chain which so binds us to Adam as to leave no freedom for individual responsibility. Confining ourselves strictly to the work of exegesis, and avoiding questions which belong to systematic theology, we find in the words of Paul that this "passing through" pertains to two points—

1. Directly "death," the penalty of sin, "passes through unto all men." This death, as we have seen, involves in Paul's teaching (*a*) physical death (1 Cor. xv. 21, 22); (*b*) conscious separation of the soul from God (Rom. vii. 9, 10).

2. The original basis of responsibility under which the first man sinned, and so originated sin, so reaches down to us, that though we could not without specific law originate sin, yet from the original moral platform of the race we are chargeable with our sins just as if they had been committed in Eden. "Upon which basis all sinned."

To sum up both points in one view. Paul's doctrine implies *a unity of the race in moral responsibility*, in virtue of which they share in the common penalty of that sin which was introduced into the world by the first sinner to the extent of being subject to physical death and conscious moral separation from God, and in virtue of which they are responsible, not merely for the moral light individually enjoyed, but also for the original heritage of moral light given to the race. But we must mark carefully the fact that Paul does not here discuss *the limits of this probational unity.* He however affirms it only of the κοσμος, *i.e.*, the present world or moral order into which sin has been introduced, and in which we pass our probation—the same world into which Christ came to save sinners. It is not asserted nor implied that our relation to Adam directly determines eternal destiny. It founds the probation of a fallen creature under penal disabilities, under which probation comes our responsibility to the law of conscience.

It now only remains to add a few notes on the verses before us. In verse 13 the adverb "until" designates the termination of a period possessing in Paul's view a peculiar moral character. On Paul's view of the relation of revealed law to human probation see chapters iii. 20, iv. 15, v. 20, vii. throughout, also Gal. iii. 19, etc. During the period prior to this intervention man's sin was chargeable in virtue of his general relation to the first man, on the basis of the light of conscience. In the axiom, "sin is not imputed when there is no law," we meet once more the word which designates the moral equation of man's probational account. This axiom applies to the absolute or original probation, whether of the race or of the individual. Without a specific or revealed law sin could never have been charged to the race, and there could have been no probation. Without such law sin cannot be charged to the individual for specific individual punishment, even though in consequence of the common probation of the race he may be amenable to the common penalty, including a personal consciousness of his individual sinfulness. The expression "when there is no law" must not be confused with the term "without" or "apart from law." The case in question is that of the entire absence of a revelation, not that of its absence from the consciousness of the individual acting. A man may be amenable to an existing law even when he neglects to recognize it.

14. Nevertheless death reigned from Adam until Moses, even over them that had not sinned after the likeness of Adam's transgression,] The expression "the likeness of Adam's transgression" here opens up Paul's meaning. That transgression was a definite sin against a positive law, to which was annexed a definite penalty. Such a transgression could only occur under a positive law, and was not possible prior to the giving of such law. The phrase "those who had not sinned," etc., thus designates, not some part of the world before Moses (as infants), but the whole world of that period.

who is a figure of him that was to come.] This represents for the present Paul's apodosis, or the second term of his comparison. He began with a strong particle of comparison, "Just as by one man sin entered into the world;" and perfect form would have required him to complete it thus, "even so by one man righteousness came and life," etc. But as he expanded the first term of the comparison the points of unlikeness came into view, as well as those of resemblance. He therefore drops for the moment the perfect and strong form of parallel and contents himself with merely saying, in this indefinite relative clause, that Adam was the figure of Christ. After he has, in the three following verses, pointed out the limitations of this resemblance, he then returns to the parallel in verse 18, where it is presented in perfect logical form. The type is literally the impression produced by the blow (as of the seal in stamping). The typical resemblance must not, however, be extended beyond the point here under consideration. On these parallel doctrines of sin and grace, see excursus at the end of this chapter.

15. But not as the trespass, so also is the free gift.] This introduces the first limitation to the analogy. The two terms used to designate the beginning of sin and of grace are worthy of note. The first is called a "fall," literally, the fall caused by stumbling against some obstruction. The term is used by Longinus to denote an age of decadence in literature. The second is a "free gift." Both terms refer to man—in one the agent, in the other the recipient. Sin is a fall, hence his own; salvation is God's gracious gift.

For if by the trespass of the one the many died,] "For" introduces or explains the divergence. Of this divergence Paul makes a threefold statement. The divergence touches a single point in each of the three statements. But the main fact of parallelism so occupies Paul's mind that even in the statement of these three points of difference he repeatedly presents the full parallel. This parallel is the same which he afterwards presents directly in verses 18 and 19. Its terms are: 1. One man, Adam, and one man, Christ. 2. The fall and the grace. 3. The many sinning, dying, condemned, and the many saved, justified, reigning in life. In rhetorical variation Paul does indeed repeat this parallel not less than five times between verses 15 and 19—first, three times incidentally, while pointing out divergences; then twice directly, *i.e.*, as his main assertion, but with important variation of point of view. In fact, the five several statements give us each a new point of view of the same grand analogy. We cease to wonder that Paul should so repeat this thought and dwell so long around it when we remember that in it lies the deepest essence of the profoundest doctrine of the Christian religion, the doctrine of the atonement. In the exposition of verses 15, 16 and 17, we must first define Paul's three points of divergence, and then note the varied views of the fundamental parallel which he has at the same time incidentally given us. In the clause before us the point of divergence is *the quantity* or *extent* of the influence of grace. It far surpasses the power of sin. This is expressed by the verb "did abound" and by the adverb "much more." This quantity or extent is not, however, numerical. It does not mean hath abounded unto a "much greater many." This would not be true. The apostle sees the objects of grace and the subjects of the fall each a countless number. He does not compare numbers. We think his point of view is such that here the number and the individuals composing that number are identical as subjects of the fall and objects of grace, *i.e.*, all mankind. He is contemplating simply the relative power of influence. The influence of the fall is definitely measured by its result, death; that of grace, Paul says simply, is far greater. We take it that Paul is here speaking of these influences from the standpoint of *probational advantage or disadvantage*. We think this because he uses the aorist tense pointing to a general historical fact of the past. Presently we shall find him using the future tense and pointing, not to the equation of probational advantages which have occurred in human life, but to the final results which are yet to occur. Whatever the universal benefits of the atonement are, as they come to us, they are something far greater than the disadvantage of spiritual and physical death which comes to us through the fall. And Paul says "they abound," *i.e.*, they flow forth to us with the most lavish freeness. They are such gifts as light of divine truth, influences of the Holy Spirit, quickening of conscience, example, love of Christ constraining us, etc. We have Paul's authority for saying that, terrible as is the power of sin by which we are dead, the power of these influences is far greater, even sufficient to awake the dead. The incidental point of view of the parallel is correspondent. The two moral forces out of which our probation is made up —sin from Adam, grace from Christ—correspond one to the other in nature of influence, each touching our probational relation to God, but not in extent, Christ's grace to save surpassing.

much more did the grace of God, and the gift by the grace of the one man, Jesus Christ, abound unto the many.] In the first clause of this verse Paul uses the term, $\chi\alpha\rho\iota\sigma\mu\alpha$, "free gift." In the present clause he seems to analyze that term. It includes "grace," $\chi\alpha\rho\iota\varsigma$, that in the divine nature which leads God to give, and "the gift," $\delta\omega\rho\epsilon\alpha$, that which divine grace gives in Christ. Both these "abound," *i.e.*, overflow toward the sinner.

16. **And not as through one that sinned, so is the gift:]** In introducing his second point of divergence Paul repeats his formula with a slight variation. The first touched the extent of influence; this touches the source or state of affairs out of which the influence flows. Hence the introduction of the expression "through one that sinned" instead of "through the fall of the one." The one that sinned is not viewed now as the author of moral evil, but simply as, in his single sin, the occasion, the starting point from which the intervention of judgment began its work.

for the judgment came of one unto condemnation,] The intervention of judgment required but one single offence from which to set forth toward its final result, condemnation.

but the free gift came of many trespasses unto justification.] As if Paul had said, "One offence was sufficient to originate condemnation, but a great many are not sufficient to prevent justification." This is the evident meaning; how does the construction express it? Simply by taking the Greek preposition $\epsilon\kappa$ in a quasi-topical sense here. The condemnation is a force starting from ($\epsilon\kappa$) the point of the first sin and pressing man towards final condemnation. Grace is a force meeting this and opposing it, and overcoming not it alone but also the condemning force of many other transgressions, and so bearing man back toward the goal of "that which fulfils the demands of law." The word "justification," though not a true translation, expresses the sense. $\Delta\iota\kappa\alpha\iota\omega\mu\alpha$ is the act which law requires, which fulfils law, and hence justifies, as $\kappa\alpha\tau\alpha\kappa\rho\iota\mu\alpha$, to which it is here opposed, is the sentence of the judge which pronounces condemnation. "Unto that which fulfils law, and so justifies," is equivalent in effect to "unto justification." Godet goes further and supposes that $\delta\iota\kappa\alpha\iota\omega\mu\alpha$ here signifies "the sentence of justification," instead of the act or conduct upon which that sentence is based. The second point of divergence becomes thus a proof of the first; *i.e.*, the fact that the act of grace wipes out many offences, any one of which was sufficient to have deserved the original penalty, proves how much more abundant is the grace than the fall. The incidental parallel again corresponds. Judgment against sin and pardoning grace, condemnation and justification, are antithetically parallel.

17. **For if, by the trespass of the one, death reigned through the one;]** This is the third point of divergence. It is, like the first point, a difference in extent of influence; but not, as there, influence measured in relation to the probation of man in the present life, but influence measured by its final results in the future. The three verses may therefore be summed up as follows:—

Grace differs from the fall—(1) in that its gifts of saving help to man in his moral probation far exceed his loss through the fall, which is seen (2) in that while the fall entails the penalty of one transgression, grace removes the penalty of many; and (3) in that the future kingdom of life will far surpass even the terrible extent of the present kingdom of death.

much more shall they that receive the abundance of grace and of the gift of righteousness reign in life through the one, even Jesus Christ.] We have interpreted "much more," both here and in verse 15, as referring to *extent of influence*, not numerically (the number of persons reached), but potentially, the power of help brought to each (verse 15), or the "weight of glory" accruing to each (verse 17). Meyer, Godet and others interpret "much more" of logical certainty, "*much more surely.*" This might hold in verse 17, where the verb is in the future tense. But it can hardly apply to verse 15, with its verb in the aorist. But if, in verse 15, "much more" refers to the surpassing potency of grace as compared with sin, then in verse 17 we can scarcely give the very same phrase an entirely different meaning. "Much more" must be taken here, as in verse 15, of extent of influence, and that measured potentially and not numerically, since under no possible conception could it be said that the number saved in Christ exceeded the number who fell through Adam. The peculiar statement of the parallelism again corresponds to the point of difference. One man (Adam) is twice mentioned to throw into more emphatic contrast the very full designation "the one, Jesus Christ." The trespass is again placed over against the grace; but mark, it is "the abundance of grace and of the gift of righteousness"—"abundance of grace" (potential extent of grace in this life, verse 15), and "abundance of the gift of righteousness" (wiping out many offences, verse 16). This clause of verse 17 thus sums up the ideas of both 15 and 16. Again, the reign of death *over us* is contrasted with *our reign* in life.

The relation of the entire verse 17 to verses 15 and 16 has given rise to great diversity of opinion. The apostle introduces the verse by "for." The second clause of verses 15 and 16 is likewise introduced by "for;" but in each of the cases the conjunction attaches directly to the first clause of the same verse—"Not as the trespass, so also is the free gift. *For*," etc. But here the introductory clause is not repeated to form the point of attachment to this third "for." But is it not clearly to be understood? A series of co-ordinate clauses, introduced by the same conjunction and all attached to the one leading clause or thought, is quite in Paul's style. Verse 17 is thus the third expansion (with γαρ explicatory) of the leading theme, "Not as the offence, so also is the free gift," which having been twice expressed is not here repeated. Godet's history of the case, and his own attempt to account for the conjunction "for" by attaching it directly to verse 16, prove the utter uselessness of all attempts to construct a logical connection otherwise. But while the grammatical connection is as stated, the thought doubtless moves forward in a natural order from verse 16 to verse 17 as from verse 15 to verse 16. We have seen already that verse 16 not only advances a new thought beyond verse 15, but at the same time supplies further proof of the thought already advanced. And so verse 17, especially by combining, as we have seen, in one of its parallel terms the ideas of both verses, advances to a climax. Grace is mightier than sin, for it in this life stems the tide not of one sin but of many, and in the life to come will raise us from being slaves under the kingdom of death to being partners of the throne in the kingdom of life. The ascent of this climax follows the line of potential influence, while numerical extent is narrowed down to the finally saved. First to the many, *i.e.*, to the all who are under spiritual death, comes a richer gift of grace reinstating them in probation. Then under that probation comes a further gift of justification from many trespasses; and finally, to those who have received (in Greek, "*laid hold of*") both the grace and the gift of justification (righteousness) there comes the "reign in life."

18. **So then as through one trespass the judgment came unto all men to condemnation;**] The apostle having thus completed his "not as," *i.e.*, the limitations or qualifications of the parallel between sin and grace, resumes the direct and full statement of the parallel by two expressive particles of connection, "*so then.*" The first of these, *αρα*, "so," signifies "under these circumstances." The circumstances are the qualifying thoughts just expressed. The second, *ουν*, "then," is resumptive. It takes up a line of thought dropped for a time, and may be represented by our phrase, "as I was saying." The two may be expanded thus: "With these qualifications, as I was saying." This gives us immediate close connection with the preceding verses, and avoids the reference back to *δια τουτο*. The particle translated "as" is not quite so strong as that first used by Paul in verse 12. While the parallel is still clear the points of difference have come into view, and the more common term of likeness is sufficient. We have already (verse 15) defined the word here translated "trespass." It certainly refers to a definite fact and act. But "trespass" limits our thought too much to the act, while "fall" would turn our attention a little too exclusively to the consequences of the act. The Greek word includes both the sinful act and its immediate consequence in the change of relation of man to God. The word "judgment" is supplied in our version from

verse 16. But this too much limits the broad scope of the original. That consists of two clauses each denoting tendency or result, and each governed by the preposition "unto," which, as we have seen, is Paul's favourite preposition to denote the historical terminus toward which a thing moves, but at which it may not yet have arrived. By "the one fall" there exists a moral power or influence moving out from the first man "toward all men," and moving "toward condemnation" in every individual case. The word "condemnation," opposed in verse 16 to "that work which justifies," is here opposed to the act of justification, δικαίωσις. This is a little wider than our term "sentence of justification." It refers to the whole process by which the judge brings forth to light the righteousness of the man who is upon his trial. But this forensic sense fails, as it always must, to bring out the full evangelical meaning. Both words, "condemnation" and "justification," are more than a process at law. They include that moral power in sin and right-doing which places a man in wrong relation to God on the one hand, or in right relation on the other; *i.e.*, the condemning power of sin and the meritorious power of right-doing. The one fall or act of transgression puts forth a condemnatory influence reaching out toward all men. So the one grand act or work of righteousness puts forth a power to justify reaching out toward all men.

even so through one act of righteousness the free gift came unto all men to justification of life.] First, what is this "one act of righteousness"? Evidently the work of Jesus Christ, and preeminently his giving himself unto death for our sins. We shall refer to an important parallel passage when we come to the next verse. Meantime let us here observe that the justifying power or value of Christ's work, or, as in chapter iii. 25, its propitiatory efficacy, lies in its being a δικαίωμα, that which fulfils the law of right. Some have held that this refers to the demand of the law for penalty, and that Christ's δικαίωμα is his suffering of the penalty, and so satisfying law. It is not clear, however, that the word will ever bear the meaning thus put upon it. We think rather that the parallel in the next verse and in the passage there referred to indicate that it was not the mere negative suffering of penalty, but *the supreme moral worth* of the act of love and sacrifice in which he bowed to suffer penalty, which constitutes the valency, or justifying or propitiatory efficacy, of Christ's death. This would give its natural ordinary meaning to δικαίωμα, "an act of right-doing." But leaving Paul in the next verse to explain the full meaning of this word we find him here asserting that from this one act of right-doing there goes forth "toward all men" that which leads toward or works toward justification of life. The supplying of the terms "judgment" and "free gift" from verse 16 is scarcely admissible. Still less so is Godet's rendering, which makes condemnation and justification the respective subjects of a substantive verb. "There was unto all men condemnation," etc. This implies an immediate imputation not to be proven from this passage or to be found in any other. "By one act of transgression (or fall) it is unto all men unto condemnation, even so by one act of right-doing it is unto all men unto justification of life." Paul's words are most carefully chosen. He does not describe nor even give a name to this condemnatory or justificatory outgoing which reaches toward all men. It is not condemnation itself but a something moving toward condemnation; not justification itself but something moving toward justification. This preposition εἰς is very carefully chosen. If the noun without the preposition were used then our thoughts would revert to the idea of a direct imputation. It is not condemnation on the one hand nor justification on the other which goes forth from the "one act," but that which leads toward these results, though each *may fall short of its end.* Individual probation is thus maintained. Neither the fall nor the atonement supersedes it. But the second εἰς introduces another guard, "unto all men"—not the simple dative "for all men," nor επι, "upon all men," but "towards all men." Here again the power of both the fall and the atonement are *universal in their range;* but the εἰς gives room for individual probation and precludes that form of universalism which has its foundation in a Calvinistic view of the nature and application of the atonement. The advocates of the Calvinistic view can scarcely escape from universalism with this passage before them. But both Calvinistic limitation on the one hand and universalism on the other are precluded by the true force of the preposition εἰς.

19. **For as through the one man's disobedience the many were made sinners,**] "For" (γαρ) is here epexegetical, *i.e.,* it explains as well as proves the preceding proposition. There are three interpretations of this explicatory clause:—(1) That they are identical, and that "all" is expounded by "many." (2) That they are identical, and that "many" equals "all." (3) That the present verse presents a particular case, well understood, of the general category set forth in the previous verse, and therefore at once explains and proves it.

The first two interpretations are mutually destructive. They both interpret καθιστημι as "imputation." In the first, if the imputation of sin is universal the imputation of righteousness must be equally universal. In the second, if the imputation of righteousness is but conditionally universal, how can we affirm otherwise of sin? Besides, such an identical reiteration would neither explain nor prove verse 18. We must therefore study the terms of verse 19 and ascertain whether they yield a sense in accord with the third line of interpretation. The verbs are in historical tenses, aorist and future. If the second refers to future historical fact the first must so refer to past. The case presented is therefore historical, past or future. The verb καθιστημι signifies to place or establish in an office, *e.g.,* in a place of trust or responsibility. But when applied to a term denoting moral character or affection it signifies, both in classical and in New Testa-

ment Greek, to make one, *i.e.*, to produce in one, such character or
emotion. (See Godet *in loco.*) Such force here would imply, not the
imputation of guilt nor yet the transmission of depravity—neither
of these need be distinctly before the apostle's mind—but simply the
more general fact that as a result of Adam's one act (without any
assertion or theory of how this took place) a vast number of men,
i.e., the "all men" of verse 12, have actually become sinners. So
the one work of Christ shall result in a vast number becoming righteous. If this interpretation, which seems to be the simple, natural
sense of the words apart from dogmatic theories, be correct, then
we have a perfect connection of thought on the basis of the third
line of interpretation. The fact that so many have actually become
sinners proves and illustrates the fact that from the one act of the
first man there went forth toward all men that which moves toward
a universal condemnation.

**even so through the obedience of the one shall the many be
made righteous.]** This must be interpreted in the same way as the
protasis just considered, and so would mean, that without expanding
or asserting theories there shall be actual results of many righteous
from the obedience of the one. The antecedent and consequent
clauses in each of these two verses (18 and 19) have thus peculiar
logical relations. Verse 18 affirms three things—the influence of
sin, the influence of grace, and the analogy between these. But the
analogy is the logical link by which the fact of the influence of grace
is deduced from the fact of the influence of sin. In verse 19 there
are also three propositions in precisely similar relations. But verse
19 is likewise the proof of verse 18, not as proving the logical process or fact of analogy, but as proving from actual and well-known
historical fact *the expressed premise* of the argument from analogy,
and so proving *pari passu* the truth of the *conclusion*, "many shall
be made righteous." At the same time the apostle takes occasion,
by variation of the terms of his thesis, to make each of his propositions more clear in itself. The general "fall" or "act of stumbling" is made more definite, and its moral desert brought to light,
by the term "disobedience." So the term "act of righteousness"
or "fulfilment of right" is set forth as "obedience." This makes it
clear that Paul has before him, not at all the substitutionary suffering of penalty, but the supreme moral worth of Christ's sacrifice of
himself as the source of the valency of the atonement. Precisely
the same view is presented in Phil. ii. 5-8, which is our best parallel
to and comment on this verse. It there appears that the obedience
includes, not merely what is called our Lord's active righteousness,
but extends to his death and to the very form of that death.

**20. And the law came in beside, that the trespass might
abound;]** We must bear in mind that the sole object which Paul
has in view in this wonderful presentation of grace in contrast to
sin is, to magnify the ground of our "rejoicing in God through our
Lord Jesus Christ." This he has done by comparing the working

out of grace with the working out of sin. But there is a still further comparison which conduces to the same effect, the comparison of the results of the law with those of grace. This Paul now introduces with a δε continuative which may be translated by "moreover" or "still further." "Moreover the *law*"—"law" here occupies the emphatic place; "came in beside," *i.e.*, beside the power of sin and the already active influence of grace which Paul has already carried back into the region of "past sin"; "in order that"—final cause, purpose, or design of God in bringing the law alongside of this antagonistic relation of grace to sin: "the trespass" ("the fall") "might abound," "be made to grow," *i.e.*, be brought out in its full natural increase or growth, as the blade, ear, and full fruit in the ear, all springing from the seed. The object of the introduction of the law is to bring out of the seed of sin its full natural fruition. This Pauline teaching in regard to the peculiar office and work of the law we have already touched in chapters iii. 20; iv. 15; v. 13. It is still further unfolded from another point of view in chapter vii. 5, 7, etc., and with especial fulness in Gal. iii. 19-25, a passage quite parallel to the present, and by which we may expound it. In that passage we find that God's design is to bring sin out distinctly *as sin*, and so shut us up to the faith of Christ, or to act as "our tutor to bring us to Christ." This tutorial office is accomplished by bringing sin out to light. The various passages referred to give us a clear view of Paul's entire thought on this subject. We cannot agree with Moule that Paul here speaks of a subsidiary aim of the law. From his standpoint of God's economy of grace this represents the one purpose of the law, not in the old time alone, but through all ages. See Wesley's sermon on "The Nature, Origin, Properties and Uses of the Law."

but where sin abounded, grace did abound more exceedingly:] The translation of two distinct Greek words by the same English term, "abound," does not give the full force of the apostle's language. The first denotes simple increase, not necessarily beyond measure or bound; the second denotes overflow, measure surpassed. What is the measure which grace thus surpasses? Evidently the measure which the moral government of God assigns to sin. Paul's teaching is that God permits sin to express itself up to full measure. This measure the law, in its variety of precepts, defines by marking the limits of responsibility for knowledge of right and wrong. The more perfect the law the wider the range of responsibility, and hence the more frequent possibility of sin. The full measure of sin is greatly extended by the giving of a high form of moral law. But the justification of this increasing responsibility, and so extending the possibility, and in like manner the occurrence, of sin, is that with its extension the measure of grace is more abundantly extended. Here lies the foundation of the duty of the church to the heathen world. Send them the gospel and greater responsibility will result, and even greater sin in neglecting or rejecting the gospel be committed; but the superabounding of grace will compensate, and more, for these incidental and temporary evils. This superabounding of grace is the occasion of our glorying in God through our Lord Jesus Christ. If the Jew "resting in the law made his boast in God," much more may the Christian "boast in God through our Lord Jesus Christ." The law served only to develop the fall and the transgression, and so "wrought wrath." The grace of God in Christ, on the contrary, brings, not only life, but life far exceeding in extent of saving power the wrath brought in by the law. Such is one aspect of the conclusion which Paul has held steadily in view from verse 11, and which he has thrown into this parenthetical verse 20. But it is not in its antithesis to the law, but to sin that the true glory of grace lies. Hence to this broader ground of our glorying the apostle immediately returns.

21. **that, as sin reigned in death, even so might grace reign through righteousness unto eternal life through Jesus Christ our Lord.**] The conjunction "that," denoting purpose, refers us back, but to what? Most commentators say, where at all explicit, to the clause immediately preceding, "grace did abound more exceedingly in order that, as sin reigned in death," etc. But this seems almost a tautology. But if verse 20 is a parenthesis thrown in by the apostle because where he touches the grounds of the Christian boasting there comes up to his mind the Jewish boasting (ch. ii. 17), then the connection of verse 21 is to be found in verse 19. Verse 21 thus completes the final summary which was commenced at verse 18. Verses 12-17 expounded the statement in its full form, with its various incidental limitations and relations, beginning with the *entrance of sin* by one and ending with the *reign* in life through one, Jesus Christ. Verses 18-21 summarize and repeat this important statement in more concise and logical form, beginning with one man's fall and ending with the reign of grace through Jesus Christ. The points of analogy from verses 12 to 18 are thus: entrance of sin, entrance of death, universality of sin and universality of death on the one hand; and on the other, the more abundant provision or gift of probational grace, the more abundant forgiveness of many trespasses, and the final reign in life through Jesus Christ. In this first statement the apostle has before him more particularly the individual probational agent. All these (one by one) have sinned. All these, even where they did not sin after the similitude of Adam's transgression, died. But to each came the more abundant gift by grace and the opportunity of justification from their many trespasses; and to those who *lay hold* of these gifts comes the reign in life through Christ. In the *resumé* beginning with verse 18 the points of analogy are more general, and presented in more perfect logical order. On the one hand we have the one fall, and disobedience and its universal penal consequence, looking to final condemnation; or, from the standpoint of moral probation, the disobedience which made many sinners, resulting in a reign of sin in death. On the other hand we

have the one grand work of righteousness, with its universal grace looking to final justification; or, from the standpoint of moral probation, the obedience which makes many righteous, resulting in the reign of grace through righteousness unto eternal life. It should be noted that in this last verse the contrast is made, not between sin and grace, nor yet between sin and righteousness, but between sin and grace working out its kingdom through righteousness. Sin is not only a controlling power in human life but a cause of guilt; and so grace brings not only redemption from the power of sin but also from its guilt.

Having thus arrived at the conclusion of Paul's statement of the occasion of the Christian's boasting in God through Jesus Christ we may recapitulate his argument from verse 11 as follows:—

We shall be saved by the life of Christ, not only having been reconciled but also making our boast in God through this Christ (by whose death we were reconciled) on this account: that as by one man's disobedience many were made sinners, so by the obedience of one shall many be made righteous, in order that as sin reigned in death, even so may grace reign through righteousness unto eternal life through Jesus Christ our Lord.

Excursus on the Dogmatic Teachings of this Chapter.

The doctrinal statements concerning sin and salvation which Paul thus brings into antithesis as the foundation of the Christian's boasting or supreme confidence in God are the most fundamental in the Christian system, differentiating it from all other theistic religions. The chapter before us furnishes us the most complete statement to be found in scripture of the doctrine of the fall in Adam, and one of the most explicit of the doctrine of the atonement in Christ. These important doctrines are not based upon this chapter alone, inasmuch as they are clearly presupposed in many other passages not only of Paul's writings but also of other New Testament authors. Nor would this passage, taken by itself alone, suffice for the full statement of either one of these important doctrines. For the doctrine of sin we must at least add the important statements of chapters i., ii. and vii.; and for the doctrine of the atonement we require important assistance from chapter iii., as well as from the second chapter of the epistle to the Philippians. But these facts do not diminish the claim of the present chapter to the foremost place in the exposition of the Biblical doctrines of sin and of the atonement. It becomes, therefore, important to distinguish clearly what is and what is not implied in the statements of this chapter. First as to the doctrine of sin, it is clearly set forth that Adam's sin is not an isolated historical fact, but bears a potential relation to the universal sinfulness of the race. This idea lies in two statements—verse 12, "upon which antecedent condition of things all have sinned;" and still more directly verse 19, "through one man's disobedience many were made sinners." But in neither of these statements is there to be found the idea of imputation of Adam's sin, nor indeed any expressed reference to any other theory of the transmission of sin from the first man to the whole race. We may fairly call in the doctrine of the hereditary transmission of depravity found in other scriptures, but we cannot quote the present passage as proof of that doctrine. Again, it is very clearly stated that the first sin is the cause of universal death. The interpretation of this term "death" as "conscious separation from God," as well as "separation of the soul from the body," we may fairly deduce from Paul's teaching in chapter vii., where see notes. Still, the foremost idea here seems to be physical death (verse 14). The statements in verse 12, "death passed through unto all men;" verse 14, "death reigned from Adam to Moses;" verse 15, "by the trespass of the one the many died;" verse 17, "by the trespass of the one death reigned," all point to the well-known fact of universal physical death, though the expression in verse 21, "sin reigned in death," would seem better interpreted of spiritual death. There is perhaps implied in this second dogmatic position at least a degree of imputation of Adam's sin, or of what is technically called hereditary guilt. If all men die in consequence of Adam's sin, then *so far* all men are held amenable to the penal consequences of Adam's sin. But because they are held amenable to some penal consequences, such as physical death, conscious separation from God, and a depraved nature, it by no means follows that they are held amenable to *all penal consequences*, still less that the *culpa* as well as the *pœna*—the blame as well as the penal consequences—can be carried forward to all the race. We are therefore by no means authorized to deduce from the passage before us an unlimited imputation of Adam's sin. But there appears a third point in the apostle's doctrine of sin contained in verses 16 and 18. "The judgment came of one unto condemnation," and "through one trespass unto all men to condemnation." This has been supposed by many to contain the doctrine of an absolute and universal imputation of Adam's sin. We have seen that it can do so only by teaching an equally absolute and universal doctrine of justification in Christ. If it does not teach the one it cannot teach the other. And if Paul uses εις here in its usual meaning of tendency or result, then in that little particle there lies the whole field of probation to be traversed between Adam's sin and the final condemnation. How the impulse from Adam's sin moves across the field of human probation towards a universal condemnation Paul does not say, nor even imply. He deals with facts, not with theories. If the impulse toward condemnation is carried through a genuine individual probation, the theory that hereditary depravity is the medium of its transmission seems much more probable than that it reaches the end at once by a law of hereditary guilt. It is, besides, much more in harmony with Paul's idea of the valency or power of sin over and among the human race, which is the prominent thought of this passage. If this be the true interpretation of Paul's thought, then the word "judgment," in verse 17, points to the penal consequences of Adam's sin, including "depravity," and conscious separation from God, as well as physical death; and these penal consequences come upon all men with a mighty power, leading to final condemnation, which would render equitable personal probation impossible were not the free gift still mightier in its moral force. Beyond what is implied in these three statements we cannot assume to read into this passage a theory of original sin. The laws of historical interpretation justify us in interpreting the ideas of any writer in the light of opinions or thoughts expressed by him in other parts of his works; but beyond this we have no right to go. With the doctrine of heart sin Paul was certainly familiar; it is a specially Pauline doctrine. With the doctrine of birth sin he could not be unacquainted; and though he does not make it as prominent as St. John, it is, we think, the doctrine of Eph. ii. 3. We may therefore fairly call in both here. But the doctrine of hereditary guilt, in its modern form of an absolute imputation, is so strange to the writings of Paul (and to the Old Testament as well as to the New, in all which the supremacy and reality of individual responsibility are so clearly taught) that we dare not force it in here beyond the plain facts of the text.

But besides laying the foundation for the Pauline doctrine of sin the passage before us contributes largely to the doctrine of the atonement. In fact, the fall in Adam and the atonement in Christ are the main themes of the passage. We have already obtained several important elements of the Pauline view of the atonement from chapter iii. We have there learned that he views it as a "redemption" or deliverance by payment of a ransom price, and that this ransom price is a propitiatory offering of his blood, *i.e.*, his life, and that in virtue of this offering God is (not merely is seen or proved to be) just while the justifier of him that believeth on Jesus. Propitiation is that in sacrifice which moves God to forgiveness, and in virtue of which he can justly exercise forgiveness. Wherein this propitiatory efficacy consists is the deepest and most difficult question of the doctrine of the atonement. The passage before us seems to touch this difficult point. It compares the work of Christ to the work of Adam. That in Adam's act which makes it the source of penal consequence to the whole race is its *guilt* or moral desert as a transgression or disobedience. That in Christ's work which makes it the source of grace to the whole race is its *merit* or moral desert as an act of righteousness or obedience. In constructing the doctrine of the atonement we might very fairly make further use of this passage and press the analogy to the extent of finding a common principle of race unity in probation in virtue of which the penal consequences of Adam's sin reach all the race, and the gracious results of Christ's righteousness reach all the race. This would lead to very important results touching the nature of the atonement in itself—its relation to the forgiveness of sin on the one hand and to the conditions of individual probation on the other. But this would lead us out of the field of Biblical into that of systematic theology. We need therefore only call attention once more to the full expansion of Paul's idea of the merit of Christ's act of obedience given us in Phil. ii. 6-8. This passage fully justifies the position we assign to our present passage in relation to the doctrine of atonement.

CH. VI. 1-23. THE ETHICAL SIDE OF THE CHRISTIAN DOCTRINE.

1. **What shall we say then?**] What practical conclusion shall we draw? Paul is here directing the thoughts of his readers to the line of duty arising out of the great truth which he has just presented. This truth was the duty of making our boast in God, not through the law, but through our Lord Jesus Christ; because where sin abounded through the law grace did much more abound through Christ. The law, by the abounding of sin, brought us to spiritual death; but the grace of Christ, through God's gift of righteousness, brings us to eternal life. We are therefore called upon to choose between continuing under the law, *which means continuing in sin*, and placing ourselves fully and forever upon the ground of grace. Which shall it be? What shall we say?

Shall we continue in sin, that grace may abound?] This question is not, we think, the boldly antinomian one usually supposed by the commentators. They have ignored the fact that Paul is addressing men who are being pressed by his opponents with the claims of the law. He has just put the grand scheme of grace before them in its relations to the whole race from Adam down, and in verse 20 has pointed out the transitory design and effect of the law as bringing the sin out to the surface, and so working wrath or death (ch. iv. 15). To those who are being pressed to commit themselves to this temporary dispensation of the law by being circumcised he puts the incisive logical question, "Shall we continue in sin," *i.e.*, by continuing under the law, or, by embracing the law instead of the righteousness of God as our hope of salvation; or, as the alternative reading is, "*May* we continue in sin?" Is it at all permissible to continue in sin by continuing under the dispensation of law? or by placing ourselves under it? That this is the real point of Paul's question will, we think, be proven by the whole following context. This question, which is a magnificent combination of rhetoric and logic, condenses a volume of argument in the simple substitution of the word *sin* for that which can only multiply sin, *i.e.*, *the law*, and thus enables the apostle to answer with a decisive

2. **God forbid.**] Such a thought cannot be for a moment entertained; not even the possibility of grace abounding can justify continuance in sin when deliverance from it is secured by grace through faith. We were indeed shut up under the law and under the dominion of sin until grace came; but now God forbid that we should

for a moment longer remain in that position. And the reason of this is clear:

We who died to sin, how shall we any longer live therein?] Here again we have an alternative subjunctive reading, which we may render "how should we any longer live therein?" In this expression, "We who died to sin," Paul brings up before his readers a definite and well-known fact in their religious life. What this was is made clear in the next verse, in his exposition of the significance and obligations of baptism. In Col. iii. 3, and in some other passages, Paul uses this same phrase and in the same sense. Probably in the administration of baptism the candidate was admonished that as this was to be a new birth to a new life, so now to the old life of sin he was to become at once and forever dead. This includes more than the mere breaking of the will with sin (Godet), and differs also from the extinction of the moral power of sin in our nature. It is the end of all *legal relation* to sin, and so of its power over us both in will and in deed. Moule and Riddle have one part of the idea, Godet another. On the various interpretations of this phrase see Godet *in loco*. Its full meaning will become apparent as we follow the apostle's own explanation of it in the verses which follow, especially verses 6, 9 and 11.

3. **Or are ye ignorant that all we who were baptized into Christ Jesus were baptized into his death?**] This clause introduces a very intricate line of thought, which is only completed in verse 11. First of all, we must determine the relation of this question, and of the line of thought which it introduces, to the question immediately preceding. It is introduced by the disjunctive "or," which seems here to present the alternative to an evasion of the preceding question. If they do not admit that in no way can they continue in sin after baptismal death to sin, then they are ignorant of the full significance of their baptism, which he now proceeds to explain. The force of the disjunctive may thus be paraphrased: "Either ye must admit that all we who died to sin can no longer in any way live therein, or ye must be ignorant that all we who were baptized into Christ Jesus were baptized into his death." Both these questions are rhetorical and equivalent to a very strong assertion of the expected answer. But the second is put in such a form as opens up a proof of the first. The only possible alternative to admitting the force of the first is ignorance of the ground upon which it rests, and which the apostle now proceeds to set forth. That ground lies in the obligation of baptism as a "baptism into Christ's death." Out of this peculiar phrase, which we think was by no means so unfamiliar and difficult to understand in Paul's day as it is now, he proceeds to elaborate his argument, showing how it leads up to the idea of the death of all our old life, and so of our death with Christ to all relation to sin. We must first ascertain what is the meaning of the phrase "baptized into his death." In answering this question we must bear in mind the fact that this preposition "into," or "unto," is the one con-

stantly used in the baptismal formula. (See Matt. xxviii. 19; Acts viii. 10; xix. 3, 5; 1 Cor. i. 13; x. 2; xii. 13; Gal. iii. 27.) Baptism was an ordinance expressive of sanctification, *setting apart*. This setting apart was from sin to God, to Christ, to the one body of his church, to repentance (John's baptism), to follow Moses (the baptism in the Red Sea), but not "to Paul," etc. The preposition thus retains its significance of the end or aim to be reached. By baptism we are made one with Christ in his death, *i.e.*, in all that is implied in Christ's death. What this is and how it leads to the end in view we shall leave Paul himself to state in the next verse. All that we need deal with here is, that baptism implies such a yielding of ourselves "*unto*" Christ as implies unity and fellowship with him in every point, even in his death. This doctrine of Paul as to baptism appears very clearly in Gal. iii. 26-28, "Ye are all sons of God, through faith, in Christ Jesus. For as many of you as were baptized into Christ did put on Christ. There can be neither Jew nor Greek," etc., "for ye all are *one man in Christ Jesus*." Here there cannot be the slightest doubt as to Paul's idea of baptism as the symbol of a perfect unity with Christ, such as does away with all old distinctions, and makes all that belongs to Christ ours.

4. We were buried therefore with him through baptism into death:] The phrase "baptism into death" is literally "baptism into the death," where we think the article, as frequently, takes the place of the personal pronoun. "The death" is "his death" just mentioned. "Baptism into the death" is thus to be taken as one united phrase. The connection of thought then runs as follows: "If by baptism into Jesus Christ we become so one with him as to be united to him in his death, 'then'" (ουν) "we enter into the grave with him through this baptism into his death,"

that like as Christ was raised from the dead through the glory of the Father, so we also might walk in newness of life.] Baptism is not the process of *burial* or entombment but the process of union with Christ in his *death*. But this implies as a necessary consequence that we, in a figurative way, go down with Christ into the grave, that so we may rise with him in the new life. The going into the grave and the rising with Christ into the new life are not baptism itself, and hence have no necessary reference to the mode of baptism. They are merely the sequence (ουν) of that unity with Christ in his death which is expressed in "baptism into his death." Baptism into Christ's death implies, therefore, as a *necessary sequence*, our rising to newness of life, and hence the utter impossibility of our continuance in sin or under its power. This argument he now proceeds to put in a condensed form.

5. For if we have become united with him by the likeness of his death, we shall be also by the likeness of his resurrection;] Here the intermediate step of burial is left out, and the decisive point alone stated. "Union with Christ in his death" (which took place at our baptism) implies "union with him in his resurrection," and hence forbids "continuance in sin." The word here translated in the revised verson "united" has been the cause of no little difficulty. "United" translates only one-half the word, the prepositional prefix συμ. In the other part of the word it is supposed that the writer brings in an altogether new metaphor to express our unity with Christ, and passes altogether away from the idea of baptism. This line of interpretation has resulted from the form of translation following the Vulgate *complantati*. As the word occurs here only in the New Testament we must depend on the classical usage. The verb signifies *to make to grow*, applied either to plants or animals, hence frequently "to beget" or "to bear." The verbal adjective may thus very naturally bear the meaning of "begotten" or "born." It occurs generally only in combination (once alone of a statue produced by nature), and where combined with συν signifies either "inborn," that which one has by nature or birth, or "*growing together*," as the lips of a wound. With this classical usage why should we call in the idea of a tree or plant. Baptism gives in itself, according to the Jewish manner of speaking of the rite at the time, the idea of *new birth*. The idea of this *birth making us one in being with Christ* is quite naturally suggested by this. We might thus translate, or rather paraphrase, the verse before us thus: "If we have grown to be one by our baptismal new birth with Christ in the likeness of his death, on *the other hand* also we shall be in the likeness of his resurrection." The idea of burial is thus quite dropped out. We have ventured to render the Greek αλλα as "on the other hand." It sets forth the necessary contrast, the antithesis to the first member of the sentence. Our baptismal union by the new birth thus places us in a relation to Christ's death which implies as its necessary sequence or antithesis the new life of separation from sin corresponding to Christ's resurrection. But this line of thought suggests a further development of the idea of our unity with Christ by our baptismal new birth.

6. knowing this, that our old man was crucified with him,] In this verse Paul takes up further the idea of dying with Christ, and makes it the foundation of an argument for cessation from sin. The first question is, what are we to understand by the "old man"? The apostle uses a variety of somewhat similar expressions—the "old man," the "new man," the "inward man," the "outer man." It by no means follows that the "old man" and the "outer man" are identical, nor yet the "new man" and the "inward man." Nor can we fairly identify either the "old man" or the "outward man" with "the flesh" or "the members in which dwells the law of sin." The most explicit passage in which Paul uses this term is Eph. iv. 22-24, "That ye put away, *as concerning your former manner of life*, the old man, which waxeth corrupt after the lusts of deceit; and that ye be renewed in the spirit of your mind, and put on the new man, which after God hath been created in righteousness and holiness of truth." Here the "old man" is evidently distinguished

from the lusts or sinful nature, through which it has become corrupt. So the renewal of the spirit of our minds precedes the putting on of the "new man." We think the "old man" is defined by the phrase "concerning your former manner of life." The preposition κατα is used of definition or description. It would thus signify the entire "old life" in its outward manifestations and works, as well as in its moral spirit and nature. To put off the old man would be thus to break away from the whole "old life," and to put on the new man would be to enter into an entirely new mode of life. This would be quite in harmony with Paul's use of the metaphor of putting on or off a garment. This, then, explains what Paul means by "dying with Christ." It is on our part the entire putting off of the old life—a much wider meaning than the simple extinction of the corrupt principle of sin within. This certainly was fully implied in baptism (see 1 Peter iii. 21), not merely promised or partially entered upon as an act of will, but expected to be carried into effect in the most thorough manner. It is not the "old man was being crucified" but "was crucified" in this baptismal sacrament, "*died*" (aorist) once and forever. The whole old manner of life came to an end. This definite act of crucifixion on our part took place for a distinct purpose:

that the body of sin might be done away,] What this body of sin is will appear clearly from the latter part of the seventh chapter, where it is also called the "body of death." It is much more accurate to designate this as the corrupt nature or sinful nature, a meaning which most of our commentators assign to the "old man." Paul says that in baptism we put an end to the entire old life, crucified it then and there with our crucified Lord; "in order that"—the conjunction expressing design or purpose—the corrupt nature "might be done away." The verb used here and frequently elsewhere does not signify an abrogation (as when applied to the law, ch. iii. 31) but a doing away with the power, effect or proper result of the law. (See notes on ch. iii. 31.) So here the body of sin is a power (ch. vii. 24) the effect of which over us (its hold upon us) is to be destroyed by this death of our old manner of life. But this breaking of the power of sin is itself the cause of a further result, expressed in Greek by the genitive case of the infinitive mood (see Winer, 409),

that so we should no longer be in bondage to sin;] Under this term "bondage to sin" Paul has in view not alone the moral power of the corrupt nature by which we are driven to do the things that we would not, but also, as appears immediately in the next verse, the legal right by which we are thus consigned to slavery to sin. This explains why this death of our old life must be in unity with Christ's death. Christ's expiatory death alone can break the legal as well as the moral bond by which we are held in the service of sin. It is thus impossible for our old life to die except with Christ. But now with Christ our old life is crucified, the power of sin is broken, and from the bondage of sin we are lawfully delivered,

7. for he that hath died is justified from sin.] This is evidently a legal maxim supposed to be perfectly plain to his readers. If it was an aphorism of law quoted by Paul, then, as Godet supposes, its original application would be to physical death, which, so far as the individual is concerned, discharges him from all legal obligations, pains and penalties. Its application here would thus be, that when, by baptism, we become united to Christ in his expiatory death, the legal claim of sin to hold us in bondage is cancelled. Paul thus intimately relates our moral renewal to our freedom from the claims of justice which hitherto has been his principal theme.

8. But if we died with Christ, we believe that we shall also live with him;] By the conjunction "but" we are at once transferred from the negative aspect of the death of our old life, and the consequent breaking of the power of sin, from whose service we are legally discharged, to the positive point of view of a new life with Christ. Baptism represented especially the dying of the old life. But Paul has full faith that more must follow. A new life must take the place of the old. The grounds of this faith he now proceeds to set forth.

9. knowing that Christ being raised from the dead dieth no more; death no more hath dominion over him;] The legal claim of death upon him, through sin, not his own but ours, is satisfied. To this Paul's readers must at once assent, though to make it perfectly clear he adds an explanation.

10. For the death that he died, he died unto sin once:] Margin, "once for all." The expression "died unto sin" cannot be identified in meaning with the crucifixion of our "old man." It is more general in meaning even when applied to us. It signifies the end of all living relation to sin. When Christ took upon him our nature he became related in life to our sin (ch. viii. 3; 2 Cor. v. 21). He was made sin for us. With his death this relation to sin came to an end once and forever. "He died to sin once for all."

but the life that he liveth, he liveth unto God.] This relation is eternal, abiding. It is *the life* of our Mediator and Head, and so ours. (See Col. iii. 3, 4, where this same idea of baptismal death and new life with Christ in God is presented.) Hence here as there the exhortation,

11. Even so reckon ye also yourselves to be dead unto sin, but alive unto God in Christ Jesus.] "Reckon," *i.e.*, put it down to your account as a matter fully and finally settled. This would not be the case if, seeking to be justified by the law, they fell away from the grace of Christ. This exhortation sums up the practical scope of Paul's entire argument in this Epistle, which was to establish the Roman church in the faith of Christ as opposed to the legal system of the Judaizers. They are to settle it forever in their minds that henceforth their life is consecrated to God in Christ Jesus, no more a slavery to sin through the law. "Dead unto sin," *i.e.*, free from all living relation to it—the reassertion of what he had implied in the question of verse 2, which he has now fully proved. But more than that, as he took care to develop in his line of proof, "alive unto God through Jesus Christ, inasmuch as unity with Christ in his death must be followed by unity with him in his resurrection. The practical outcome or expansion of this we next turn to consider (verses 12-14).

12. **Let not sin therefore reign in your mortal body, that ye should obey the lusts thereof:**] The conjunction "therefore" presents this exhortation as the outcome of the positions already advanced, proved, and finally summed up in verse 11. The entire section must, however, be read in close connection with the last clause of verse 14. This entire discussion was introduced by the mention of the law in chapter v. 20; it returns to the mention of the law in verse 14. Taking chapter v. verses 20 and 21 together, we see the point to which Paul is thus coming back. Then through the coming in of the law the trespass abounded and *sin reigned in death*. "Let not sin thus reign in your mortal bodies." Under the dominion of death they still are, but not under that of sin. To see what this means in Paul's mind, and its relation to the law, compare 1 Cor. xv. 56: "The sting of death is sin; and the power of sin is the law." "Let not sin reign in your mortal (or dying) bodies, for ye are not under the law but under grace." Godet well says the word "mortal" must have some logical connection with the line of thought here, and such connection we thus find in Paul's own words. We need not thus import into the exhortation ideas which deprive it of all its power. The "mortal body" is not the body as the field of the power of sin, or as not yet fully delivered, and so still under the power of sin. This is exactly what the apostle says must not be. Nor is the *reign* contrasted with the *occasional outbreak* of sin as an abnormal thing. "Let not sin reign" equals "ye are dead to sin." The apostle's exhortation is not a loose generality admitting unlimited exceptions, but *an absolute standard of holiness*. Paul holds that our will, our reckoning, must place sin in fact just where our new gracious relation to Christ places it in right, *i.e.*, in complete separation from us. Nor is there any covert for the hiding of sin in the phrase "that ye should obey the lusts thereof." Even this expression does not imply the continued "presence of sin in the mortal body of the justified." It may be true that such is the case, but that is quite outside the line of Paul's thought here; and he is so very far from affirming its necessary continuance that his words demand its instant and complete cessation. The lusts of the body are those desires and appetites which sin has so long used as its servants. When we obeyed the servants we obeyed their master. But all this is now to cease—not only our slavery to sin, our obedience to the servants or instruments of sin in the desires of our own bodies, but the very relation of those appetites and desires to sin. Hence Paul immediately adds,

13. **neither present your members unto sin as instruments of unrighteousness;**] Sin is clearly to be put out of the body as well as out of the will. These members as instruments of sin are the

seat of the lusts, *i.e.*, sinful desires. They become the instruments of sin by their power over the will—not in a merely external way. This is implied in the Greek word for instruments, in the margin and literally, "weapons." Sin, by these members warring against the soul, conquers the will, and so enslaves us. Paul's point of view is, that in the past, under the law, before we died to sin, "sin reigned," making our members, through the lusts of the body, the weapons by which it took us captive. But far from comtemplating this state of things as necessarily continuing even in part, he commands it *all* to cease. God's command implies the power to obey; and if in faith we reckon ourselves thus fully and forever dead to sin, even in the members of our "mortal body," dead we surely shall be.

but present yourselves unto God, as alive from the dead,] This is the positive sequence of Paul's argument. We are dead with Christ and raised to new life with him, and hence with him are called to live to God. This presentation to God is not the mere will to do good while evil is still present. It goes far beyond that. The very "members" in which sin reigned as a law of sin and death are to be included in the presentation.

and your members as instruments of righteousness unto God.] The mortal body, far from continuing to be the seat of sin, henceforth is itself to be the seat of righteousness. Its members, *i e.*, its natural desires, now sanctified to the new service, are to be the weapons of righteousness as they once were the weapons of sin. No higher ideal of holiness can be presented than this, that the very desires (members) which once led to sinful acts now, changed under the new life, lead to holy acts of God's service—"become the instruments of righteousness unto God."

If it be asked how Paul can speak of all this as at the command of our will the reply is,

14. For sin shall not have dominion over you: for ye are not under law, but under grace.] The legal claim of sin is broken, and, as Paul takes for granted, with the legal claim the moral power. It is henceforth in our own will, for we are "not under the law, but under grace." Were we under the law sin would necessarily reign, as Paul will show presently; but under grace we are delivered from its power, and hence free to will ourselves from sin and unto God.

15. What then?] This formula, as in chapter vi. 1, marks a new direction in the argument. In verse 1 that direction was determined by the mention of the purpose of the intervention of the law and its relation to the reign of sin and the reign of grace. Here the direction of the argument is determined by the statement which closes verse 14, "Ye are not under law, but under grace." "What then?" *i.e.*, what follows from this?

shall we sin, because we are not under law, but under grace?] "Shall we sin" must not be taken as identical with "shall we continue in sin." Were it so there would really be no advance in thought.

"Shall we continue in sin" refers to our *general moral position*, our status before God, which must be either under grace, dead to sin, or under the law, servants to sin. That question Paul has settled: "Sin shall not have dominion over you; for ye are not under law, but under grace." But out of this very new relation, which delivers us from the dominion of sin by transferring us from the law to grace, there arises a new danger, the danger of yielding to *individual acts of sin*. Paul doubtless was well aware of the tendency, so often since his day marked in human nature, to feel satisfied with the gracious assurance that we are delivered from the bondage of sin, especially in regard to guilt, and so to be less watchful against occasional transgressions. To the question he therefore replies, God forbid.

16. **Know ye not, that to whom ye present yourselves as servants unto obedience, his servants ye are whom ye obey;]** "Know ye not" equals "are ye ignorant," of verse 3—a repetition of logical formulæ peculiar to Paul, and introducing here, as there, the grounds for his strong assertion. The dominion of sin is not a mere ideal matter, a legal fiction or hypothesis; it is a matter of practical life. It is determined by our actions—we are the servants of the master whom we obey in *the acts*, the living service of our lives. An antinomian carelessness of life, under a supposed privilege of grace. in reality returns us to the bondage of sin.

whether of sin unto death, or of obedience unto righteousness?] These individual sins must *end* in death. Grace covers no wilful persistence in sin. On the other hand, if we are to maintain the right relation to God, obedience alone leads to righteousness. Mark the contrast between "death," separation from God, and "righteousness," right relation to God. We are instated in that right relation by faith, but that relation can only be maintained by obedience, by a "faith which works by love." What the nature of that obedience is Paul proceeds at once to state. Meantime the principle is laid down here in the most absolute manner, that grace will not shield us from the result of sin in death, nor dispense with the necessity of "obedience unto righteousness."

17. **But thanks be to God, that, whereas ye were servants of sin, ye became obedient from the heart to that form of teaching whereunto ye were delivered;]** Notwithstanding the uncompromising fidelity and seeming severity with which Paul maintains the ethical obligations of religion against a morally inefficient legalism on the one hand, and against an antinomian abuse of grace on the other, he is not unmindful of the truly gracious and sincere character of his readers. This moves his heart, for Paul was a man of strong feelings, of stern zeal against sin, but of tenderly loving appreciation of all that is good. Hence this outburst, "Thank God." "'That ye *were*." The emphasis is on the verb in the imperfect (past historical) tense, hence implying that they are no longer "servants of sin." This does not imply a legal or Jewish state preceding their

conversion. Paul is here dealing with practical bondage to sin in any form, not with that particular type of doctrine which only serves to make that bondage more sorely felt. He frequently refers to the complete practical slavery to sin from which the Gentile converts were delivered (1 Cor. vi. 11; Gal. iv. 8; Eph. ii. 2, 3; Col. i. 21). "But ye obeyed from the heart," the aorist pointing to the definite time of their conversion. This was not a superficial change likely to degenerate into antinomian indifference, but obedience "from the heart," hence full of the true holy spirit of the gospel. "That type of doctrine unto which ye were consigned," *i.e.*, in the order of God's providence. "Type of doctrine" is quite Pauline, both as a rule of faith and also of life. It doubtless refers to the Pauline form of the gospel as distinguished from the gospel of the circumcision given to Peter (Gal. ii. 7). To this type of doctrine God had in the dispensation of his grace assigned the Gentiles—"unto which ye were delivered." The Roman Christians were still further and more particularly "given over" to this type of doctrine by its being in the providence of God the form of the gospel under which they were converted. (See Introduction.)

18. **and being made free from sin, ye became servants of righteousness.**] This was the sequence of their hearty obedience to the gospel. The obedience of the heart to the gospel is everywhere with Paul synonymous with true and "saving faith." (See Rom. i. 5; x. 16; xvi. 26; 2 Thess. i. 8.) "Being made free from sin" thus implies the full saving power of the gospel, that justifying as well as sanctifying grace which Paul has just expounded. This includes, as we have seen, the new life to God, "servants of righteousness," as well as the death of the old life in sin. Of the reality of such an experience on the part of his readers Paul entertains no doubt. He sincerely thanks God for it. But the reality and sincerity of their religious experience does not deliver these Roman Christians from that moral weakness which Paul designates as "the flesh."

19. **I speak after the manner of men because of the infirmity of your flesh:**] This exhortation is rendered necessary in this human form because of the infirmity of the flesh. What is "the manner of men" in which Paul says he here speaks? and what is the "infirmity of the flesh" which renders this manner of speech necessary? Philippi, Meyer and Godet all refer this to the expression "ye became slaves of righteousness." Godet goes so far as to explain how the service of righteousness was to some extent a slavery, through opposition and weakness of the flesh, which he regards as moral weakness, the flesh in the sense of the corrupt nature. Meyer thinks the "weakness of the flesh" intellectual weakness, and that the very strong metaphor of slavery is employed in condescension to mental weakness. But both of these explanations are unsatisfactory. Meyer's is especially so. Paul elsewhere compliments the Roman Christians on their knowledge; and if he accommodated himself to their intellectual weakness he would not be very likely to tell them

of it, though fidelity would demand that he should not spare a moral weakness. Godet's idea of the service of righteousness being really a slavery through moral weakness takes away the point of the phrase "I speak humanly," and is, besides, out of harmony with Paul's universal doctrine of the glorious liberty of God's children from the law of sin and death in the members (ch. viii. 2, 3). But is this form of expression "bondservant," which Paul repeatedly applies to himself (see ch. i. 1), so objectionable that it needs an apology? Does it not express Paul's idea of the ethical spirit of Christianity—the complete subjection of our whole nature to the new spirit of righteousness. If so then the use of this metaphor is not "the human manner of speaking" to which Paul refers. We think it rather lies in the stern, forceful manner of exhortation which he had just used (verses 15, 16) and which he is now about to repeat (verses 19-21), and in the use of an appeal to human considerations. This severe method of legal precept might well be called the human method, rendered necessary by the moral weakness of the flesh.

for as ye presented your members as servants to uncleanness and to iniquity unto iniquity,] "For" here, as frequently, introduces the explanation or statement of this human manner of speech. So the ancients, although they thought the humanness lay in the lowering of the demands of holy law rather than the childlike preceptual manner of enforcing it. On the members as servants of sin see verses 12 and 13. The terms "uncleanness" and "iniquity" designate the positive and the negative side respectively of the opposition of the flesh to right. The end of this service is "lawlessness," used by John as the definition of sin.

even so now present your members as servants to righteousness unto sanctification.] Even on "human" principles this is only a fair thing. The service of righteousness demands no more than did the service of sin. Not that thereby the Christian law of righteousness is lowered, for sin, as a taskmaster, exacted the full tale of brick. Sanctification is the sanctified state, the state of saints, consecrated to God. This lower human method of enforcing the obligation to Christian holiness is still further expanded by γαρ in the next verse:

20. For when ye were servants of sin, ye were free in regard of righteousness.] "For"—a reason, *more humano*, for the exclusive service of righteousness. Sin obtained exclusive service. It excluded all claims of righteousness. Give now the same measure to the new master. You are justly called upon to do so, for what were your wages under that former master?

21. What fruit then had ye at that time in the things whereof ye are now ashamed? The conjunctive "then," ουν, is not equivalent to therefore, but serves, as Grimm states (Lex. *sub voce*), to attach this question in a general way to the preceding statement. It might be rendered "furthermore." The adverb "at that time" must not be dropped out of sight. It distinguishes the fruit from the final result, "the end," to be mentioned presently. The fruit is the immediate benefit. The interrogative used is not "What kind of?" but simply "What?" This would require as answer either a direct negative, "none," or a specification of the fruits. The former alternative Meyer adopts, rendering the final clause as a part of the question, as in both our English versions. A large number of translators and expositors adopt the latter alternative. (See Godet.) This we think more in harmony with the strong thought at which Paul has now arrived. The answer to the question is then in the middle clause, "Those things of which you are now ashamed," or to imitate more closely Paul's sententious style, "What you are now ashamed of." The next clause then presents the reason for this shame.

for the end of those things is death.] It is now evident to their enlightened conscience that the end of every sinful pleasure or indulgence is death, therefore they are ashamed of them. This is in harmony with Paul's customary use of the word "fruit" to denote the acts flowing from a principle or spirit of life (Gal. v. 19-23).

22. But now being made free from sin, and become servants to God, ye have your fruit unto sanctification, and the end eternal life.] From the new position of life the fruits, *i.e.*, all the actions, tend—the usual force of the preposition—to holiness, the passive form of this word, hence denoting the state, not the active principle, of sanctification. These fruits do not sanctify us, but constitute the sanctified state into which we are led and in which we are maintained by them. The end no less than the fruits is in contrast with sin; it is not "death" but "eternal life."

23. For the wages of sin is death;] "Wages" signifies originally, as Godet observes, payment in kind. It includes both "fruit" and "end," the whole outcome of sin.

but the free gift of God is eternal life in Christ Jesus our Lord.] Salvation, summed up as eternal life, is not a payment in kind of aught that we can do; hence the term "free gift of God" is expressly chosen. "Eternal life" is in Christ Jesus, reminding us of our Lord's words (John x. 28 and xiv. 6). In this magnificent concluding sentence Paul sums up the two fundamental ethical axioms of Christianity: the first excludes all antinomianism, the second opens the way to the true eternal righteousness. The present chapter thus enforces the ethical obligations of Christianity, first as against an unethical legalism (compare the Augustinian doctrine that the Christian must necessarily continue to sin), and secondly against an antinomian interpretation of grace. Against both the one and the other the twofold aphorism of the last verse is conclusive.

CH. VII. 1-4. THE RELATION OF THE BELIEVER TO THE LAW.

1. Or are ye ignorant, brethren] This formula has before occurred (ch. vi. 3 and 16). In each case it follows a logical question, "What then?" And in each case it introduces the proof of Paul's answer to this question as a thing of which they cannot possibly be ignorant. Here our "What then?" is to be found in verse 21, "What fruit then had ye at that time?" To this Paul answers directly, "Things whereof ye are now ashamed, for the end of these things is death;" but adds immediately in contrast, "But now being made free from sin, and become servants to God, ye have your fruit unto sanctification, and the end eternal life." It is to this obverse of the answer to his question that the present verse attaches itself—or if ye do not acknowledge this, if ye are disposed still to plead for continuance in sin by clinging to the law, "are ye ignorant, brethren?" We have already seen, in the logical attachment of chapter vi. 1 to chapter v. 20, that when Paul speaks of continuance in sin it is in his mind connected with continuance under the law; and we have called attention to the passages in which his doctrine on that point is expanded at full length. This same idea—continuance in sin results from continuance under the law, and deliverance from sin can only be effected by release from the law—we meet with in chapter vi. 14. Here again it is the mentally-supplied link which joins chapter vii. 1 to chapter vi. 22.

(for I speak to men that know the law),] This parenthetical clause does not imply that the address is to Jewish Christians. It is not to "that part of you that know the law," but "to you all as knowing the law." The Gentile Christians were generally those who had already a "devout regard" for the Old Testament scriptures. Even where that was not the case, as Christians they could not have failed after their conversion to make themselves acquainted with the Old Testament.

how that the law hath dominion over a man for so long time as he liveth?] This is the proposition upon which Paul is about to found his argument in support of the thesis propounded in verse 22. Its force for this purpose is not immediately obvious. It must be explained. This explanation consists of an example, a particular case in point, and is introduced in the following verse by $\gamma a \rho$, "for."

2. For the woman that hath a husband is bound by law to the husband while he liveth;] The relative clause "that hath a husband" scarcely fully represents the force of the single Greek word which it translates. It might be somewhat awkwardly rendered "the husbanded" woman. It implies the present actual existence of the relation. The same thing is implied in the predicate, where the phrase "while he liveth" is represented by the present participle. The clause "so long time as he liveth," in the first verse, fixes attention and emphasis all the way through upon the element of time in all these adjective words. The example before us is thus to be taken as an example of the time limit to the binding power of the law. That time limit is life. If the law binds two parties to mutual obligations, then the limit is the life of the party to whom the obligation is to be performed, or of the party by whom the obligation is to be performed. Which of these mutually related parties is mentioned

as dying makes no difference to Paul's argument. His point is, *death is the time limit of the binding power of the law.* He passes indifferently or as may suit his analogy from the death of the person bound (verse 1) to the death of the person to whom bound (verse 2), and again to the death of the person bound (verse 4). The principle is the same throughout—*death ends the binding power of the law.* But we must carefully distinguish what Paul asserts in this proposition. It is not that death ends obligation to moral principles, to holiness, or to righteousness, or to godliness. It is to "*the law,*" *i.e.*, to that *code* of precepts introduced into human probation for a definite moral purpose, "that the transgression might abound." This law it is which binds only so long as life lasts. Many precepts or moral principles might extend to eternity, but the law as a whole, as a code, as a rule of life by which man is to serve God, ends with human life. The illustration selected by Paul in proof of this proposition is therefore taken from a field in which it is self-evident, the relation of husband and wife. The law itself was specific on that point (Deut. xxv. 5); marriage was clearly permitted to a widow. The law claimed to regulate human conduct only within the limits of human life. The aptness of Paul's illustration will appear from the manner in which this very question had been handled by the Sadducees, who projected this law into the future life (Matt. xxii. 24). His illustration is, however, chosen with another purpose in view, *i.e.*, to illustrate by the marriage relation itself the relation of the human spirit both to the law and to Christ. Were it not for this he might have selected some other legal precept the legal obligation of which evidently ends with life. But he selects this particular precept of the law that it may serve both as an example to prove the general thesis of verse 1, and as an analogy to confirm the particular conclusion of verse 4. It is the necessity arising from this peculiar logical combination which forces the apostle to pass from one form of statement to another in verses 1, 2 and 4. Verses 1 and 4 correspond in form, each speaking of the death of the person bound; but verses 2 and 3 vary from both in order to be true to fact as a particular instance of verse 1, and in order to select that particular fact which serves for analogy in verse 4. The apostle makes no attempt to obviate this awkwardness of expression, but sacrifices perfect form to the line of thought. His logic is perfect even where the rhetorical form fails. Paul's mode of argument may be compared to the argument from precedent in law. The precedent must involve *the general principle,* and the cases must be clearly *analogous.*

but if the husband die, she is discharged from the law of the husband.] This is the special point of this illustrative example as proof of the general thesis of verse 1. The law which governs human life continues to bind only while that life continues. It ceases with the cessation of the life which it governs.

3. So then if, while the husband liveth, she be joined to another man, she shall be called an adulteress: but if the husband die, she

is free from the law, so that she is no adulteress, though she be joined to another man.] This is a full statement of the precedent in its double form. In its positive form it concedes the limited claim of the law. In its negative form it denies the indefinite extension of that claim. The last clause looks especially to the analogy of the precedent to the case in hand. This analogy covers more than the general principle. It covers the peculiarities of its application to which Paul now proceeds.

4. **Wherefore, my brethren, ye also were made dead to the law through the body of Christ;**] The form of the conclusion is not governed by the deductive argument, *i.e.*, from the general principle of verse 1, which would require ovv, "therefore," nor yet by the simple analogy which would require $όντως καί$, "so also," but is stated as a (divine) purpose in a past event, which purpose governed the event in harmony with both the general principle and the analogy. "So that" ye died to the law, or rather "ye were made dead to the law" (passive voice), "to the end that," etc. $Ώστε$ co-ordinates what follows with what precedes, and represents it, not as an effect in the rigid sense, but as proceeding in a general way from it. Here the ordinance of God which unites us to Christ and makes us dead to the law is based on the principles and analogy stated. "Ye also were made dead to the law" signifies, as in chapter vi. 2, 11, etc., the cessation of all living relation. This takes place "through the body of Christ." This is supposed to be synonymous with the death of Christ in chapter vi. 3, 5, etc. This is on the supposition that our death to the law is identical with our death unto sin. But is there not a distinction? Is not our death to the law necessary to our death to sin—the means by which it is practically effected? Then there is a marked difference in the apostle's mode of expression (ch. vi. 2) and that used here. There the form is active, here purely passive. There reference is made to the voluntary covenant of baptism, here to God's purpose in something which has taken place seemingly without our consent. The death of Christ's body on the cross ended his relation to sin as the bearer of its penalties. It likewise ended his relation to the law. During his earthly life he "was made" not only "in the likeness of sinful flesh," but also "under the law." Both these are Pauline ideas. At death he ceased from both the one and the other. When, therefore, in baptism we died with Christ to sin, we were at the same time made dead to the law. This was God's order for a most important purpose.

that ye should be joined to another,] In Paul's conception union with Christ and with the law as a means of salvation are as incompatible as that a woman should rightly be the wife of two men while both are living. (Compare Gal. v. 4.) God had therefore to make us dead to the law that we might so be united to Christ.

even to him who was raised from the dead, that we might bring forth fruit unto God.] The reference is very slight, if at all, to the fruits of marriage union. The apostle is not governed by the metaphor but by the line of spiritual things which he is considering. This severance from the law was demanded by the statement of chapter vi. 22. The circle of thought there suggested is here completed, calling in once more the resurrection of Christ, as in chapter vi. 4, 8, 9, 11. The fruit unto God is the fruit unto holiness. But why should we be thus severed from the law in order to be united to Christ? Why are the two so incompatible? This leads Paul to enunciate once more the doctrine of the practical effect of the law, and to elucidate its working in God's economy of salvation.

CH. VII. 5-25. THE RELATION OF THE LAW TO MAN'S MORAL NATURE UNDER THE FALL.

5. For when we were in the flesh,] This and the following verse belong to the preceding, and at the same time to the following, context. They complete the preceding line of thought by assigning a reason for our severance from the law in order to our union with Christ. But that reason lies in the very relation of the law to our fallen moral nature. The statement of that relation in general terms we have (in verse 5) thrown into contrast to the new relation of our moral nature to grace in verse 6. But as that statement is liable to two very important misconceptions the apostle opens up these misconceptions by "what then" in verses 7 and 13 respectively, followed in each case by the full presentation of the truths involved. The remaining part of the chapter is thus only an expansion and explanation of what is stated in verse 5. This verse therefore forms the most natural point of departure for the new subsection.

"When we were in the flesh" defines the characters of whom the apostle speaks. It has been a matter of very earnest discussion as to whether this seventh chapter of Romans describes the condition of the regenerate or of the unregenerate. The Calvinistic interpreters, following Augustine after the Pelagian controversy, maintained the former; the Arminians and others, the latter. The apostle's words here are, however, so definite that there is no longer any dispute as to the application of the passage as far as verse 13. It describes the action of the law upon our moral nature "when we were in the flesh." The terms throughout correspond with verse 5. A few, however, still hold that from verse 14 onward, where the apostle changes to the present tense, he is describing his own present regenerate experience. (So Moule. On the contrary, compare Riddle's intermediate and much more tenable position.) The probabilities are certainly in favour of the view that Paul is throughout describing the effect of the law upon our unregenerate moral nature. His statement in verse 5 is unmistakable. His argument from verse 7 to verse 12 is intended directly to guard that statement from misconception, and maintains throughout the same fundamental line of thought. That, however, again involves a position liable to be misconstrued to the disparagement of God's law. That misconstruction is anticipated and prevented in verse 13, and the whole argument from 14 to the end is the proof of what is there advanced. The line of argument is thus continuous from verse 5 throughout, and so important a change as that implied in the Augustinian view is not to be supposed except on clear evidence. We may note here that already in verse 5 the apostle passes from the second to the first person plural, thus identifying himself in this common experience of the effect of the law. In verse 7 he passes from the plural to the singular as clearly the vividness of the subject in its relation to personal experience grows upon him. This, however, by no means makes it an exclusively personal experience. He still describes the common experience of the effects of the law. It may be that he here adopts the first person singular inasmuch as the experience of the effects of the law was peculiarly his own. His Gentile readers, while to some extent sharers, could but partially understand what was the legal state of those who, like Paul, had tested the power of the law to the utmost. So in verse 14, when enunciating a general principle (the law is spiritual), he is obliged to use the present, the same increasing force of vivid conception carries him forward in the use of the present to the end. His whole discourse from this point onward is also the enunciation of general facts in fallen human nature, hence expressed in the present tense. This vividness of conception on the part of the apostle may well be explained by the fact that few men had more profound experience of the effect of the law on fallen moral nature than he. But it by no means follows that because we recognize the apostle's reference to his own experience we should therefore, in opposition to the clear requirements of his argument, transfer that experience from his unregenerate state under the law to his new position under grace. In fact, so clear is the incompatibility of this position with the unity of the argument that Hodge, Barnes and others are obliged to construct at verse 14 an entirely new section of the Epistle, extending from verse 14 to verse 25, and supposed to describe "the effect of the law upon the mind of a believer." To this there are the following weighty objections:—

1. The section thus introduced is without logical or grammatical connection with the preceding or following discourse. The apostle has been replying to an objection taken to his statement that in his unregenerate state the law, *i.e.*, the Mosaic law, excited his sinful nature, and thus led to death. What is the connection of this with the effect of the law on the mind of a believer? Again, how can the glorious regenerate experience of chapter viii. be logically deduced from the forlorn regenerate experience of chapter vii.? But the grammatical structure presses still more strongly against such a construction. The introductory "for" directly demands a close grammatical and logical connection with the context directly preceding.

2. The doctrine thus extorted from this supposed distinct section of the Epistle is out of harmony with Paul's entire conception of the true moral relations of the believer.

Barnes gives the following summary of arguments in favour of the position which he takes that here is described the experience of the believer:—

1. "Because it seems to me to be the most obvious." This may be true of one who has embraced the Augustinian theology; but the best answer to such an assumption is the fact that this passage was read and expounded in the church for three hundred years before this interpretation occurred to anyone, and then only under the pressure of controversy.

2. "Because it agrees with the design of the apostle." The apostle's design can only be gathered from his own words, which all point, as we have seen, to the other interpretation.

3. "Because the expressions which occur (verses 15, 22) are such as cannot be understood of the impenitent sinner." Very true, but still such as can be understood of the convicted sinner struggling for freedom from sin by the help of God's law.

4. "Because it accords with parallel expressions in regard to the state of conflict in a Christian's mind." The passage referred to seems to be Gal. v. 17. The expression ἵνα μὴ ἂν θέλητε ταῦτα ποιῆτε denotes something very different from the statement of *actual facts* in Rom. vii. 14, etc. ἵνα, followed by the subjunctive mood, denotes, not the *actual* consequence or result, but the intended result, the purpose which exists as yet in thought. But as the preceding part of the verse makes mention of a double conflict in which the opposing powers have directly opposite purposes in view, both these purposes may be included in ἵνα μή, etc. Thus the entire verse but pictures to us the inward conflict without stating how it terminates. But the apostle does not leave us in doubt as to the side on which he expects the victory to turn in the case of these regenerate Galatians. "Walk in the Spirit, and so ye shall surely not fulfil the desires of the flesh," is Meyer's emphatic translation of verse 16. And in like manner verse 18 says, "If ye are led by the Spirit" (indicative mood, implying actual fact) "ye are not under the law." Certainly the apostle here expects the Spirit and not the flesh to be conqueror. On the other hand, in Rom. vii. "the flesh" and not the law of the mind is conqueror. This we take (with Wesley) to be the characteristic difference between the awakened sinner and the regenerate believer. The parallel passage referred to does not thus lead to the opinion that Paul here speaks of the regenerate.

5. "Because there is a change here from the past to the present tense." If, as Barnes asserts, this change were inexplicable on any other supposition than that the writer here passes from his past to his present experience, then this argument would be conclusive. But we have already seen that this change occurs by a natural form of expression under very vivid thought, the present tense being first introduced by the absolute necessity of expressing the idea contained in the first clause of verse 14, and continued as an expression of what is universally true of fallen human nature.

6. "Because it agrees with the experience of Christians and not of sinners." Here we must take direct issue with Barnes. Even Riddle (an Augustinian) admits that in so far as it applies to believers it applies to them only as living under the law and not under grace, *i.e.*, in so far as they are not yet believers in the full evangelical sense.

We may therefore accept the conclusion of Riddle, that the entire seventh chapter treats of the legal state, a state influenced by God's Spirit, it is true, but not the normal condition of those who believe on the Lord Jesus Christ for justification. The phrase "when we were in the flesh" therefore fixes the point of view of this entire discussion. It treats of the relation of the law to man's moral nature under the fall. On the term "flesh" see below.

the sinful passions, which were through the law,] "The sinful passions" are the impulses or desires towards sin. These were through the law, *i.e.*, were not originated *by* the law, but were quickened into activity by its agency. The preposition indicates, not the author, but the instrument.

wrought in our members to bring forth fruit unto death.] The members are here, as in chapter vi. 13, the natural capacities and powers of our being. In our unregenerate state these are the seat of sinful passions, *i.e.*, impulses to transgression excited by the restrictions of the law. These "wrought," put forth active energy, in our members. "The fruit unto death" are the acts of transgression by which the sinful passions break through the fetters of law. Death is the conscious separation of the soul from God, the sentence of which appears in the conscience. In this verse we have the comprehensive statement of the relation of the law to our moral nature under the fall. This is fully expanded in verses 7–11.

6. But now we have been discharged from the law, having died to that wherein we were holden;] The "now" is the new life in Christ. "We have been discharged." The verb here is a favourite one with Paul, previously used chapter iii. 31, where it is said the law is not made of none effect. It signifies the ending or cessation of power, effect, claim, etc. The law is not abolished, but we have come to the end of its claim upon us. By the death of Christ we died to it. Until then it held us. It must be borne in mind that the law here is not moral principle or obligation—we cannot die to that—but that code of moral and positive precepts by which the Jew sought his salvation, the law as an instrument for the regeneration of humanity and as a means of acceptance with God—from this "we are discharged."

so that we serve in newness of the spirit, and not in oldness of the letter.] Literally translated this would be "so as to serve;" ὥστε, with the infinitive, denotes the object or end aimed at, the purpose to be effected. Moral obligation, holiness of life, is still the purpose aimed at; but aimed at, not by the old letter of the law, "thou shalt" and "thou shalt not," but by the "new spirit," or as

Paul phrases it when, after his explanations, he brings us back again to this point, "the *law* of the *Spirit of life*" (ch. viii. 2). This verse is the text of chapter viii. 1-11 as verse 5 is the text of chapter vii. 7-25. In these two verses we have the contrast of the ethical foundations of the old dispensation and of the new as the reason for which God hath made us dead to the old that we might be united forever to the new. But the old dispensation, the law, was still of God. What Paul hath said, therefore, as a reason for our release from it, must be guarded against possible misapprehension.

7. What shall we say then? Is the law sin?] The introductory question is the apostle's usual method of calling special attention to a difficulty. The difficulty is here stated in the second question, "Is the law sin?" *i.e.*, is the law immoral in *its nature?* He does hold that it results in the increase of transgressions. Does this prove that it is wrong in its nature? To this he replies decisively, **God forbid.**] This Old Testament dispensation of religion Paul recognized as of God. To insinuate that it was immoral would be to impugn the holiness of its author.

Howbeit, I had not known sin, except through the law:] While Paul denies the false inference from the general statement of verse 5, he at once, by the adversative conjunction, proceeds to place before us the true explanation of what he had there stated in general terms. Sin here is "the sin," *i.e.*, *sin as a moral force*, opposing itself to right. Sin as a course of evil conduct, of individual transgression, he might know, with all its attendant misery. But the sin, the moral power of evil in our nature, is only known, brought out into distinct consciousness, by the opposition of law. Of this he instances an example:

for I had not known coveting, except the law had said, Thou shalt not covet:] Coveting is one of the passions of sin referred to in verse 5. These are excited through the prohibitions of the law, and thus we become aware of "the sin" of which they are the outcome. "The sin" is conceived as a personal being who makes his presence and power felt in these lusts. "Lust," sinful desire, must here, in Paul's conception, be distinguished from mere natural desire. Lust is natural desire *opposing itself to God's law*. Sin is not manifest in mere natural desire. Only when law sets before us the restraints to be imposed upon natural desire does "the sin" which lurks there appear as rebellion against law.

8. but sin, finding occasion, wrought in me through the commandment all manner of coveting:] The personification of sin here becomes very distinct, and is carried through the discussion. "Finding occasion"—in the relation of the law to the various circumstances of life in which natural desire might arise. The words signify "seizing a point from which to push forth for attack"—a military figure. "All manner of coveting." Every form of natural desire breaks out into sinful desire, through the commandment—not merely the law but the particular form of law as command ("thou shalt" and "thou shalt not") which places direct restraint upon all natural desire. That element in natural desire which makes it sinful is its refusal to submit to law, its insubordination. This can only be known through the commandment.

for apart from the law sin is dead.] In the Greek here the article is wanting, and we are disposed to interpret the sentence in harmony with this as an axiom of our moral nature. The change to the present tense, or rather to the simple universal predicate, favours this view. This axiom may have been a common dictum of the schools in Paul's time. If so it here asserts, in general form, what Paul has just presented in detailed example. "Dead" is not thus to be taken in the absolute sense, nor even in the strong sense in which Paul has used it in the preceding discussion, but as a proverbial metaphor. (Compare ch. iv. 15.)

9. And I was alive apart from the law once:] This life cannot be interpreted of carnal or Pharisaic security, but must refer to the innocence of the young of conscious transgression. This period was clearly marked to the young Jew. At twelve years of age he became definitely responsible for the observance of "the law." Such a definite period well within his personal recollection is implied in the historical tense and the adverb "once." "He was alive," *i.e.*, free from the conscious sentence of death which transgression brings.

but when the commandment came, sin revived, and I died;] This points to the time of probational maturity. At twelve years of age the young Jew was brought face to face with the precepts of the law. Then sin "rose up to life," the form of expression used of a rising from the dead, and also of the springing into life of a seed, aptly describing the first consciousness of "the sin," *i.e.*, the natural opposition to God's law. "I died," then and there passed into a state of conscious separation from God.

10. and the commandment, which was unto life, this I found to be unto death:] The pronoun translated "this" is emphatic, "the very commandment," "which was unto life." There is no verb in the original, simply the attributive article with the adjunct "unto life." This preposition denotes, as usually in St. Paul, aim or tendency, without implying that the intended result is or is not reached. The old version "was ordained" is scarcely too strong; we may render "which aims at life." To this intended result is opposed the actual result, "was found by me (in my experience) to lead to death."

11. for sin, finding occasion,] (See note on verse 8.) The opposition of the law to natural desire gives added force or impulse, by its reaction, to the natural desire for the forbidden object.

through the commandment beguiled me,] The reference here is evidently to the temptation of Eve. The woman "was deceived" (1 Tim. ii. 14). There is a momentary deception in every temptation. For the moment the strength of the excited passion blinds to all else; and thus indirectly the very command which excites the passion blinds us. But it is only for a moment, for there follows in swift sequence,

and through it slew me.] No sooner is the sin committed than the same command speaks (in conscience) the sentence of death.

12. **So that the law is holy, and the commandment holy, and righteous, and good.**] This conjunction sets forth (as in verse 4) the result, not as springing from the efficient cause, but as determined by circumstances. It draws a conclusion from the varied discussion of many facts which lead up to it, but no one of which determines it. The conclusion is the answer to the question of verse 7, holy, not sinful, both law and commandment; and further, "righteous and good" in its intent, *i.e.*, promotive of justice and of man's highest well-being. The mention of this last point starts a new objection.

13. **Did then that which is good become death unto me? God forbid.**] How can the beneficence of the law be reconciled with the actual result? Only by a clear understanding that the law was merely the occasion, not the efficient cause, of the malign result. The efficient cause is to be sought elsewhere.

But sin,] This is the real efficient cause, and the law is made the innocent occasion of its action for a definite purpose,

that it might be shewn to be sin, by working death to me through that which is good;—] The malignant character of sin is shewn in the very perversion of that which is good in itself. The very law which provokes by resisting sin exhibits sin's real nature. This is God's design in the giving of the law, to unmask sin.

that through the commandment sin might become exceeding sinful.] This second statement of the intention of the law is more specific and emphatic. By the commandment each outbreak of sin not only appears as sin but becomes more guilty, "exceeding sinful." This is the true statement, in general terms, of the office of the law in God's economy. (Compare Rom. iii. 20; v. 20; Gal. iii. 19, 23, 24.) But the ground of this order of God lies in the nature of sin as dwelling in me, its relation to the spiritual elements of my nature, and the relation of the law to those same spiritual elements. That is, God hath appointed the law to this office in harmony with what may be called the moral psychology, or as we should perhaps rather say, the pneumatology of human nature. From verse 14 to verse 25 we have an exposition of those grounds in general terms applying to fallen human nature universally, as it is brought into full moral development in contact with the law of God. This is perhaps the most profoundly metaphysical passage in St. Paul's writings, involving in itself a complete system of psychology. He is no longer discussing definite historical experiences either of himself or of his readers, but general principles applying to fallen human nature as such; hence, while as himself the representative of humanity he retains the first person, he passes from the aorist to the present.

14. **For we know that the law is spiritual:**] "We know" introduces an admitted truth, one which the apostle expects his readers at once to recognize. "The law is spiritual." Here we meet the first

of Paul's psychological terms, "spiritual," in its source or nature belonging to the spirit; but what spirit? Most commentators say to the Spirit of God. Some, holding the doctrine of the trichotomy, say the spirit of man. But is it not better to say that Paul here uses the term in a generic sense, including both. The spirit of man which, whatever else it may include, at least includes conscience, the understanding of the Old Testament, that which discerns right, is made in the image of God. Thus we have a genus spirit, a type of spiritual nature sharply contrasted with the *somatic* by Plato, and with the *psychical* by Paul, and here directly opposed to the carnal. The sense of right is an attribute of this nature. It is this nature in God which founds and maintains the right, and this nature in man discerns and approves the right. Out of this divine type of nature came the law of God, and wherever this type of nature is to be found in man or angel that law commands its assent.

but I am carnal,] not "fleshlike" but "of flesh," the better reading. The "I" is the *person* which consciously embraces both natures, and of which the spiritual nature is the most important part. (See verses 17 and 20.) The word corresponds exactly to "the spiritual" just used. Both terms are used in a moral sense. Both define a moral character. This moral character lies not in the physical constitution of mind or of matter, but in their relation. The flesh as the servant of the spirit is holy; as controlling the spirit and subjecting it to bondage, unholy. Moral character is always determined by relation. The terms, therefore, "flesh" and "spirit," or "carnal" and "spiritual," as applied to moral character, derive their significance from the relation of each to our personality. The ruling element determines the designation; and as the reign of the flesh is sin, *i.e.*, breach of God's law, so "carnal" signifies sinful, and *vice versa*. This ethical significance dates back beyond the New Testament age. (See 4 Macc. vii. 28.) The "flesh" in this ethical significance must be distinguished from "the outer man," "the old man" and "the natural man," though related to each of these. It is to be remarked that Paul never uses the word "flesh" alone as designating the principle of evil in man. This is always expressed by adjectival forms derived from or including the noun, *e.g.*, "carnal," "in the flesh," "after the flesh," "the mind of the flesh." All this is in harmony with the idea that evil is not either in the organization of the body or in matter, but in the relation of the body to the personality, the I. It is upon this relation that Paul fastens attention when he says, "I am carnal."

sold under sin.] a bondslave under sin. This Paul himself fully explains in verse 23. Here he is sold into this slavery; there taken captive in war. The variation of metaphor is unimportant; the slavery is the point to which our attention is directed.

15. For that which I do I know not:] The word here translated "do" should be more fully rendered "am working out." "For what I am working out I know not." The verb "know," which seems never to bear the meaning of "allow" or "approve," here has its proper significance. The slave knows only the work of the hour, the master alone understands what is being *wrought out*—a life-like picture of the sinner, who acts with no intelligent recognition of the ends of life, but under the momentary commands of his masters, the sinful passions.

for not what I would, that do I practise; but what I hate, that I do.] The distinction of the revised version here between "practise," the habitual act, and "do," the act of the moment, is well taken. The apostle does not assert that man *never does* what he would, but that he does not steadfastly follow it. It is not even frequent enough to be called his practice, his habit of life. On the contrary, his actions are isolated doings of things which he hates. The "would" here includes both the approval of conscience and the effort of the will, such as it is. The hatred is the moral hating of a wounded conscience. We cannot, with Moule, so interpret the teaching of Paul as to exclude the possibility of such activity of conscience as is here described on the part of the still unregenerate man.

16. **But if what I would not, that I do, I consent unto the law that it is good.**] We should express the idea of the first clause in English idiom by making the relative clause the principal. This is indicated in Greek by its emphatic position. "If I *will* not" (in the sense of "approve" and "aim at") "that which I do," "I assent" (emphatic assent, implying full agreement) "unto the law that it is good." Here we meet for the first time that term so often employed by the Greek philosophers to express their admiration of moral excellence. Το καλον was a designation of moral beauty, and καλοκαγαθος a title of the perfect man. The clause thus expresses the strong feeling of righteous approval which the law extorts in that very act by which, in our conscience, we condemn our own conduct.

17. **So now it is no more I that do it, but sin which dwelleth in me.**] The particles here are not temporal but logical in their force. "Now," under these circumstances; "no longer," *i.e.*, "not any more." The conjunction δε is not adversative but continuative, and we may paraphrase the whole clause thus: "And in this case it is therefore not I." Here again the word "work out" is introduced—"Not I who am working out this course of conduct, but sin which dwelleth in me." He does not deny personal responsibility, for the conscious agent is responsible with the principal. But he proves the existence of a stronger personality within, whose law rules and works out death. The proving of the existence of this inner personality of sin, not the denial of his own responsibility, is the end at which he aims. This conclusion he proceeds to present in another form.

18. **For I know that in me, that is, in my flesh, dwelleth no good thing:**] This reproduces verse 14 in the additional light gained at the conclusion of 17. He had there said, "I am carnal." But

meantime he had learned to distinguish the impelling power of sin in his flesh from the personality which it controls; hence the present form of expression, "in me, that is, in my flesh" (the lower nature which controls me). He does not retract the "in me," but explains it by fixing attention on that part of the personality which rules. "There dwelleth no good thing." Looking through this lower nature he finds in it no impulse free from the taint of sin—no voice of good. This again does not imply the denial of the power of conscience in the higher nature. The "will" attests that; but inasmuch as the lower nature rules, it is that which dwells in this lower nature which determines moral character. Even the form of denial is peculiar. It is not the absolute "nothing good" (ουδεν αγαθον). It is not even "the good" (το αγαθον, goodness), but simply "a good." According to ordinary grammatical principles this could only mean "some good," *i.e.*, some part of the universal good. This may signify, as below, "a good act," or it may be that the article is omitted here as before the names of virtues and vices, the neuter adjective being treated as if a substantive. It would thus be equivalent to "the good," and the force of the sentence would be, "in me the ideally good, or the principle of goodness, does not dwell." We do not think that the Greek will bear a stronger rendering than this. The exact sense will appear more clearly from the next clause.

for to will is present with me, but to do that which is good is not.] The will, which includes approval, choice, and at least purpose, though not necessarily immediate putting forth of effort or act, is present, literally lies right beside me, quite at hand, but "to do the good" not so, *i.e.*, "to work out the good." By "good," therefore, in the preceding clause, Paul must mean that sympathy or harmony with goodness which is needed to give effect to our good purpose or choice. This dwells not in me, *i.e.*, not in my flesh, not in that lower nature through which every purpose must be carried into effect, *i.e.*, wrought out.

19. **For the good which I would I do not: but the evil which I would not, that I practise.**] This is very far from being a mere repetition of verse 15. We may paraphrase thus: "For what I approve and purpose, a good thing (as approved by conscience), I do not," *i.e.*, do not perform; "but what I neither approve nor purpose, an evil thing, I practise." Here "good" and "evil" are used again without the article, not of abstract goodness or evil, but of individual acts of goodness and evil. If we take this same sense in verse 18*a*, then we should translate thus: "I know that in me, that is, in my flesh, a good act (the performance of the good) does not dwell;" 18*b* becomes then the explanation: "for though the first part of the act (to approve and purpose) is ready enough at hand, the full performance is not. For this good act which I approve and purpose I never accomplish; but some evil act which I neither approve nor purpose I find myself continually practising."

20. **But if what I would not, that I do, it is no more I that do**

it, but sin which dwelleth in me.] Here again we arrive at the conclusion already announced in verse 17. But there it is reached in view of his *habit*, "practice," which proves that he is "carnal, sold under sin." In verses 18, 19, 20, the same conclusion is reached by following up a single act. "A good act (*i.e.*, the power to perform it) does not dwell in me." This corresponds to the general statement, verse 14, "I am carnal," etc. This specialization of the individual act, followed through its stages as above, again demonstrates what he had already deduced from the general character of his practice. "But if what I do not approve or purpose, that I actually do, it is no longer I who work it out, but the principle of sin which dwelleth in me." He has thus, by two distinct lines of thought—the one following the general character of his actions, and the other tracing up the failure in each particular act—brought out into distinct consciousness the personified principle of indwelling sin, by which this failure of good and practice of evil is effected. This he now proceeds to set before us, not as a separate personified will, but as a general authority or power controlling the will—a law.

21. I find then the law, that, to me who would do good, evil is present.] This verse has presented almost insurmountable difficulties to the commentators from the fathers downwards. The difficulties arise both from the construction and as to the meaning of the word "law" here. Heretofore it has borne the one meaning, "the Mosaic law." But immediately afterward it is used in a new sense, "another law," "the law of sin." A large body of modern commentators, from Luther down, understand here this "other law." But the fathers, with Meyer, Olshausen and others of late, held to the meaning "Mosaic law." Their reasons are, not that it gives a better sense, but that the principles of sound exegesis require that we adhere to the established meaning of a term unless there be some specifying adjunct or other evidence that the author uses it in a new sense. But in the construction which they adopt they find no such adjunct. Again, they contend that the article prefixed to the word "law," without any specifying adjunct, requires that it be taken as the law so often before spoken of. To obviate this very strong objection we must find a simple, natural, grammatical construction of the sentence which will specify the new sense of the word "law," and account for the use of the article. The construction adopted by Godet and by the revised version is liable to the objection urged by Meyer. We therefore (with diffidence) propose the following: (1) We make τον νομον the subject accusative of ειναι understood. (2) We make θελοντι εμοι ποιειν το καλ. ον an adjunct of τον νομον. (For example of similar adjunct in the dative σκολοψ τη σαρκι see 2 Cor. xii. 7). (3) We take οτι εμοι το κακον παρακειται as the predicate after ειναι understood. By the adjunct and by the predicate clause the new sense of νομον is clearly specified, and the presence of the article is accounted for by the fact that νομον is the subject limited by an adjunct. The sense of this construction may be expressed as follows:

"I find then that the law which governs me when I wish to do good is, that evil lies at hand to me." This sense, which is virtually the same as that of the revised version and Godet, seems much more in Paul's line of thought than either of the following given by Meyer, and all taking "the law" in the sense of the Mosaic law:—(1) "I find then in me, who am desirous of doing the law (namely, the good), that evil lies before me." (2) "I find therefore the law for me, who am disposed to do good, because evil lies before me." (3) "I find therefore the law, when I desire to do what is beautiful, how it (the law) lies at hand to me as evil." (4) (which Meyer adopts) "It results to me that while my will is directed to the law in order to do the good, that evil lies before me."

22. **For I delight in the law of God after the inward man:**] There are two expressions in this verse which have been held to apply only to the regenerate man, and hence to determine against us the proper application of this entire passage. The first is, "I delight in." This word ($συνηδομαι$) corresponds to $συμφημι$ in verse 16, "I consent with" and "I rejoice with." With what? Some say "with the law"; others, "with other good men, to or in the law." Better Godet, who interprets the preposition $συν$ of the *inwardness* of the assent or feeling of joy. The words are thus after the analogy of $συνειδησις$, *con-science*. If this is the correct significance, then this word is but an expanded term for what we have already in conscience; and to deny the possibility of this to the unregenerate man would be to deny the existence and activity of conscience prior to regeneration. The second term, "the inner man," is supposed to be equivalent to "the new man" or "the regenerate man." It is found in one other passage, Eph. iii. 16, and a similar expression, "the inward man," in 2 Cor. iv. 16. Both these passages present the inward man, not as *the result* of regeneration, but as *the sphere* in which regeneration is wrought. The strengthening is not *of* the inward man but *unto* the inward man, reaching to our inward nature. Again, it is this inward man which undergoes the process of renewal day by day. In the very next sentence Paul calls this the "mind," *i.e.*, that higher part of our nature in which moral law makes itself manifest. Both terms, therefore, apply to man as such without implying a previous regeneration.

23. **but I see a different law in my members, warring against the law of my mind,**] We have seen, in chapter vi. 13, that "the members" constituted the weapons by which sin maintains dominion over us. They are therefore to be taken as those passions by the aid of which sin is strong. The law in the members is therefore the force or power of the passions. This is opposed to the "law of my mind." The mind ($νους$) translates the Hebrew "understanding," that power of our nature which discerns moral right and wrong, the moral judgment. *The law* of the mind is the *conscience*, that which gives constraining power or force to the moral judgment.

and bringing me into captivity under the law of sin which is in

my members.] We have in the verse before us four laws. The term "law" is in each case used to denote a ruling or controlling power. These laws are contrasted two and two, and allied two and two:—(1) The law of God opposed to the law of sin. (2) The law of my mind opposed to the law of my members.

The law of God is allied to, but not to be identified with, the law of my mind; the one being objective, the other subjective; one the outward moral rule of life, and the other the inward moral motive of life.

Again, the law in my members, the controlling power of passion, is not identical with the law of sin, but is so closely allied to it that the members (the passions) are the seat of the law (controlling power) of sin. These distinctions are of the greatest importance in tracing the psychological process here described by Paul, and deducing from it the materials for a doctrine of depravity. The law of sin takes possession of the captive, but the law in the members does the fighting and furnishes the weapons. The law of God furnishes the true standard of right; the law of my mind assents to, yea, delights in this.

Logically, verse 25 should follow here, and must be so interpreted; but ere he completes the argument he gives voice to the feelings of the heart, contrasting the vivid remembrance of the past with the blessed experience of the present.

24. O wretched man that I am! who shall deliver me out of the body of this death?] Literally, "O worn-out man," worn out and ready to sink in the conflict—"Who shall rescue me?" still keeping up the military figure—"Out of the body," not without reference to the members in which the law of sin resides. As these members belonging to the physical body are now members of sin, so they are considered as belonging to a body of sin and "of death." Death is here clearly the spiritual death which directly follows sin. "The body" which he would have called a body of sin (ch. vi. 6) he now calls a body of death, as the full result of sin is plainly before him.

25. I thank God through Jesus Christ our Lord.] A momentary anticipation of the glorious doctrine of chapter viii. As the whole passage is the expression of deep emotion the best attested reading is in every way to be preferred. This sentence is of itself sufficient proof that the apostle has been describing, not his present personal experience as a Christian, but the universal relation of the law to man's moral nature as he had tested it in his own experience. To this he now returns, summing up all in a single sentence—

So then I myself with the mind serve the law of God; but with the flesh the law of sin.] The two conjunctions with which this sentence opens express—the first, the resuming or summarizing of the preceding discourse; the second, the conclusion. Of the term "I myself" (American revisers, "I by myself") three constructions or renderings have been proposed: (1) "Even I," *i.e.*, "I, Paul," hence how much more other or all Christians (so Philippi). (2) "The same I" (Olshausen). (3) "I, of myself" (Meyer, Godet). The second is not grammatically tenable, and the first is out of harmony with the line of thought as we have followed it. The last is both grammatical and pertinent. In the preceding sentence the apostle had returned to the standpoint of his freedom "in Christ Jesus." When therefore in this final sentence he returns to sum up, the conscious contrast of the old life in himself with the new life in Christ Jesus brings out this αυτος, "myself." The mind is, as before, the inner, or, as we would say, the higher nature, the moral principles. He here uses the strongest term of the relation of this nature to God's law. He had said (1) that it assents to the law, (2) that it delights in the law; now (3) it serves the law. The antithesis is "but with the flesh," evidently contrasted with "the mind," hence pointing, not to depravity (which is none other than the sin which dwelleth in me), but to that nature in which depravity, *the sin*, has its special seat, just as the law of God has its special relation to the mind, the moral nature. If this distinction is valid then the apostle clearly recognizes a basis of moral life and of the influence of truth and of the Holy Spirit even in the unregenerate man. It is to be especially marked that it is with this lower nature that the law of sin is served. The relation of sin to the higher nature is represented by death, blindness, sleep, etc.

EXCURSUS ON THE DOCTRINES OF CHAPTER VII.

It only remains to summarize the very important dogmatic teachings of this passage. They relate (1) to the moral constitution of man; (2) to his responsibility, in relation to the law of God; and (3) to his depravity, in relation to moral law. In the moral constitution of man Paul everywhere distinguishes two fundamental elements. These are variously named as they are considered in various forms of activity, or in various moral relations. The broadest distinction is expressed by the terms "flesh" and "spirit" employed in the next chapter. These are not merely two opposed moral states but two fundamental elements of human nature. As we have seen in the present chapter, they designate moral states only as they control the ego, the personality. The *pneuma*, or spirit, is that element in man's nature by which he is related to God; the flesh is that element by which he is related to nature. The flesh is more than the body. It is the body with all its living powers, and especially the desires, passions, etc., by which its activities are controlled. In their relation to man's moral nature those desires and passions make up the flesh. Hence it is, in this moral relation, that the flesh is the seat of sin. Not that sin is confined to the flesh, but that its primary impulses are here first felt. The control or dominion of the flesh is always sinful; so are the lusts, *i.e.*, the inordinate, or insubordinate, desires of the flesh.

1. The spirit, as the power of moral discernment, distinguishing

right from wrong, is called the mind; the acts of the mind are *sunesis*, understanding, or *suneidesis*, conscience. That which this understanding apprehends is το αγαθον, the good, or το καλον, the moral beauty. This whole spiritual nature of man is the seat of the operations of the Holy Spirit, and is intimately related to the regenerate nature as its natural basis. The new nature finds its possibility in the spirit of man, just as sin finds its possibility in the natural antithesis of the flesh to the spirit. A very careful study of the use of these two terms by Paul will, we think, make it evident that he does not identify the new nature with the spirit, nor the old evil nature with the flesh, though they are respectively so intimately related that terms derived from the one are applied to the other. But we shall consider this more fully under the third head.

2. As to man's responsibility, the apostle does not fall into the line of our modern psychology and base this upon free will. He does not abstract the act of willing, as we are accustomed to do it. With him there are, in fact, two wills—the will of the flesh, and the will of the spirit or the true self. Will is simply the outgoing of the nature toward action, and is supposed to be the free expression of the nature which wills. It is the moral character of the nature which wills that determines the moral character of the will. Man is responsible in virtue of his nature as a spiritual being. The subjective basis of his responsibility lies in his power to know, approve, and choose or will the right. In other words, it lies in conscience, in its twofold power of moral understanding and moral motive to action. Paul takes it for granted that wherever conscience exists there is responsibility, or at least the subjective basis for it. But while he recognizes this higher will power in conscience as the basis of responsibility, he at the same time recognizes a will power, an impulse to action, from the lower nature. Sin seems to lie in the antagonism of this lower will to the higher, which we shall consider presently.

The objective basis of responsibility is, according to Paul, the presence of law. "Sin is not imputed where there is no law." Law is the revelation to man of moral principles in the form of positive commands. The presence of law lifts man out of the state of mere instinctive action, which has in itself no moral character, *i.e.*, it may be good, but it is not virtuous; or it may be bad, but it is not sin. With the presence of law comes the conflict of the two wills, or rather, natures, and the distinct consciousness of the spirit or conscience as opposed to the flesh. Our subjective basis of responsibility becomes efficient only through the presence of law. Two conditions are thus necessary to responsibility—the possession of a nature capable of the moral activities, and the presence of a law calling for the regulation of the lower nature, and thus calling this higher nature into conscious exercise.

3. We are thus prepared to define Paul's view of depravity, or the sin of our nature, as distinguished from the sin of act. It is such a state of the lower nature as refuses to obey law, and carries its lower

will into act in the face of the higher will of conscience. The origin of this abnormal state (this warfare in ourself) is stated in chapter v. 12, etc. In the present chapter Paul deals with its nature, its manifestation and its extent. As to its nature, he calls it $επιθυμια$ (lust), he fixes its seat in the flesh (the lower nature) and in the members (the natural passions, etc., of that nature). Hence we may safely infer that "the sin" of our nature lies primarily, or in part at least, in the undue strength of all those lower desires and appetites which conscience should control. In other passages Paul goes further, and shews us that the mind and conscience may be darkened (Eph. iv. 18) and the sensitive feeling of obligation blunted (1 Tim. iv. 2). Perhaps Paul refers to a moral state even more terrible than this in Titus i. 15, 16, where the higher nature is not only enfeebled but actually prostituted to sin. It may, however, be questioned whether Paul contemplates it as an actual fact, or even a possible case, that any man should be born in this deeper form of depravity. In the passages referred to it is presented rather as the result of a course of personal transgression. On the other hand, in the present chapter we have depravity described as it manifests itself in one man from the beginning of his moral development, he being taken as a type of all others. We may thus take the depravity here described as the measure of the extent of that depravity which is common by birth to all. This measure of extent we find in the fact, *the will of the flesh rules.* The true self constantly fails to maintain its prerogative. The apostle does not directly say that it cannot. He does not say, "The good that I would I am not able to perform," but simply, "I do not." He does, on the other hand, affirm a "cannot" on the part of the will of the flesh (ch. viii. 7, 8). This mind of the flesh has in itself no self-regulating power. It has lost its original subordination to law. It cannot please God, nor can those do so who are in the flesh, *i.e.*, who resign themselves to its power. If, therefore, Paul does not assert a moral inability on the part of that higher nature which "approves," "delights in," and "serves" God's law, he seems fairly to imply as much, as also in the expressions "sold under sin" and "making me captive." The moral inability is, however, to complete action, to the "working out" of the good, not to the effort or even struggle towards it. But here again we must remember that the case described is that of an actual man *under the law*, not of a fallen being left absolutely to himself. Paul never discusses such a theoretical fiction. But the question now arises, How far does this natural bondage to sin affect responsibility? In answering this question we must first note that Paul is here discussing the case of a man who is in full possession of both requisites to responsibility. He has a moral nature and he is under the law. Prior to the coming of the law Paul does not say that he is responsible. Yet he does recognize responsibility arising from even the lower forms of law in the Gentile world (ch. ii. 14, 15). But God's law is never a mere objective condition of responsibility. It is not a mere rule by which a man may measure the extent of his obligations. It is spirit and life. It awakens conscience, removes its blindness, increases its sympathy with the right, and adds moral force to its mandates, and thus changes the subjective conditions of our moral nature. On the other hand, it creates a moral crisis in the other direction as well. As conscience was mere latent moral capacity till the law came, so also with sin. Not that it did not previously exist, but it needed this opposing force to react against, and so render sensible, its activity. If it be said that all this implies a redemptive interference, and so does not answer the question as to what is man's condition under the fall prior to 'redemption, we can only reply again that Paul knows no such abstract fiction. He takes man as he is and traces his development under the fourfold law—(1) of his mind, his higher nature; (2) of his members, his lower nature; (3) of God; and (4) of sin. Such a man, under existing conditions of moral development, he certainly holds to be responsible in the presence of *the hope of redemption*.

But Paul leaves room for degrees of responsibility. His typical man is a Jew in whose case the objective conditions of responsibility are most perfectly satisfied. Still, he recognizes the responsibility of the Gentiles, leaving room for Christ's supplementary teaching, "It shall be more tolerable for Tyre and Sidon," etc. His view of the process of moral development would also lead us to the conclusion that where the external conditions are favourable moral development may take place very early in life. On the other hand, under less favourable conditions the process may be *slow* as well as imperfect.

CH. VIII. 1-11.—THE TRIUMPH OF THE SPIRIT OVER THE LAW OF SIN AND ULTIMATELY OVER THE LAW OF DEATH.

1. **There is therefore now no condemnation to them that are in Christ Jesus.**] The conjunction "therefore" points back to a preceding statement of facts from which it draws a conclusion. These facts are not contained, as Meyer thinks, in vii. 25*b*, but are called up again in 25*a* from vii. 6. The present section is a comment on vii. 6, as the preceding section was on vii. 5. The "newness of the spirit" in vii. 6 is the "spirit of life" in Christ Jesus of viii. 2. But to this 25*a* adds the idea of deliverance from the bondage of the law of sin. These are the facts which our conjunction gathers up in the conclusive statement of this verse, and which are stated in the way of explication by the γαρ ("for") of the verse following. The "now" of this verse is opposed to the "when" of chapter vii. 5. The condemnation is the sentence of God's law against sin, spoken in the conscience, and finally executed in the day of judgment.

2. **For the law of the Spirit of life in Christ Jesus made me free from the law of sin and of death.**] If our view of the connection be right then the "law of the Spirit of life" must be defined in accord with the idea already presented in verse 6 supplemented by verse 23.

In verse 25 we find a "law" (a regulative power) of the mind, *i.e.*, of the higher moral nature, but insufficient to set free. In verse 6 we find a reference to "newness of the spirit." In this same Epistle (ch. xii. 2) the author speaks of "the renewing of the mind," and in Eph. iv. 23 of being "renewed in the spirit of your minds." This by no means excludes the office and work of the Holy Spirit, but it shews us that Paul regards the Holy Spirit, not as working by an outward constraint, but through the spiritual basis of our nature, renewing it and making it the regulative power of the new life. "This law set me free," a clearly defined historical experience at a definite past time. "From the law of sin and death." This is clearly defined as the law of sin in chapter vii. It is at the same time the law of death as working death (ch. vii. 13). The expression "hath set me free" turns the thought back to the question of verse 24.

3. **For what the law could not do, in that it was weak through the flesh,**] We have here in the Greek a peculiar, suspended construction. It might be rendered "the impossibility of the law." It may be taken as a substantive in apposition with the entire sentence following, especially verse 4. It thus prefixes an important statement concerning the great fact there mentioned. It was a thing impossible to the law. This had been fully proven in chapter vii., and the reason for it fully explained, which Paul here briefly recapitulates, "in that it was weak through the flesh." The governing impulses of the lower nature, constituting the law of sin in the members, are here presented as the cause of the failure of the law.

God, sending his own Son in the likeness of sinful flesh and as an offering for sin,] The participial clause here, as frequently, sets forth the means by which the act of the principal verb is accomplished, *i.e.*, in the case before us the redemption of man from sin. This consists of three elements—(1) "God sends *his own* Son." Here the pre-existence and divinity of our Lord are clearly recognized. Here also Paul unites with John in ascribing the fundamental and initial act of human redemption to the love of the Father. (Compare ch. v. 8; John iii. 16; 1 John iv. 9.) (2) "In the likeness of sinful flesh." This is the second step in the accomplishment of the redeeming work. The redeemer must be one of the race to be redeemed, as was the author of their sin. The same law of probational unity governs both. (See ch. v. 12-19 and Phil. ii. 6-8.) In the present clause, however, Paul goes further than usual. He says not merely "in the likeness of men," or "was made flesh," but "of sinful flesh"—literally of this very flesh possessed by sin—"of flesh of sin." The genitive is not, we think, here properly rendered by an adjective which would imply attributes or quality. That would be to attribute to our Lord's human nature sinfulness, in opposition to Paul's own teaching (2 Cor. v. 21). We cannot, with Riddle, escape from this through the word "likeness." There is in that word no docetic idea. Paul everywhere uses it to express the specific form of the nature itself, not a mere resemblance to the nature. But if we adopt the marginal rendering we have the idea that the very flesh which sin had made its stronghold, and which on account of sin was under the curse and subject to death, was the flesh which Christ entered. This justifies our definition of the word "flesh" in the last chapter. It cannot here mean, and we think it does not anywhere mean, "sinful nature," or depravity as such, but that element of our nature through means of which sin rules, and *the predominance of which over the mind and spirit* constitutes depravity. Christ took upon him this very nature under its law of sin and penalty, *though specially sanctified for him by the operations of the Holy Ghost.* The nature is not in itself sin—it is capable of being the servant of God and the instrument of righteousness. Christ then took this nature sanctified from personal sin, but still the very nature of fallen man, and subject, as also his sanctified followers still are, to all the pains and penalties, trials and temptations, which its relation to sin has imposed. (Compare Heb. ii. 14-18.) (3) "And as an offering for sin." This is an interpretation rather than a translation. The original reads, concerning sin, $\pi\epsilon\rho\iota\ \dot{\alpha}\mu\alpha\rho\tau\iota\alpha\varsigma$. This expression is used in the LXX. in reference to sin offering. (See Lev. xvi. 6, 11, etc.; Num. viii. 8.) It is similarly used in the New Testament, especially in the Epistle to the Hebrews. (See Heb. v. 4; x. 6.) The use of the phrase in this form is so distinct that—especially as Paul uses it only here, and as where he wishes to express the more general idea he uses the preposition $\dot{\upsilon}\pi\epsilon\rho$—we feel inclined to take it in that more limited sense of expiation. If it bears the broader meaning of "on account of," and includes "all the relations of Christ's work to sin," then this of expiation is certainly the most fundamental.

Out of the three integral elements of the redemptive work thus presented, viz., (1) the divine person of the Redeemer, (2) his unity with the sinful humanity to be redeemed, and (3) his expiatory offering, we have finally the result of this work from the Godward side, "condemned sin in the flesh." This predicate is capable of two constructions. The adjunct "in the flesh" may be taken in immediate relation to "sin." The article would favour this—"The sin in the flesh." Or it may be taken directly with the verb—"In the flesh condemned sin." "The sin" will thus be generic, sin as a power in the moral world. The first construction, though in harmony with the particular line of thought before us, is more restricted, and fails to bring out so fully the idea that the triumph over sin is in that very nature through which and in which sin triumphed. This becomes more important when we ask, as we must, what is the meaning of the expression "condemned sin." It cannot be taken as a mere variation in expression for conquered or overcome sin, nor for destroyed sin. Paul is too precise and direct in the use of language to admit of any such interpretation. We find, however, a precise meaning attached to this form of expression in two passages of the

New Testament. The first is in Matt. xii. 41, and is repeated in Luke xi. 31, etc. The second is in Hebrews xi. 7. A parallel to these is found in John iii. 19. The same idea is applied by our Lord to his own work in John ix. 39. The thought in all these passages is, that sin is judged and condemned in the light of righteousness. If Christ's work is a supreme act of righteousness whereby it comes unto all men unto justification, then that act of righteousness is of itself a supreme condemnation of sin. That act of righteousness is wrought out in the very nature which had sinned, yea, by the very submissive obedience of that nature "even unto death." The flesh which had by arrogantly ruling over the spirit made itself the instrument of sin, in Christ yielded itself to the "willing spirit" that "God's will might be done." Here again the apostle touches the deepest mystery of the atonement. (Compare Heb. v. 7, etc.) As this supreme act of righteousness includes the suffering of death as the penalty of sin, the condemnation of sin, $i.e.$, its judicial sentence of judgment before the whole universe, became complete when the Son of God himself submits the flesh which he had made his own to suffer the penalty of God's law, but which as our sinful flesh was held to suffer this penalty. (Compare 1 Peter ii. 24.)

4. **that the ordinance of the law might be fulfilled in us,]** This is the central point of this entire sentence. This is "the impossibility of the law." It is here introduced as the final purpose of the great redemptive work set before us in the preceding verse. That redemptive work is contrasted with the law; this glorious result with the failure of the law. The word "ordinance" is as far aside from the meaning of $δικαιωμα$ in the one direction as is the word "righteousness" in the other. It signifies that which law requires; not the statute which makes the requirement on the one hand, nor the character acquired by fulfilling law on the other, but the manner of doing the right acts which the law requires. This very manner of doing which the law demanded and which our minds approved, but which we failed under the law to "do," is now filled out to the full, not only in letter but in spirit, by the same us.

who walk not after the flesh, but after the spirit.] Here, if at all, the word "flesh" is used in a purely ethical sense, $i.e.$, as a designation of sinful human nature as such. We think, however, that even here the contrast is not so much between "the flesh" and "the spirit" as between "the walking *according to* the flesh" and "*according to* the spirit." The "walk according to the spirit" is God's order; the "walk according to the flesh" is the subversion of God's order. The flesh as ruler of the man is the minister of sin and corrupt; the same flesh as the instrument of righteousness is the holy temple of the Holy Ghost. We doubt, therefore, whether even here Paul uses the word "flesh" as the designation of an ethical state. It is rather the adjectival expression derived from it, "after the flesh." The corresponding expression, $κατα\ πνευμα$, is likewise adjectival. We have before seen that Paul recognizes a spiritual nature in which God and man unite. "After the spirit" describes a life controlled by this nature. In bringing this about the Spirit of God works, but through and in the spirit of man.

5. For they that are after the flesh do mind the things of the flesh;] "They that are after the flesh." are the persons ruled by the flesh, and who have thus reversed God's order of their being. The word "mind" is a peculiar one. It is derived from the Greek name for the diaphragm, and like heart, reins and bowels, is used as a psychological term. It designates a peculiar mental state, including intellectual elements as well as desire and will. It is to apply the thoughts to a thing with strong emotional elements, usually of a lower moral character, though not always so—the eagerness of natural desire or passion. This very eagerness, however, may, like all natural things, be sanctified. (Compare Col. iii. 2.) It is used by Paul in this passage to denote the great end of life. This with those who are governed by the flesh is to gain the things of the flesh.

but they that are after the spirit the things of the spirit.] Compare Phil. iv. 8, where the things of the spirit are presented as an objective course of life. In Gal. v. 22 they are given as an inward character. In Col. iii. 1–4 we have them as hoped for in the future. We have thus designated two classes of men, two distinct sets of ruling aims of life, representing two distinct moral states, and having their starting point in the right or wrong relation to will and conduct of the two fundamental elements of man's nature. He now adds the two final results to which they respectively lead.

6. For the mind of the flesh is death;] The aim of life which is based upon the flesh, the lower nature, leads to death, inasmuch as the very fact of ruling the life makes the flesh a breaker of law. God's law subordinates the flesh to the spirit. If the beginning of depravity lies in the *insubordination* of the flesh (its lusts, see on ch. vii.), then the apostle has carried this idea consistently through, making depravity and sin everywhere *moral* and not physical in their nature. The mind of the flesh is the moral impulse which is governed by the flesh. Moral impulse, *i.e.*, impulse governing the will, should always be spiritual. To resign this high prerogative to the flesh is death.

but the mind of the spirit is life and peace:] Because in harmony with God's order and law of our being. All moral law is natural law, as duty. All natural law which guides the conscious acts of a moral being becomes moral law through his intelligence and conscience. Hence Paul adds at once as the reason,

7. because the mind of the flesh is enmity against God;] Paul does not say that the "flesh" is "enmity against God"; but "the motive," that entire aim or direction of life which springs from the flesh, is enmity, *i.e.*, is a warlike opposition to God. It must be so, inasmuch as it is directly contrary to God's order.

for it is not subject to the law of God,] That is this "mind" or direction of life which springs from the flesh. It is, as we have be-

11

fore seen, this insubordination which constitutes its sinfulness. The word translated "subject" signifies to reduce to order under authority or law. God's law prescribes the order and limits of the flesh, its true office as the servant of the spirit. But by presuming to direct the life it has broken loose from this order.

neither indeed can it be:] Even the revised version neglects the force of the particle γαρ, "for," which is found in this clause. We should render thus, supplying the ellipsis in full from the preceding clause: "For indeed it cannot possibly be subject to God's law." What cannot possibly be subject? Not the "flesh," but "the mind of the flesh." In its very nature it is a breach of God's law.

8. and they that are in the flesh cannot please God.] The expression "in the flesh" is here repeated from chapter vii. 5; but as it has now become a familiar term the article is dropped. It corresponds to "after the flesh" in verse 4; but the preposition there used and repeated in verse 5 is suited to the idea of "direction of the conduct according to a rule prescribed by the desires of the flesh," which idea is found in both these verses. The present preposition points rather to *the permanent moral condition* of those whose life is governed "according" to the flesh. These are said to be "in the flesh," a term corresponding to the adjective "carnal" (ch. vii. 14). On the expression "please God" commentators are divided, some taking it as a mild way of saying "are under God's wrath"; others regarding it as equivalent to "cannot acceptably serve God." The first sense requires us to connect this clause with the first clause of verse 7, thus, "the mind of the flesh is death," etc., "because the mind of the flesh is hostile toward God; and on the other hand, those that are in the flesh cannot be pleasing to him," *i.e.*, are the objects of his displeasure. So Meyer and Godet. The decidedly active significance of the word, as signifying effort or active desire to please, is, however, rather in favour of the other interpretation, which would connect this clause with the middle clause of verse 7 (making the last clause a parenthesis), as follows: "The carnal mind is hostile to God, for it is not subject to God's law, and they that are in the flesh cannot please him." There may be a "will of the mind" to do so, but it is never carried into effect, "wrought out." Verses 5, 6 and 7 become thus a *resumé* of chapter vii.

9. But ye are not in the flesh, but in the spirit,] By means of the adversative conjunction contrasting the condition of his readers with that just described, the author returns to the point which he had reached at the end of verse 4, in which he was expanding the text already given (ch. vii. 6). The expression "in the spirit" here is equivalent to in "newness of the spirit" there, and to the adjective "spiritual" elsewhere; and as the phrase "in flesh" describes the permanent moral condition of the unregenerate, so the phrase "in spirit" describes the permanent moral state of believers.

if so be that the Spirit of God dwelleth in you.] With these important words the apostle opens up a new aspect, before untouched in this Epistle, of the process of our moral regeneration in Christ. This is nothing less than the personal agency of the Holy Ghost, who "abideth with us and shall be in us" (John xiv. 17). The distinct personality of the Holy Spirit is scarcely less prominent in this passage than in the later writings of St. John. We may note, further, the expressions "the Spirit of God dwelleth in you," "the Spirit of him that raised up Jesus from the dead," "as many as are led by the Spirit of God," "the Spirit himself beareth witness." All these, in the light of parallel passages of St. Paul as well as of St. John, the church has interpreted of the Third Person of the Trinity. (See Gal. iv. 6; 1 Cor. iii. 16; Eph. iv. 30, etc.)

But if any man hath not the Spirit of Christ, he is none of his.] The Spirit of Christ is not the Christ-like spirit, but the Holy Spirit, the Comforter promised by Christ. This designation of the Holy Ghost is common with Paul and Peter. (See Gal. iv. 6; Phil. i. 19; 1 Peter i. 11). The reference to the promise of the Spirit (Eph. i. 13) and the fact that our Lord's promise was recorded by Luke (Acts i. 4, 8), and that its fulfilment was clearly recognized on the day of Pentecost, make it almost certain that the Holy Spirit is called the Spirit of Christ in all these passages, as promised by our Lord and proceeding from him. The possession of this promised Comforter is absolutely essential to the Christian. No stronger form of language can be found in the New Testament than this: "'This one is not his," *i.e.*, Christ's. He may be a servant of God under the law; he is not Christ's.

10. **And if Christ is in you,**] This passing from the Spirit of Christ to Christ himself is in harmony with the language of the promise. (Compare John xiv. 16-18.) Christ manifests himself unto us and in us by his Spirit (John xiv. 23, 26, etc.)

the body is dead because of sin;] Our two English versions omit the corresponding conjunction μεν, which, with δε following, connects this clause with the next. It may be rendered thus: "*it is true that* the body is dead because of sin, but." (See Liddell and Scott's Lex.) The reference here is clearly to physical death as the penalty of sin. How, even from that, we shall be finally delivered he will tell us presently. Meantime the body is still subject to death on account of sin, *i.e.*, the sin reaching the race from Adam.

but the spirit is life because of righteousness.] "The spirit" is our spirit as contrasted with our body. This becomes life, *i.e.*, our true life, controlling our whole living being. While the spirit is here clearly the regenerate nature, yet the word does not bear this meaning taken alone. It is as the subject of this predicate "life" that it designates the new nature. "On account of righteousness"—not on account of Christ's righteousness, as the procuring cause of this life; nor for the sake of working righteousness, as the final cause of this gift of life—but on account of our new right relation to God, in connection with the bestowment of which (*i.e.*, our pardon or justification) God's Spirit bestows this life. The two things—

the gift of righteousness, or *justification*, and the new life of our spirit, or *regeneration*—are inseparable concomitants. The second is given on account of the first and with the first.

11. **But if the Spirit of him that raised up Jesus from the dead dwelleth in you, he that raised up Christ Jesus from the dead shall quicken also your mortal bodies through his Spirit that dwelleth in you.**] The concessive clause in verse 10, "the body, it is true, is dead," had called up to Paul's mind the great doctrine of the resurrection. On Paul's view of this subject see 1 Cor. xv. The present passage is important as bringing the regenerating work of the Holy Ghost into direct relation to the resurrection of the body as a forepromise of that final deliverance (compare verse 23 and Eph. i. 14), and also as indicating a still more intimate connection between the regenerating work of the Spirit and the glorification of the resurrection body which will be a *spiritual* body (1 Cor. xv. 44). The alternate reading, "for the sake of his Spirit that dwelleth in you," is not so well attested. It would favour the identification of the Spirit of God with that of man, the body being raised again for the sake of this spirit, *i.e.*, to be its eternal habitation. This reading is as old as the Macedonian Controversy, and was used by the heretics of that time. The reading of the text represents the Holy Spirit as the agent of the resurrection of the saints in glory.

EXCURSUS ON THE DOCTRINES OF DEPRAVITY AND REGENERATION.

In the larger section of the Epistle here completed, extending from chapter vii. 5 to chapter viii. 11, and embracing two subsections—the first on the relation of the law to our fallen moral nature, and the second on the relation of grace to that same fallen nature—we have incidentally presented the moral nature of man in the light of the two dispensations, (1) of the law, and (2) of the gospel. We may therefore here supplement the data as to the doctrine of man's fallen nature or condition derived from chapter vii. That which in chapter vii., in contrast to God's law, was there designated as a law of sin and death, is here, in contrast to the new governing principle of the spiritual life, called "the mind of the flesh," *i.e.*, an aim or controlling principle of life derived from the flesh, *i.e.*, from our lower nature. The persons governed by this impulse are said to be "after the flesh" and "in the flesh." This impulse or controlling motive of life is not only opposed to God's law but is further hostile to God himself, and insubordinate to his revealed will in his law; and in its very nature must be so. And as a result it is not possible for those who are in this moral condition to please God, *i.e.*, to work out a course of life acceptable to him. And the end of this impulse is death, as was the end of the law of sin. The process of regeneration is the quickening into new life of man's spiritual nature. This nature, even under the flesh, existed as the law of the mind, assenting to, delighting in, and even willing to serve the good; but now, under the regenerating grace of God, it becomes the mind of the Spirit, *i.e.*, a governing power of life founded in our spiritual nature. This spiritual nature is restored to life in harmony with God's gift of righteousness, *i.e.*, pardon as received in the conscience, delivering us from condemnation or the sentence of death against sin. So that the emancipation of the conscience from the sense of guilt is at the same time the restoration of its power to govern the life, *i.e.*, not any emancipation, such as a delusive carnal security, but the emancipation which God gives us in Christ. Regeneration is thus the restoration to man's spiritual nature of its power to control the whole man, which thus in all its activities becomes a new man in Christ Jesus. But this regeneration is effected by the indwelling of God's Holy Spirit, the promised Comforter, whose office it is to reveal to us the things of God (1 Cor. ii. 9-12). Hence the harmony of Paul's doctrine with that of Peter, who says that we are born of the word of God (1 Peter i. 23; see also James i. 18). In the immediate context Paul calls especial attention to the revelation by this Spirit of God's adopting love, the testimony of God's Spirit that we are the children of God. The communication of this testimony is thus most intimately associated with the work of regeneration.

CH. VIII. 12-17. CONCLUDING STATEMENT OF OUR HIGH OBLIGATIONS, CULMINATING IN THE PRIVILEGES OF CHRISTIAN SONSHIP.

12. **So then, brethren, we are debtors,**] The two conjunctions here used sum up and resume the preceding argument. "So," *i.e.*, under these circumstances; "then," resuming the discourse and carrying us back to the main line of thought. But what is the main line of thought? and to what point are we carried back? The word "debtors" gives us the clue. It carries us directly back to chapter vii. 5, 6, and thence to chapter vi. 21-23. The whole intervening discourse, as we have seen, is but the expansion and demonstration of chapter vii. 5, 6. The conjunction "so" sums up this entire expansion of the main thesis of chapter vii. 5, 6, to which the deductive "then" directly attaches the present practical conclusion.

not to the flesh, to live after the flesh:] The constant thought of the apostle is to guard his readers against return to that Jewish legality which will place them once more under the dominion of the flesh. He does not say that we have no debt to the flesh; we owe it food and raiment, but we do not owe it the rule of our lives.

13. **for if ye live after the flesh, ye must die;**] This was the central thought which the apostle's "so" (verse 12) summed up, and to which his "then" carried us back, already placed before us in chapters vi. 23 and vii. 5, and subsequently repeated at the conclusion of each subordinate line of argument.

but if by the spirit ye mortify the deeds of the body, ye shall live.] The adversative conjunction advances the apostle's thought to the new step toward which he is now leading us, the blessed privilege of living in the spirit. The "spirit" is here probably our spiritual nature quickened into new life by God's Spirit. The deeds of the body which, by the authority of the spiritual nature, are to be put to death, *i.e.*, put out of existence, are enumerated in Gal. v. 21. These are the "deeds" or "works" of the flesh, *i.e.*, the acts which result from its control over the will. The substitution of the word "body" for the "flesh" shews us that in the apostle's vocabulary the word "flesh" is not identical with depravity. The life promised is the real life with Christ in God, which the apostle proceeds to set forth in the verses following.

14. **For as many as are led by the Spirit of God, these are sons of God.**] We have already seen that at various points in his discourse the apostle opens up a new field of thought by a "for," making it the reason or expansion of something going before. Here the whole doctrine of Christian sonship is opened up in illustration of the promise, "ye shall live." The idea of sonship comes directly out of the idea of new "life" now before the apostle's mind; though Paul presents the sonship rather as an "adoption" than as a "regeneration." (Compare ch. ix. 4; Gal. iv. 5; Eph. i. 5.) The idea of new birth is with him, as in the Jewish mind generally, connected with baptism (Titus iii. 5). The proselyte who sought admission among the covenant people was first baptized, which was reckoned a new birth. Then by circumcision he was instated in all the privileges of the covenant, *i.e.*, adopted as a son. This term, received by Paul from Roman law, designated, not so much an individual relation between father and adopted son, as with us, as a tribal or family relation. In the case of the Jews, a national relationship, in which all shared in common in the covenant promise, "Ye shall be my sons and daughters, saith the Lord Almighty," is presented before us. This verse therefore constitutes the turning point at which the apostle passes from the great question of "righteousness," in its relations to the law and the gospel, and in its moral obligations and the helps afforded by the two dispensations, to the covenant privileges of those who are accepted as righteous before God. In chapter ix. 4 Paul acknowledges that the adoption belongs to the ancient covenant people; and it is there placed at the head of the catalogue of the covenant privileges. As up to this point he has, by comparison of the law and the gospel, vindicated for believers the claim to righteousness before God, such as could never be attained by works of law, so now he quietly proceeds to claim for them all the covenant privileges of the ancient people. We may therefore paraphrase the verse before us thus: "For as many as are led by the Spirit of God, *these* (and not mere natural descendants of Abraham, or those who are outwardly under the law), *these* are the true *sons of God*. On the title "son," as designating the chosen people, compare Ex. iv. 22; applied to their anointed head, 2 Sam. vii. 14; 1 Chron. xvii. 13. (See also Hosea xi. 9; i. 10; Isaiah xlv. 11; Jer. xxxi. 9.) The text is therefore the announcement of a most important principle, putting

the whole catalogue of covenant privileges upon the basis of inward character, of spiritual (not mere legal or external) relationship to God. The carrying out of the position which Paul takes in the verse before us fills out the rest of this chapter and calls for chapters ix.-xi. Sons, heirs, partakers of suffering, sharers of glory, to which we are predestinated and called, and toward which all things work, and so instated in a relationship to God from which nothing in time nor eternity can move us—these are the golden links of the covenant privileges which are ours in Christ, and of which we have the first now before us. The fully expanded thought of Paul in this connection we have in Gal. iii. 26-iv. 7, where our interpretation as related to the ancient covenant and its sonship is fully borne out. Paul summarizes here what is given in full there.

15. For ye received not the spirit of bondage again unto fear;] "The spirit of bondage" is the spirit of a mere servant, as distinguished from that of a son. The word "spirit" here designates our spiritual nature in its relation to God. This nature may stand towards God in a relation of servitude, "unto fear," *i.e.*, leading to the fear of God, reverential dread of God as a holy God. This was not the relation in which they were placed by faith in Christ Jesus. The reference is to a definite experience on the part of his readers at a particular point of their religious history. But the adverb "again" implies that they had *previously received* the spirit of servitude to fear. The attempt to restrict the adverb to the phrase "to fear" does not invalidate this conclusion, unless it can be shown that there is such a thing as religious fear apart from this spirit of the servant. But does this spirit of bondage refer to the law? Our present passage taken by itself alone would not warrant such a reference, although the entire scope of the Epistle, as everywhere throwing the law into contrast with the gospel, might strongly suggest it. But in the light of Gal. iv. 23, etc., such a reference becomes unavoidable. There we are told that the old sonship under the law was only the sonship of *children in ward*, which differs nothing from the condition of the bondservant so far as the present is concerned (Gal. iv. 1, 2). Thus the condition of God's people under the law was also one of bondage until, "in the fulness of time, God sent forth his Son," etc. (Gal. iv. 4, 5). In the light of this parallel passage we must therefore interpret the adverb as follows: "Ye received not the spirit of servitude again (as those under the law formerly received it) to fear."

but ye received the spirit of adoption, whereby we cry, Abba, Father.] The spirit of adoption is here beautifully defined as that relation to God out of which our spirits "cry, Abba, Father." In the parallel passage in Galatians this act is represented as that of the Spirit of God's Son crying in our hearts, *i.e.*, in the seat of our moral judgment and affections, Abba, Father. The next verse will bring the two into harmony. It is, however, to be noted that Paul everywhere uses the expression "spirit of *adoption*, and not the term "spirit of *sonship*." Even in the case of ancient Israel, who were sons in virtue of birth from Abraham, he uses the same term. The term is therefore chosen, not so much in view of the fact that these Gentiles received the adoption in a way differing from the "Israel after the flesh," as that this sonship is everywhere God's gift, a privilege *conferred* under the covenant. The spirit of adoption is therefore not the spirit or disposition which characterizes a son, though it may include that, but the spiritual relation to God conferred in the very act of adoption, by the gift of the Spirit of God's Son in our hearts.

16. **The Spirit himself beareth witness with our spirit, that we are children of God:**] Paul does not say "the same spirit," *i.e.*, the aforesaid spiritual state or relation growing out of God's act of adoption, but the Spirit himself. The pronoun is emphatic, and leaves us without possibility of doubt as to the distinction between our own spiritual nature and the personal Spirit of God who dwelleth in us. "The Spirit himself" can be no other than the personal Spirit of God's Son referred to in Gal. iv. 6. This Spirit beareth testimony with our spirit that we are children of God. Our spirit receives the testimony which this Spirit gives. How this testimony is given Paul does not say; but its outcome is that we cry Abba, Father. This cry is at once the cry of our spirit, and of God's Spirit in and with our spirit. Like every other truth given directly in our spiritual nature, this cannot be defined; it can only be known in conscious experience, and to their own conscious experience Paul refers his readers—"ye received."

17. **and if children, then heirs; heirs of God,**] This was another title of God's people. (Compare ch. ix. 4 with Gal. iii. 29.) This was one of the great truths specially revealed to Paul. (See Eph. iii. 6.) This heirship makes us heritors of all the promises of the ancient covenant. But these promises were given not only to the covenant people but especially to their covenant head, the Messiah. (See Isaiah xl.-liii., and compare 1 Peter i. 11.) That this was a thoroughly Pauline conception appears from Eph. i.-iii., where Paul has fully expanded this subject, setting forth Christ's heritage in the saints (ch. i. 11, 18, 20-23) and our inheritance with him (ch. ii. 7), and finally the unity of the Gentiles with the Jews in this inheritance (chs. ii. 11-iii. 11). Hence he adds,

and joint heirs with Christ;] Elsewhere he puts it, "All things are yours, and ye are Christ's, and Christ is God's (1 Cor. iii. 23). On our Lord's inheritance see Phil. ii. 9-11. But Christ inherited through suffering, and so must we.

if so be that we suffer with him, that we may be also glorified with him.] On this Pauline idea of fellowship with Christ's sufferings compare Phil. iii. 10, 2 Cor. iv. 10-18—where, as here, it is followed by fellowship in glory—and 2 Tim. ii. 11, 12. This presents the theme of the next subsection of the Epistle.

Ch. VIII. 18-30. THE CONTRAST OF THE SUFFERINGS AND THE
GLORY OF OUR HEIRSHIP AS SONS.

18. For I reckon that the sufferings of this present time are not worthy to be compared with the glory which shall be revealed to us-ward.] The theme thus announced—"the sufferings of this present time" and "the glory to be revealed"—may be compared with Luke xxiv. 26, 27, and with 1 Peter i. 11. From both these passages we learn that the mind of the whole infant church was cognizant of the fact that the ancient prophecies depicted, both for the Messiah and for his people, a course of suffering, to be followed by glory. How fully Paul had apprehended this great prophetic thought appears as well from the passage before us as from others to which we have already referred. The conjunction "for" here expands the thought of verse 17 into the new section upon which we are now entering, and of which the present verse states the theme. The expression "I reckon" is used by Paul when about to present a great general statement of truth. (Compare chapter iii. 28.) There it presents the truth founded upon preceding investigation. Here the reckoning follows, being introduced by "for" in the next verse.

19. For the earnest expectation of the creation waiteth for the revealing of the sons of God.] This verse contains the first proposition upon which Paul founds his reckoning—the universal suffering of creation, which, of course, must mean sentient creation, as it alone is capable of suffering. This universal suffering leads all creation to watch with "head uplifted," as the animals are accustomed to do when attracted by a coming object. The creation here we take to be the sentient physical world, of which man's body, referred to presently, is a part. This gives us the necessary contrast between the sons of God and the creation. It fits the predicates of verses 20, 21 and 22, and gives the needed point of connection for verse 23. The revealing of the sons of God is the glory that shall be revealed in us. (Compare 1 John iii. 2, and for a similar Pauline view Col. iii. 4.)

20. For the creation was subjected to vanity,] This expression "subjected" designates, in Paul's use of it, a dispensation or arrangement of God. The vanity is presently designated as a "bondage of corruption" and a "groaning and travailing in pain." It would thus seem to include all physical suffering in nature as a dispensation or ordering of God.

not of its own will, but by reason of him who subjected it,] All agree here that the expression "not of its own will" must signify not by any act of its own, nor even by consent to or conscious implication in the act of another. We should therefore look in the antithetic clause for the mention of the one by whose act or on whose account it was subjected. The preposition used (διά with accusative) is in harmony with this, and both would point to man (Adam) as referred to. But the relative clause makes the one referred to the subject of the verb, and it can only be said of man indirectly that he "subjected it." The dispensation is undoubtedly of God. The moral cause is in man; and as the moral cause of an act is often said to do it, we may perhaps be most safe in accepting this interpretation.

21. in hope that the creation itself also shall be delivered from the bondage of corruption] On the foregoing construction of verse 20 "in hope" must be made an adjunct of the first clause of that verse, "was subjected in hope." "The bondage of corruption" seems to signify physical death and the decay which leads up to it and which follows it. Deliverance from this does not imply a resurrection of the lower life, which lives in the species rather than in the individual.

into the liberty of the glory of the children of God.] The liberty here referred to must correspond to the bondage; and as that included suffering, decay and death, so is this liberty at least deliverance from these. It is the liberty of the glory of God's children because attained at the time of their glorification, and also in itself a part of that glorification. (See 1 Cor. xv.; Phil. iii. 11.) But does this apply to the whole sentient physical creation? So it would seem unless the word "creation" is here to be limited to the physical nature, i.e., the bodies, of believers. There are not wanting intimations of this universal glorification of nature elsewhere. (See Isaiah lx. 17, etc.)

22. For we know that the whole creation groaneth and travaileth in pain together until now.] This is Paul's proof from an open fact of his first proposed proof of the greatness of the glory that shall be revealed in us. It contains a most magnificent generalization and interpretation of the fact of suffering in nature. This suffering is *universal;* it takes place in virtue of the *unity* of nature (together); it is the presage of a new birth into a higher good. Every one of these conclusions is substantiated by the best conclusions of biological science. On the scientific difficulties of this view see Godet. And as the suffering still exists the higher good which it portends is still to come, and hence it is the first ground of our hope.

23. And not only so, but ourselves also, which have the firstfruits of the Spirit,] The first ground of assurance of the great hope announced in verse 18 lay in the phenomena of universal suffering in nature, which all point to the, to them, unconscious hope of a higher good. We now turn to the second ground—the phenomena of our own conscious experience as the children of God.

even we ourselves groan within ourselves, waiting for our adoption, to wit, the redemption of our body.] Our adoption Paul himself explains as the redemption, i.e., the resurrection, of the body. He repeatedly uses redemption in this sense of the final consummation of Christ's work at his second coming, in the resurrection glory (Eph. iv. 30; i. 17), although at other times, of the work accomplished on the cross. Our sonship and adoption is only complete when the body is finally redeemed. But now "we groan, waiting,' especially in our share of this universal dispensation of suffering. This suffering hope is proof number two.

24. **For by hope were we saved:**] The word "hope" here, occupying the emphatic position in the sentence, sums up the experience just referred to. This hope is equivalent to faith. It is the permanent faith by which we are saved, looking out of present suffering into the promised future.

but hope that is seen is not hope: for who hopeth for that which he seeth?] This interjected parenthesis serves the same purpose as the "until now" of verse 22, *i.e.*, in this second proof it demonstrates that the good, which corresponds to our groaning, is not already attained, but still in the future, and hence he adds,

25. **But if we hope for that which we see not, then do we with patience wait for it.**] The strength of our hope is measured by our patience. This repeated reference of the Christian hope to the eternal future and to the things unseen (2 Cor. iv. 18) may well be taken in contrast to the purely temporal and material hopes of those under the old dispensation.

26. **And in like manner the Spirit also helpeth our infirmity:**] The "in like manner" we take as referring to the two lines of hope already described as each pointing to the glory to be revealed. Of this glory the physical creation is only unconsciously hopeful in its suffering. We are consciously hopeful, but with very *infirm* perceptions of our needs. But God's Spirit, in revelation to us of the future, helps this infirmity. The infirmity is specifically mentioned in the next clause, as also the specific character of the help afforded.

for we know not how to pray as we ought;] The old version, "what we should pray for as we ought," is nearer the original. The reference is not to the manner of prayer, but to its subject matter—"what we should ask, according to that which it is proper to ask."

but the Spirit himself maketh intercession for us with groanings which cannot be uttered;] Instead of referring this to mystic, unintelligible desires, we think the best comment upon it is to be found in Paul's own words (1 Cor. ii. 9, 10, etc.), "Things which eye saw not, and ear heard not," etc., "what God hath prepared for them that love him. But God hath revealed them unto us by his Spirit," etc. Note that in this passage Paul has specially before his mind "the glory" which God had "foreordained" (1 Cor. ii. 7) for "them that love him" (1 Cor. ii. 9)—expressions which he here repeats in this immediate text and context. "The searching," the "mind of the Spirit," etc., are all ideas present in both passages. The apostle is speaking, not of the *immediate wants* or prayers arising out of our sufferings, but of their final result, "the glory that shall be revealed." This which the revealing Spirit has unveiled only in symbols, and which we see now only in a mirror darkly, is the object of our hope and the subject of the unutterable desires prompted by the Spirit. On this term "unutterable," as applied to the unseen world, see 2 Cor. xii. 4, where a similar form is used. The Spirit then has helped our infirmity (lack of knowledge) by this revelation of the future which, though literally "inexpressible" in human language, is "mirrored" to us so as to be the object of our desires and the subject of our prayers.

27. **and he that searcheth the hearts knoweth what is the mind of the Spirit, because he maketh intercession for the saints according to the will of God.**] "The mind of the Spirit" in this verse must be taken as in verse 6, where it denotes the moral impulse or aim which springs from the Spirit—there our renewed spiritual nature; here the promptings and revelation of God's Spirit. God sees in our hearts the φρονημα (desire and aspiration) given us through his Spirit's outward and inward revelation of the things unspeakable; he understands its full significance, though we do not (we "know in part;" see also 1 John iii. 2), "that" (rather than "because") "it is according to God," *i.e.*, "God's purpose" or his working. This he proceeds to expand in the next verse.

28. **And we know that to them that love God all things work together for good,**] See 1 Cor. ii. 9, "Whatsoever things God prepared for them that love him." We may in our text read, "he worketh," or with some very weighty authorities, "God worketh." The things work, not of themselves, but God worketh them. We think even the revisers' text is better translated with "he" (God) as subject rather than the plural "all."

even to them that are called according to his purpose.] For the meaning of this word "called" see chapter i. 7. If, as we have there argued at length, it signifies that abiding relation of God's people to himself in virtue of which they are responsible for holiness of life, then it is synonymous with the "saint" of verse 27, and with the expression "them that love God" in the clause preceding. The "purpose" according to which this calling takes place is explained by the verse following. In its general meaning this word "purpose" is applied (1) to the "calling" of God's people (here and 2 Tim. i. 9); (2) to their heritage in and with Christ (Eph. i. 9-11); (3) to their election (Rom. ix. 11); and perhaps in a still wider sense (4) to the dispensation of divine grace in Christ (Eph. iii. 11), and to the atonement (Rom. iii. 25). Now, in all these passages there is express reference to the method or principle upon which God from age to age designated the chosen people as his church upon earth; *e.g.*, in chapter ix. 11 it is said to be of God's purpose that Jacob was chosen to be the head of the chosen people rather than Esau; in Eph. i. 9, and presumably 11, it points to the extension of these privileges to the Gentiles. (Compare verse 9 with ch. iii. 3-6, the same idea being carried forward to verse 11.) Now, the call to be a holy people, *i.e.*, a people separate to God's service, was one of the peculiar distinctions of the ancient people. Hence the call according to God's purpose would seem to have distinct reference to this plan of

God regarding the continuity of his church, or his *separated people*, as through Enoch, Noah, Abraham, Israel redeemed from Egypt, and finally by a church gathered from Jews and Gentiles alike, he carries forward his purpose of grace for the world's salvation. We must, however, carefully distinguish what is and what is *not* included in this purpose. We cannot find that this purpose extends back of the mission of Christ. The purpose is "in Christ"—Christ includes the purpose. When God so loved the world that he gave his only begotten Son, the gift included a purpose as to when and how his work should be carried into effect. But the gift of his Son, even Christ, is behind the purpose. God's love is behind the purpose as it was behind the Christ. The purpose, therefore, cannot be held to limit either God's love or Christ's atoning work, both which are declared to be as wide as the world (Rom. v.; 2 Cor. v. 19). On the other hand, the purpose *gives effect* both to God's love and Christ's mission. Thus in Paul's conception the purpose includes all the means and agencies by which the grace which is in Christ Jesus is to be administered, or as he phrases it, "the dispensations." Nor can we find, on the other hand, that the purpose of God covers the salvation of the individual. It does cover everything that lies between God's love in Christ and individual salvation. But we can find no passage which makes the purpose intrude *beyond the line of individual ethical responsibility* which, as we have seen all along, is the very essence of Paul's doctrine. The Jewish idea of salvation by covenant privilege *did so intrude*. Paul has overthrown that doctrine for the very purpose of *putting Jew and Gentile alike upon the ground of personal responsibility before God*. It is inconceivable that after he has done this he should overthrow his own work by re-establishing a conception of salvation upon a basis of metaphysical prerogative quite as unethical in its tendencies as was the old Jewish idea of national prerogative. Such a conception made its first appearance in the church in the teaching of Augustine, who was led to it by the logical necessities of the thoroughly Jewish doctrine of sacramental salvation. And once introduced it has been maintained in the church by a misconception of the scope of chapters ix.-xi., with which we shall deal presently. God's purpose defines the atoning work of Christ (Rom. iii. 25); defines the dispensations through which God prepared the world for his coming (Eph. i.-iii.); defines the fulness of times in which all the privileges of the separate and covenant people are opened to Jew and Gentile alike, on the probational condition of faith; and finally defines the holy work or holy discipline by which all who believe are fully and finally glorified with Christ after having suffered with him. It is this last element of the divine purpose to which the apostle now specially calls attention, as he proceeds to explain in the next verse, connecting by ὅτι, "because," or as it might be fairly rendered, "that."

29. **For whom he foreknew, he also foreordained to be conformed to the image of his Son,**] If "the called according to God's

purpose" are the body of God's people separated from the world, holy to the Lord, for his service in the salvation of those who are not so called, then those "whom he foreknew" must be this same body. If the purpose according to which they are called does not collide with individual responsibility neither does the divine foreknowledge. We need not at all limit that foreknowledge to the foresight of faith and good works. It must include all the general facts upon which God's purpose was based as well as the particular facts which directed that purpose along particular lines in the divine predestination. And it guards both the purpose and the predestination from being arbitrary. It does not interfere with God's sovereignty, as we shall see in chapter ix. But that which is founded upon knowledge is founded upon reason, and cannot be arbitrary. That which is founded upon God's knowledge is founded in perfect reason, and perfect reason violates no truth, principle or fact. Hence this word "foreknew" secures both the universality and impartiality of God's love on the one hand, and the fulness of human responsibility on the other. It is this divine foreknowledge which directs the purpose of God to this, that or the other body of men. But as the divine purpose was not directed toward them irrespective of foreknowledge of what they were as fit instruments of God's purpose, so neither does it compel their individual salvation even when it reaches them. But on this point see further below. But these who are thus foreknown "he also foreordained." This word "foreordained" includes two ideas: first, of the persons included within the boundaries; secondly, of the boundaries within which they are included. The boundaries or "marked out limits" here are defined in the next clause, "to be conformed to the image of his Son." This is the emphatic idea of the text. (See Cremer on $\pi\rho oo\rho i\zeta\epsilon\iota\nu$.) *The persons are not designated by "predestination" but by "foreknowledge."* The discipline is predestinated, i.e., "conformity to the image of his Son." This is in harmony with Paul's idea of the purpose. The purpose is the divine method of carrying Christ's saving work to its full completion for the world's salvation. Individual men or bodies of men are included in that purpose, not merely with reference to their own salvation (they are rather included as themselves already *foreknown as saved*), but as *co-workers* with Christ as his body the church, whether patriarchal, Mosaic or Christian, as those who are his representatives or agents, set apart, *i.e.*, sanctified or holy, to God for his loving purpose toward the sons of men. It is therefore fitting that, like their master who was made a perfect Saviour through suffering, they should share in his sufferings. (For this Pauline idea see besides ch. viii. 17; 2 Cor. iv. 10, 11; 2 Tim. ii. 10-12; Phil. iii. 10; and especially Col. i. 24, 25, where these sufferings are peculiarly presented as part of the dispensations of God in the mystery of the gospel.) On the relation of our Lord's own sufferings see Heb. ii. 14-18 and v. 8. (Compare the excellent essay of the Rev. J. S. Evans, D.D., on this subject.) "Conformed to the image of his Son" is thus not to be taken solely in its widest sense, but with special reference to "the fellowship of his sufferings." Riddle, Moule and the Calvinistic expositors generally, by making the predestination unto individual salvation, make this conformity refer to the purity of Christ's character, or to partaking of his final glory. The latter is pertinent to the apostle's line of thought, but we are predestinated unto suffering with him *that* we may be sharers with him in glory, or as Paul puts it here,

that he might be the firstborn among many brethren:] The reference here is probably to the glory of the resurrection. (1) In the immediate context (verse 23) he has spoken of this as "the adoption"; (2) in Col. i. 18 our Lord is called "the first begotten from the dead." The association of our resurrection glory and of our Lord's resurrection with the idea of Sonship of God is thus clearly established as a Pauline idea. In fact, this is the only Sonship common to us with our Lord, unless it be either the sense in which all men are sons of God, who is the Father of Spirits, or the sense presented by Godet, that the eternal Son is the type after which we were originally created, and to which we are to be conformed in renewal. But we fail to find evidence that this idea is Pauline. In the Epistle to the Hebrews we become his brethren by virtue of the fact that he unites himself to us in our human nature. In reference to the eternal Sonship it is said, "My Father and your Father," implying a distinction rather than unity. This idea that those who are sharers in the toils and sufferings of Christ's kingdom upon earth shall be in a special sense partakers of his resurrection glory and exaltation (throne) is frequent in the New Testament, and especially in the Apocalypse, where Christ is also called the first begotten from the dead (Rev. i. 5).

30. **and whom he foreordained, them he also called:]** It does not follow that all the finally saved are either thus foreordained or called. If the calling is unto special responsibilities and sufferings it does not at all belong to infants, nor (unless in a subordinate sense) to those who may be saved under the dispensation of the Gentiles. But the chosen people, Israel of old, and the church now, are "chosen in the furnace of affliction." We shall see more of this in the study of Isaiah's doctrine of the Lord's chosen servant, upon which Paul has so largely founded his evangelical conceptions.

and whom he called, them he also justified:] As this is the justification of God's called ones, who, as we have seen, are the same with the "saints" who "love God," it cannot be identified with the "justification of the ungodly" of the preceding chapters. It is rather the justification of God's elect of verse 33. It is to this same final justification that Paul refers in 1 Cor. iv. 1-5, where again it is closely associated with the suffering of God's called ones—(verse 9) justification before "the world, angels and men." If this be taken of the process of salvation then we have the anomaly that the process of sanctification is provided for before the call and before justification.

and whom he justified, them he also glorified.] (See verse 17, "That we may be also glorified together.") This glorification is not entrance into heaven, or final salvation. It is more than that It is reward—a reward which even a Paul struggled to attain (Phil. iii. 12). The aorist is used throughout this exposition of God's purpose. This brings the whole matter into the field of history. It cannot be arbitrarily transferred to the sphere of the eternal. But why not use the future to the last step, glorification? Because the apostle is looking at past history, and especially at the whole past history of the chosen people as summed up in Christ the head. The historical facts of the past, already realized in the body of the people of God in part, and in full, even to the glory, in their Head, is the pledge to those who still remain that so it shall still be. That Paul regarded the ancient covenant people as *having been* glorified in the past is clear from such passages as chapter ix. 4. But the glorification of the chosen people of each dispensation was the entrance into that which followed. The patriarchal was glorified in the promised land, the Mosaic in the Messiah, the Christian shall be in the resurrection. Paul thus takes up the Christian believers as a body into the line of God's chosen ones of all the ages, and in these two verses marks out the law which governs their life as God's elect, a law ordained of God beforehand, but lighting down on such as in the foreknowledge of God were the fit instruments to receive this call and bear its responsibilities, and so to share its glory. The law is, first suffering, then glory—the sufferings of Egypt, the glory of Canaan; the sufferings of Babylon, etc., the glory of the Christ; the sufferings of the Christ and his glory; our sufferings and the glory that "shall yet be revealed." The last Paul has already anticipated in verse 18, and has here only finally decisively proved by this historical *resumé* of the law of God's elect. The "we know" of verse 28 is the "we know" of a historical induction, and thus introduces the fourth of Paul's magnificent inductive proofs of the great thesis set forth in verse 18. This proof thus complete he turns to a triumphant hymnal recapitulation of the blessed truths which must follow.

CH. VIII. 31–39. THE TRIUMPHAL HYMN OF THE CHRISTIAN CHURCH.

31. What then shall we say to these things?] This form of question is Paul's device for fixing special attention upon a salient point, whether the demolition of some objection of his opponent, or as here, the culmination of his own argument.

If God is for us, who is against us?] "We," that is, the Christian church, are thus assumed to be the called and chosen people, the heritors of the Abrahamic promise. "God is for us" inasmuch as his "plan" (πρόθεσις), unfolded in his promises, "works all things together for good" to the people whom he loves and who love him. And *that being so*, "*who is against us?*" Men may seem to be so, but they cannot foil God's purpose. It shall stand, and the very wrath of man shall praise him. At the time when this Roman church was just about to enter the furnace of persecution how precious this encouragement!

32. He that spared not his own Son, but delivered him up for us all,] The writer opens this clause with the emphatic form of the relative, "Who indeed," equal to "The very God who." The great gift of this God to man he puts in both its negative and positive forms, "spared not" and "gave him up." The greatness of God's love and gift are presented in a startling anthropopathism which throws into the divine nature the intense parental emotion of man, and correspondent to which is the expression "his own Son." The mystery of these words, "spared not but delivered up his own Son," who can fathom? Paul is perfectly one with John in making the infinite love of God the sole source of the atonement. "For us all," the "all" extends the "us" to the whole race to which we belong. There is no contrast among the called people which could suggest a need for this word "all." It must therefore have been suggested by the apostle's thought embracing, with the mention of God's gift, the whole race for whom the gift was given. We cannot therefore say with Riddle, "all believers." Paul never imagined it necessary to say that Christ died for all believers; but he asserts, in opposition to Jewish exclusiveness, that Christ died "for all men" (2 Cor. v. 14, 15).

how shall he not also with him freely give us all things?] This was a favourite idea of Paul's. Because we are Christ's all things are ours. The love that embraces all the persons takes cognizance of all the circumstances and wants, and giving the greatest gift will not withhold the less.

33. Who shall lay any thing to the charge of God's elect?] One's thoughts readily turn here, with Moule, to the case of Job and "the great accuser" (Rev. xii. 10). The various accusations suggested by Godet seem scarcely apposite, "conscience," "the law," "persecutors," etc. On the other hand, we find it a common conception with Paul that misfortunes are God's judgments on the ungodly world (1 Cor. xi. 30-32). The very afflictions which to God's people are a means of glory, or at most chastisements, are God's judgments on the ungodly. It is this idea of God's judgment in afflictions which leads Paul to use the technical term for accusation. He probably has no special accuser in mind; in fact, he affirms that none can be found, since

It is God that justifieth;] This justification is not the initial justification of the ungodly attained by faith, but the continuous justification of "God's elect," a justification finally completed in the great day. This idea of a continuous judgment of men by God, an abiding state of condemnation of all who believe not, a reiterated declarative justification of God's people, throughout their probation, finally consummated in the great judgment, runs through both Old and New Testaments. It is more especially associated with the application of the truth to the conscience, and with God's providential afflictions (John iii. 17-21; ix. 39; xii. 48. See also 1 Cor. xi. 31, 32). It is this question of the afflictions of life as a divine process of judgment that Paul has before his mind. In them God justifies his people, *i.e.*, declares their righteousness. It is God's elect who are thus justified. This election belongs to the body. (See below, preliminary excursus to ch. ix.) Each individual is affected as sharing in the common privileges of the body. But the collective justification in God's providence of the despised, calumniated and persecuted body of Christians is perhaps even more in the apostle's mind than the individual justification of any one member.

34. who is he that shall condemn?] If they cannot even be accused before God, much less shall they be condemned. The participle here used may be either present or future, the difference being a matter of accent. If the justification is the continuous justification of God's people through the whole course of their probationary discipline, then the condemnation must be parallel and the present participle used. (So the American Com. of Rev.) If the apostle had reference to the single act of final condemnation at the great day, then the future indicative would seem to be the proper tense. God is to the wicked every day a condemning judge. But "there is no such condemnation to those who are in Christ Jesus." The apostle's "who" is therefore not to imply that he had a condemning judge before his mind, but that no such judge is to be found, because

It is Christ Jesus that died, yea rather, that was raised from the dead, who is at the right hand of God, who also maketh intercession for us.] This is not an enumeration of "the four great saving facts" (Riddle). That would be pertinent if the apostle were speaking of the initial justification of the ungodly, and not of the declarative, continuous justification of God's people. As this is declarative it requires not so much a basis or procuring cause as *a proof*. The four facts enumerated are therefore four proofs of our righteousness. "Christ died for us," proving that our sins are expiated. "He was raised from the dead," God's seal of acceptance of this expiation and his public declaration of acceptance of sinners in Christ. (See note on ch. v. 25.) "He is at the right hand of God"—glorified as our representative and forerunner—proving that we shall be glorified with him. "He also maketh intercession for us," giving still greater emphasis to the fact that our acceptance in him is secure. There is thus but one great saving fact, the death of Christ. But the resurrection (God's seal), the ascension to glory (the reward), and the intercession (the outcome or application), form with the death a fourfold climax of proofs of our righteousness, and are in themselves a continuous justification of God's people. On Paul's doctrine of the exaltation compare Eph. i. 19-23; Phil. ii. 9-11; Col. i. 15-20. On the intercession see the Epistle to the Hebrews vii. 25 and ix. 24; 1 John ii. 1, and John xiv. 16. These passages are the full expansion of the great doctrine here mentioned.

35. Who shall separate us from the love of Christ?] Not our love to Christ, nor our sense of Christ's love to us, but Christ's love to us, *going forth in beneficent activity* - Christ's love as blessing us. Christ's love is not a mere subjective feeling in his mind toward us, to be delightfully recognized by us, but it is the fountain from which flows forth all the wondrous provision of grace, securing our present, eternal and perfect well-being. Nothing can *bar the way* of this active love as it comes forth to bless us.

shall tribulation, or anguish, or persecution, or famine, or nakedness, or peril, or sword?] Each of these had been a matter of actual experience, and that repeatedly (2 Cor. vi. 4, etc.; xii. 23, etc.). Nay more, they had been the experience, as scripture records, of God's people in the past as well.

36. Even as it is written,
For thy sake we are killed all the day long;
We are accounted as sheep for the slaughter.

The quotation is from Psalms xliv. 22, a psalm descriptive of some one of the many afflictions of the ancient chosen people, but of the afflictions which came not as judgments (see verse 17) but for the Lord's sake, or "for the love of him." It illustrates, therefore, the kind of suffering which Paul has in mind—not penal suffering but holy suffering.

37. Nay, in all these things we are more than conquerors through him that loved us.] The strong adversative "but" of the Greek is very well translated "nay," an implied "no," followed by "but on the contrary, in every one of these things we ($\dot{v}\pi\epsilon\rho\nu\iota\kappa\tilde{\omega}\mu\epsilon\nu$) are more than conquerors," a word perhaps invented by Paul and used by the later ecclesiastical writers to designate the triumph of the martyrs over death and suffering. It calls to mind Paul's "far more exceeding and eternal weight of glory." The figure may not be military but, perhaps rather agonistic, the victory in conflict for a prize, or forensic, victory in vindication of innocence "Through him that loved us" looks back to "the love of Christ" in verse 35. That love, far from being hindered by the intervention of these afflictions, carries us triumphantly through them, more than vindicating our cause.

38. For I am persuaded,] The conviction of a perfect faith founded on the great facts adduced in verse 34, confirmed by his own experience, and that of God's people in every age (verses 35-37), and now looking out with assured confidence to every contingency of the future.

that neither death, nor life, nor angels, nor principalities, nor things present, nor things to come, nor powers,

39. nor height, nor depth, nor any other creature,] An enumera-

tion of all possible contingencies of opposition beyond that hitherto experienced. The terms are therefore chosen in logical pairs which form, taken together, *universally exhaustive categories*. Death and life include all forms of our own existence; angels and principalities, all forms of unseen creation, lower or higher; things present, things to come, and powers include all historical circumstances through which we may pass, however powerful or influential; height and depth include every contingency of position or station in which we may be placed; and finally, to include all else, he adds, nor "any other created thing." We may then paraphrase Paul's enumeration thus: No changes of our existence, no opposition of spiritual beings, no variation of surrounding circumstances, no power which can affect us, no position in which we can be placed, in fact no created thing—
shall be able to separate us from the love of God, which is in Christ Jesus our Lord.] Note that "the love of Christ" (verses 35, 37) is here "the love of God which is in Christ Jesus our Lord." To Paul's conception the Father and Son are perfectly identified in the loving motive toward redemption. "Separate us" must be understood as in verse 35. It is not "make God cease to love us," which implies a thought so monstrous in itself that it could not occur to Paul to mention it. Nor is it, on the other hand, "cause us to cease to love God," an idea which would lie right athwart Paul's entire teaching as to personal responsibility. But it must be taken in reference to that of which Paul has been treating throughout, the providential orderings and outgoing of God's love in Christ towards his people. Nothing *can bar that*. "God worketh all things for good." Out of them all comes "a far more exceeding and eternal weight of glory." And nothing in God's created universe can be so evil in itself, so obdurate or intractable, so powerful in counteracting influence, as to thwart God's love, or prevent its reaching us with its exceeding weight of glory. But it must ever be borne in mind that the "us" is the body of the people of God, the church, the elect, the called, the saints, the separated possession. From this body we individually, by unfaithfulness, may become reprobates, and then the promises of the elect are no longer ours. As a supplement, therefore, to the glorious teaching of this chapter, as well as an introduction to the sad case of reprobation which Paul turns next to consider, we must pause to study Paul's doctrine of election.

EXCURSUS ON THE DOCTRINE OF ELECTION.

While in the preceding Epistle St. Paul has been discussing the terms of individual probation, he has throughout tacitly assumed that to those who, upon these terms, are admitted into God's favour there accrue all the prerogatives of the covenant people. The doctrine of the rights and privileges of the covenant people had at this period assumed a very definite form. The people of God, in the Jewish idea, were exactly defined by *the circumcision and the observ-*

ance of the law. They were the seed of Abraham, called of God to be a separate or holy people, an elect race, a royal priesthood, a people for God's own possession, to whom belonged the adoption or sonship, the manifestation of the divine glory, the covenant, the giving of the law, the worship of God, the promises, who, descended from the fathers, were to be the progenitors of the Messiah. It will be seen at once that these prerogatives belong, not to any one individual, but to the nation or body, and to the individuals only through the body. As they are enumerated by Paul (Rom. ix. 4, 5), and further by Peter (1 Peter ii. 9, 10), Paul makes no objection against their scriptural character.

But associated with the scriptural claim to these prerogatives of the covenant people were certain fundamental errors most fatal in their influence upon the moral and religious character of the covenant or chosen people. These were—

1. The belief that they possessed, as a nation, an indefectible right to these covenant privileges. This right they based upon the covenant and promises given to Abraham.

2. That membership in this covenant body was based solely upon the natural descent from Abraham, the only exception being the proselyte who, by baptism and circumcision, was born again into this covenant family.

3. That the covenant was purely a covenant of exclusive privilege or prerogative, ignoring entirely the very important duties or responsibilities involved therein.

4. That one of these prerogatives was the absolutely assured salvation of every individual member of the body, it being considered impossible that any child of Abraham should perish. This prerogative they seem to have held to be exclusive as well as inclusive. Salvation was of the Jews. Only by incorporation with the chosen people could a Gentile be saved, while the chosen people could not fail of salvation whatever might be their moral character. Only the utter apostasy of worshipping false gods could imperil this security.

Through these false conceptions of the election the Judaism of our Lord's time had become external and formal, pharisaic, and antinomian in its entire spirit, the very antipodes, in one respect, of the idolatrous proclivities against which the old prophets contended, and yet scarcely less immoral in its results than that outward ungodliness. John the Baptist was the first to attack this state of things, "laying the axe to the root of the corrupt tree" by his preaching repentance and saying, "*Think not to say within yourselves,* We have Abraham to our father," etc. Our Lord's life-work as a teacher was largely the uprooting of this corrupt antinomian doctrine. The ministry of the twelve in the Jewish Christian church was for the time so gloriously full of the positive factors of the Christian faith, remission of sins and the gift of the Holy Ghost, that this preparatory work of overturning the false in order to build up the true seemed almost to drop out of sight till Paul once more took up the work and set forth both the positive spiritual and new truth and the negation of all corrupt forms of error. One of the most important parts of Paul's work was the correction of the old doctrine of election. The fundamental error of Judaism was the building of personal salvation upon the covenant of election. This Paul completely overturned by shewing that even Abraham, the first of God's elect, the very father of the elect race, was not justified by virtue of the covenant, but received the sign and seal of the covenant in virtue of the righteousness of faith. Paul thus entirely separates the matter of individual righteousness before God, *i.e.*, personal probation, and salvation, at least in its initial stage of justification, from the privileges of election. These do not in any way dispense with or supersede the personal probation and righteousness by faith. This he further intimates in the fact that membership in the true body of the chosen people implies more than outward circumcision or natural descent, even the circumcision of the heart and the inward character of the Israelite indeed. Instead, therefore, of making the outward election supersede the individual probation, he makes the individual probation the foundation of the true election. That individual probation he founds upon faith in our Lord Jesus Christ and the renewing of the Holy Ghost. Up to this point the work of Peter and of Paul was one. It was the "purification" of the outward and visible election "through faith" in Jesus Christ. But Paul sees further that there is to be a new outer and visible election; that God's people can no longer be limited to natural descent and the circumcision. Peter himself recognized this great truth (Acts xv. 8, etc.), but does not seem to have felt called to work beyond the sphere of the old election (Gal. ii. 7-9). This extended view of Paul it was which brought him in contact with Jewish prejudice. It contradicted not only the antinomian position of the infallible salvation of every member of the elect body, but also the proud national conceit of the Jew that the election was forever to be the exclusive monopoly of his race. Nay more, it implied *the rejection of the old elect body*, inasmuch as the great body of them had rejected Christ, and the substitution of a new election founded on the personal probation of faith. These positions constitute what we may call the unexpressed postulates of Paul's teaching in this Epistle. The great body of the Epistle treats of personal righteousness, and only indirectly touches the question of the election which relates, not to the individual probation, but to the privileges of the collective body. But when, in chapter viii., he would establish the believer in all the full privileges of his new personal relation to God as one justified by faith, he leads up to all the prerogatives of the collective body, such as their being "sons of God," "heritors of God" and "with Christ" of the "coming glory," and directed in all things by a divine p'an leading up to that glory. It is along this line, where the collectively elect and the individually justified by faith coincide in the new Christian order, or rather are so parallel as to appear as the two opposite sides of one and the same line, that *we* require *the most accurate definition* of the interrelations and distinctions of the personal probation and the collective election. In Paul's day the solidarity of the collective elect body was in danger of completely concealing, and leading men to ignore, the personal responsibility. Hence Paul bends all his energy to the work of bringing out into full light the personal responsibility, especially in chapters i. to vii. In our day again the idea of the election has been magnified, not to the destruction of individuality, but as an individual and no longer a collective prerogative. Paul's opponents never dreamed of an indefectible individual election. They thought only of an indefectible national or collective election, which so swallowed up the individual responsibility as infallibly to secure salvation, one sin only excepted, that of utter apostasy from the true God. But this false idea landed them in pharasaic pride and antinomian immorality, which, as Paul saw, was only to be cured by the calling of a new people and the rejection of the old election. But to suppose that Paul would have built up a new election of a personal character, *like the old completely destroying the conception of personal responsibility*, is utterly untenable. He overturned the false assumptions attached to the old election by bringing to light the true universal doctrine of personal responsibility as illustrated by good men of all ages. The doctrine of personal responsibility must therefore be laid down as the fundamental plank in the platform of the new election. First, men are personally justified, and thus are of the elect in Christ Jesus; his idea of election never losing its concept of solidarity so familiar to the Jewish mind and so difficult to ours. (Is it this concept which led to the παν, neuter singular, of John vi. 37, etc.?) The mistake of our age lies, we think, in supposing that because Paul individualized personal responsibility he therefore individualized the election. He separated the individual in personal probation to make him the unit out of which the elect people should be built up, but it still continued to be the elect people, the body of Christ, *assimilating new units wherever found and rejecting any old that became unfit*. But this entire conception of the election as based upon individual probation was so different from the old conception based upon natural descent that, especially when taken into connection with the fact that the Gentiles were admitted without circumcision, it was equivalent to the rejection of the old body and the creation of a new. This Paul fully understood and this is the theme of the next three chapters. We may summarize Paul's doctrine of the election as follows:—

1. The election was a solidarity, the body of God's people.
2. It was originally constituted and continuously purified and rebuilt on the basis of personal responsibility.
3. This election involved a collective responsibility of the entire body as well as an individual responsibility of the units.
4. The Christian dispensation involved, not only a widening, but, on account of the unfaithfulness of the old body, an entire reconstruction of the election.

It is of interest to note that the same view of the election is found
in the writings of Isaiah, from whom Paul quotes in his defence of
the divine procedure in regard to the election which we are now
about to study. In Isaiah's first commission the purified election is
represented by "the remnant," who are "the holy seed," the "vital
substance" of the tree, the main trunk of which has been felled
(Isaiah vi. 13). This remnant alone saves the people, the body, from
utter destruction (ch. i. 9). Out of this remnant or still living root,
represented in David its Messianic head, there is to spring a new
"shoot," through which God's purposes are to be accomplished in
the universal establishment of righteousness and overthrow of wickedness (ch. xi. 1–5). This is in harmony with the original promise
of the election covenant (Gen. xii. 3), and points out clearly *the responsibility* of the election. It is not a monopoly or a prerogative
but a sacred trust which, far from excluding all nations from a share
in its blessings, is constituted for the very purpose of *blessing them*.
This appears more clearly in the second part of Isaiah, where "the
remnant" or "root of the holy seed," with its Messianic "shoot,"
becomes "the Lord's servant," "elect" and "called." (Compare
Isaiah xli. 8, 9; xlii. 1–4; xlix. 3–9, etc.) Even Paul's doctrine *of the
suffering of the elect people with their Messianic Head* runs through this
part of Isaiah, culminating in the well-known fifty-third chapter.
The term "servant" is the key to Isaiah's conception of the election.
The elect people is Jehovah's servant, and under its Messianic
Head is to be "for God's salvation unto the ends of the earth."
*The elect are elected for the sake of the non-elect, that they, too, may be
saved.* The only reprobation which this election knows is the reprobation of those who have proved unfaithful to the responsibilities of
their election. Only by God's mercy has it happened that the ancient
Israel have been saved at this very time from this rejection (Isaiah
xli. 9; l. 1; liv. 6, 7). It is very interesting to compare with this
teaching of Isaiah Paul's faith that the present rejection of the ancient people will in like manner be but for a time (Rom. xi. 26, etc.).
In studying the part of the Epistle upon which we now enter we
must therefore keep steadily before us the concept of the election in
the apostle's mind, as a solidarity, an elect body of people the individual members of which are still amenable to all the laws of personal
responsibility. What he says in regard to the election or rejection
of this body belongs to their collective responsibility, and neither
ensures nor bars their individual salvation. The reprobation of the
Jewish people does not prevent the salvation of individual Jews any
more than the reprobation of Esau prevented his salvation. He was
apparently a much better man than perhaps the majority of the elect
race, yet was not found *fit for God's purpose*. It is this purpose of
God in the election, viz., the world's salvation, which lays the foundation of Paul's first thought (in ch. ix.), that in the election God is
sovereign. It is the failure to fulfil that purpose on the part of the
Jews which forms the basis of Paul's second thought (in ch. x.), that

in their rejection God is *just*. And it is the final success of this purpose in the ultimate salvation of both Jews and Gentiles which lays the foundation of his third thought (in ch. xi.), that in this whole work of carrying forward his purpose concerning the election God is infinitely *wise and good*.

CH. IX. 1-29.—GOD'S SOVEREIGNTY IN THE ELECTION OF HIS PEOPLE.

1. **I say the truth in Christ, I lie not, my conscience bearing witness with me in the Holy Ghost,**] The apparent abruptness of this introduction is only seeming. The apostle could not call up before his mind, as he has just done, all the privileges of the election, and so claim them for the Christian church, without remembering those who were losing those privileges. The alternative to this, the elevation and widening of the old Israel into the new Christian church, he sees now to be clearly impossible. Perhaps it was to this that the church of the circumcision clung so long. Paul had already abandoned it as hopeless, but with great sorrow of heart. This sorrow he asserts, not as a matter of mere pretence, but as a part of "the truth in Christ," revealed by the Holy Ghost in his inmost spirit. The apostle here stands before us in the very position of the old prophets. The revealing Spirit of Christ has opened up before him the clear intuition of the moral and spiritual relations of Jew and Gentile in Christ, and that not as a mere intellectual conception but as an overwhelming tide of feeling, filling him now with joy and again with sorrow; and the feelings and the truth by which they are excited are alike a part of the revelation "in Christ" given by the "Holy Ghost."

2. **that I have great sorrow and unceasing pain in my heart.**] The apostle has chosen the strongest terms in the language to designate his feelings. On the inexpressible painfulness of the divine revelations of wrath compare Isaiah vi. and Lam. v.

3. **For I could wish that I myself were anathema from Christ for my brethren's sake, my kinsmen according to the flesh:**] "I could wish" (the imperfect indicative) expresses that which is impossible of realization (Winer, 353). It thus means that were it possible the apostle would himself bear their penalty, if so be they might receive the fulness of his blessing in Christ. This identification of himself with the sinning and miserable people is again thoroughly in the prophetic spirit. The expression "anathema away from Christ" can scarcely be reduced to any mild significance, and the force of the imperfect tense obviates the necessity for this. But it expresses, not the state of hardness and unbelief, but the penal consequences of that state. This he could even suffer for their sakes if their unbelief could be removed. This love is grounded in his relationship to them. In the mind of all Hebrews the ties of kin were very strong; but with Paul this feeling was sanctified and deepened by God's grace.

4. who are Israelites;] This is the beginning of Paul's enumeration of the prerogatives which are now passing away from the ancient people. The title "Israel" included all else. It signified "prince" or "prevailer with God." This title was given, not as a personal or national prerogative, but as the seal of God's covenant with Jacob in virtue of which he was to be the father of a people "that could not be numbered for multitude." When he was brought face to face with Esau it was not his own merits but the covenant promise which he pleaded (Gen. xxxii. 12), and this name was God's answer to his prayer establishing the covenant with him. It became therefore *the covenant name* of his descendants.

whose is the adoption,] This prerogative also appears first on a most memorable occasion (Ex. iv. 22). God called *his son* out of Egypt. This was a fact recognized by the elder prophets (Hosea xi. 1); and the later prophets claimed the same prerogative for the new covenant (compare Jer. xxxi. 31 34), recalling the deliverance from Egypt in connection with the first covenant.

and the glory,] The shekinah or manifested presence of God. A symbol of special relation to God, both in regard to his providence and his grace. On the high value placed on this manifestation see 1 Sam. iv. 21 and 1 Kings viii. 10; and on its relation to the Messianic future see Isaiah iv. 5 and Haggai ii. 9. The absence of the visible shekinah in the second temple led to the more spiritual conception of the later prophets, who find in the glory *the revelation of God's nature.*

and the covenants,] They were the heritors of all the covenants. Those recorded were with Noah, Abraham (repeated to Isaac and Jacob), Moses for all Israel, and finally David. All these from the beginning followed the line of the chosen people. These again the prophets projected into the Messianic age in a new and more perfect form. (See as above Jer. xxxi. 31, etc., and also Ezekiel xxxvii. 26.)

and the giving of the law,] This in its widest sense included the whole trust of divine revelation, which Paul regarded as the greatest of all their advantages (ch. iii. 2). Paul, however, regards this as a sacred trust.

and the service of God,] This word included the whole outward form of divine worship according to the Levitical ritual established among the chosen people. They are thus spoken of as God's priests, a royal priesthood; and in the age of universal conceptions of the mission of Israel this priesthood was conceived of as exercised on behalf of the whole world, and all nations were called to join in the worship of God's people. (See Psalms xcvi., c., etc.)

and the promises;] These promises were very familiar to the Jewish mind. (See Acts xxvi. 6.) They were the covenant heritage from Adam, Noah, Abraham and David downward, and fully expanded in the prophets. It is these promises of which Paul says that they "are all yea and amen" in Christ Jesus (2 Cor. i. 20).

5. whose are the fathers, and of whom is Christ as concerning

the flesh,] These two facts occupy a peculiar place. This people sprang from the fathers with whom God first formed this covenant and inaugurated this wonderful process of his grace; and from them sprang the Christ in whom the manifestations of God's grace culminated. From the fathers to the Christ represents the history and course of two thousand years, in which God prepared his work for the world's salvation. Such is Paul's catalogue of the prerogatives of the elect people of old. It will be seen that they do not in anywise cross the matter of individual responsibility. They are prerogatives belonging to the body, not to the individual, except as a member of the body; and they all have respect to the office which that body was chosen to fulfil in the economy of the world's salvation. The greatest of these is the Christ, over whose pre-eminent dignity Paul dwells.

who is over all, God blessed for ever. Amen.] Of this famous passage there are four renderings, varying not in text but in mere punctuation. These are (1) the text; (2) placing a period after "flesh," "He who is God over all be blessed for ever"; or (3) "He who is over all is God blessed for ever"; (4) placing a period after "all," "Christ as concerning the flesh, who is over all. God be blessed for ever. Amen." The only guide in choosing between these constructions is the connection of thought. After the preceding enumeration of the privileges of the ancient Israel the only conceivable reason for the introduction of such a thought as is expressed in No. 2 as a benediction, or in No. 3 as a direct assertion, is, that Paul stands confounded in the presence of the sovereignty of God, which conferred such peculiar privileges on this people to the disregard of others, and so feels called upon to explain by the assertion that God is over all and must be blessed for ever. But we do not conceive that Paul felt himself face to face with any such difficulty. If, as we believe, Paul viewed the ancient election as the preparation of God's purpose of grace for all the nations, and for every man, then there was no modern doctrine of reprobation to be defended, or covered over by an assertion of God's sovereignty. Paul's only reprobates were the unfaithful elect, or those who, by a long course of rebellion, had made themselves vessels of wrath fitted for destruction. The assertion of God's sovereignty seems, therefore, here quite out of the line of the apostle's thought. So also is the benediction included in both (2) and (4). First of all, this is not the Greek form everywhere used to express benediction or doxology. But even more striking is the fact that the man here speaking is not exulting and praising God for the gifts of his grace to his people, but mourning with broken heart over their loss. We are therefore led to fall back, with all the ancient and the large majority of modern expositors, upon the first rendering as both apposite and grammatical. The mention of the flesh in antithesis to the Godhead, as in John i. 14 (Godet), prepares the way for the presentation of the higher nature of the Christ. This is in Paul's mind familiarly associated with his descent from the fathers (Rom. i. 4). And it was this higher dignity which gave its glory to the Messianic descent as "*God with us.*" The common association of Pauline ideas and the requirements of his present argument thus combine to point to the old rendering which for fifteen hundred years alone held place in the church. For a very able and exhaustive discussion of the arguments see Godet *in loco*. The true idea of the text may be paraphrased with Godet thus: "Who is exalted over all things *as God*, to be blessed (or worshipped) for ever. Amen. So let it be." Christ is thus presented to us as the *divine* Head of the Messianic kingdom. The text is thus parallel in thought with Phil. ii. 6, 9, 10.

6. But it is not as though the word of God hath come to nought.] With these words Paul strikes into the very heart of his subject. They imply the terrible fact which he leaves unspoken: "All these privileges they have lost, but still the case is not such an one that God's word hath fallen to the ground." It was absolutely incumbent on St. Paul to prove this in order to vindicate the divine right of the new gospel of salvation by faith. This gospel, if true, practically resulted in the rejection of the Jews. Its opponents urged that very fact in proof that this gospel was at variance with God's word, and hence untenable. Hence the pertinence, in a letter addressed to the Gentiles for the confirmation of their faith in this universal gospel of the uncircumcision, of a demonstration of the harmony of this gospel, *and of this special result of it*, with the Old Testament promises to the ancient Israel. Even this fact of the rejection of the Jews does not involve the failure of God's covenant word of promise.

For they are not all Israel, which are of Israel:
7. neither, because they are Abraham's seed, are they all children: but, In Isaac shall thy seed be called.] This reason strikes at the root of the main deception of Judaism They "thought to themselves that they had Abraham to their father." Their trust for salvation was in the mere carnal descent from Abraham. But Ishmael was so descended, and yet they held him to be on a level with sinners of the Gentiles. This was an unanswerable argument. But Paul proceeds at once to evolve the principle contained in this clearly acknowledged fact.

8. That is, it is not the children of the flesh that are children of God;] The direct contradiction of the Jewish false confidence. By "the children of God" we are here to understand the children whom God recognized as his elect people. It would be a fatal mistake here, if we took this phrase in its modern or Christian significance of personal adoption into the family of God's regenerate children. The apostle is speaking, not of the rejection of *individual* Jews as Jews, but of the rejection of the *people* as a *people*. We must therefore take the term children here in the sense of the national adoption of verse 4. This is clear in the antithesis of the last clause,

but the children of the promise are reckoned for a seed.] Here, instead of the ambiguous term "children," he uses the term "seed," a term exactly fitted to his purpose. This was the term of the promise to Abraham (Gen xv. 5, etc.), and used by Isaiah to designate the body of God's elect (Isaiah vi. 13). This seed, God's adoption, was marked out by the promise (Gen. xvii. 21 and xviii. 10).

9. For this is a word of promise, According to this season will I come, and Sarah shall have a son.] But what are we to understand by Paul's expression, "the children of the promise." The simplest explanation would be, the children pointed out or designated by the promise. But several expositors (Riddle, Hodge, Godet) take it to mean the children born in virtue of the promise, *i e.*, through faith in it. But this fails to apply to the very next example adduced by Paul. And this calling in of Abraham's faith in the promise, about which Paul here says not a word, destroys all the force of Paul's argument. In chapter iv., where he treated of Abraham's personal responsibility and justification, the subject of Abraham's faith was pertinent. But here, where he is justifying God's sovereignty in the election of his people, it has nothing to do with it. We therefore take the term "children of the promise" to mean the children pointed out by the promise. Now, in giving a promise God is perfectly free. He can give it such form and limitations or extensions as in his wise and beneficent sovereignty may seem to him best. If those not embraced in the promise were excluded from salvation, if there were in the promise anything which traversed the rights of their personal probation, objection could at once be made to the limitations of the elect seed to the promise. But the promise simply points out the body of men through whom God is about to reveal himself for the salvation of all the world. This outside world, therefore, who in them are to be blessed, cannot complain because God so directs his promises as to secure the very end which the promise contemplates, *i.e.*, the blessing, not of this or that individual and specially privileged man, but of "all nations." When Paul therefore uses the term "children of the promise" he virtually affirms the just, wise and beneficent sovereignty of God in designating by promise the chosen seed. The next example is to the same point.

10. And not only so; but Rebecca also having conceived by one, even by our father Isaac—] This peculiarity is introduced to cut away the last refuge of those who trusted in the descent after the flesh. They might say, these were the children of the bondwoman. But in Paul's next example both father and mother are the same. The natural descent of the twins is identical. The election is absolutely independent therefore of natural descent; and not only so, but also of everything else that might prejudice the freedom of God's choice, and so he adds in a parenthetical clause—

11. for the children being not yet born, neither having done anything good or bad,] This is introduced to obviate another subterfuge. It might be said that the action of Esau in selling his birthright excluded him. Paul aims at maintaining the absolute sovereignty of God in this matter. The responsibility of the Judge of all the earth to do right admits of no personal claim which may bias his action by the influence of personal favour. He therefore represents the designating promise as prevenient to every act and even to the birth itself.

that the purpose of God according to election might stand, not of works, but of him that calleth,] We beg first of all to submit to the judgment of our readers a modification of this translation. The Greek phrase ἡ κατ ἐκλογην πρόθεσις admits equally well of two distinct translations, "the purpose according to election" and "the purpose concerning election." The first translation makes the election precede the purpose as the rule or norm according to which the purpose is constructed. The second makes the purpose stand first as the norm or rule by which the election is directed. The election, like the calling, is according to God's purpose. We submit that this is the true Pauline conception. (See Rom. viii. 28; Eph. i. 4-11; 2 Thess. ii. 13; 2 Tim. i. 9.) On the grammatical propriety of this version see Winer, p. 500, on the general figurative use of κατα to denote "relation" or "influence" or "more exact definition." Again, the verb of this sentence signifies, not to stand fast or strong, but simply *to continue to remain as it had been*. This quality or attribute in which it is to continue is defined to be, "not of works," *i.e.*, not directed by the obligation of justice or merit which works might create, "but of him that calleth," *i.e.*, directed by the will of him that calleth. The preposition ἐκ here signifies the root or source out of which a thing springs, and which so determines its nature and form. We may therefore paraphrase as follows: "In order that the purpose of God concerning election might continue to be directed as it was at first, not by any claim of any individual man, but simply out of the wise, holy and beneficent will of God, who calls this or that body of men as his chosen instrument.

12. it was said unto her, The elder shall serve the younger.] This was a clear designation of the line of God's election, confirmed ever.after, as appears from the further declaration of scripture.

13. Even as it is written, Jacob I loved, but Esau I hated.] We need not adopt any doubtful interpretation of "I loved less," etc. The passage (Mal. i. 2, 3) is a plain historical statement of God's election between the two nations as represented by their progenitors in the two brothers. In regard to this choice God "loved Jacob and hated Esau." This by no means implies that Esau was personally, as an individual, excluded from God's grace and saving love. Paul is not here considering God's election of individuals unto personal salvation (we shall consider the bearing of election upon this presently), but the determination of the line of election of his separate people. In this determination Esau was refused. Paul has thus demonstrated from the facts of the case the sovereignty of God in his election as free from every trammel of personal obligation to man. But if God so determines the line of election without regard

to personal rights or claims, is he not unrighteous? This is Paul's next question.

14 **What shall we say then?**] The question with which he calls attention especially to his discussion of an objection.

Is there unrighteousness with God?] This is the natural objection of those who regard election as a matter of personal claim and prerogative securing *individual salvation*. It is a perfectly pertinent question on the part of one who believes that election is a matter of personal salvation, when told that election is of God's sovereignty. We must therefore carefully consider Paul's answer.

15. **God forbid. For he saith to Moses, I will have mercy on whom I have mercy, and I will have compassion on whom I have compassion.**] Paul's indignant denial is supported by a quotation from Ex. xxxiii. 18. In this passage God asserts to Moses his right, not to save whom he will and leave to perish whom he will, but *to select as he will the objects of a special mercy*. This mercy was what Moses had requested—*a special revelation of the divine nature*, such as the Jews held no man could see and live. Such a mercy God says he will confer on whom he will. But few are such as God chooses for such a purpose. This case is therefore perfectly analogous to the election of a line in which God should accomplish his great Messianic purpose for the world's salvation. In regard to both these matters God is in his election sovereign, that is, the principles upon which he determines them lie beyond the personal or individual claims or merits of any one man or set of men. They affect the reward of Christ, the highest and eternal welfare of the whole human race, the interests and well-being of all God's moral creatures, and the final perfect manifestation of the divine glory. God therefore holds these matters in his own hand to be wisely, righteously and beneficently determined as he *sees best*. Paul's quotation of this instance of this very special revelation to Moses proves this, that these matters are too high to be determined by any will or desire of man, even such a man as Moses; or as Paul puts it,

16. **So then it is not of him that willeth, nor of him that runneth, but of God that hath mercy.**] Isaac willed this prerogative to Esau, Esau ran to obtain it, but God directed as seemed him best. Had it been the matter of the personal salvation of Jacob and the perdition of Esau, this riddle of God's permitting the duplicity of Jacob to succeed would have been a hard one indeed. But in reference to the wider and no longer personal question of the election God could overrule his sinful deception of his father for final good, and yet punish him for his personal sin. The matter here in question, that is, of being the elect progenitor of the chosen Messianic people, is not of man's willing or seeking but of God's compassionate will or purpose. To draw from these words the inference of Riddle, "that the participation in any or *all* the effects of God's mercy and compassion does not depend on human will or effort, but on the will of God," is to draw from a particular premise a universal conclusion.

It is not correct to say that "neither the preceding context nor the scope of the argument suggests any limitations" of the application of the quoted words of Exodus. The original context clearly applies them to *a particular matter;* and with equal clearness does the scope of the argument limit their application here, and more than that, the limitations are analogous in both cases. But Paul has another equally clear example at hand to prove the same principle, *i.e.*, the sovereignty of God in the selection of his instruments for the accomplishment of his great providential purposes.

17. **For the scripture saith unto Pharaoh, For this very purpose did I raise thee up, that I might shew in thee my power, and that my name might be published abroad in all the earth.**] This is a case taken from the opposite side of God's providential purpose, *i.e.*, his revelation of righteous judgment against sin. First of all, the passage quoted requires careful attention. The quotation is from Ex. ix. 16. The Hebrew text of verses 15 and 16, which belong together, may be rendered as follows: "For now indeed had I stretched forth my hand and had smitten thee and thy people with the pestilence from the earth. But peradventure for this very purpose have I let thee stand, to show in thee my power, and to proclaim my name in all the earth." With the revised version before us it is scarcely necessary to justify the foregoing translation by reference to Ewald, Driver and other modern grammars. (See Driver, p. 184, sec. 141.) The meaning of the original Hebrew text is therefore not that God created Pharaoh for this purpose of judgment, but that after he had repeatedly sinned against God's warning, and had deserved immediate destruction, God had still continued him in existence upon the earth to make him a more conspicuous example of his power to punish the sinner, and to make him a means of revealing his holy name in all the earth. Now many a wicked man as bad as Pharaoh is not selected by God for this purpose. God reserves, with reference to these examples in his providence of the punishment of sin, the right to choose from among all obstinate sinners those whom he thus will make conspicuous examples of his judgment; but our Lord guards us against supposing that the final destiny of such is worse than that of others. "I tell you nay; but except ye repent, ye shall all likewise perish." The final personal penalty determined by individual probation is not affected by the use which God may thus make of the sinner in time for the revelation of his righteous judgments among men. Here then again is the proof of the sovereignty of God in the selection of those whom he makes conspicuous in human history, by choosing in them to reveal his justice. The reasons for this again are above the question of personal merit, but at the same time do not contravene the rights of personal probation. And hence Paul safely concludes that along both lines God exercises his sovereign wisdom.

18. **So then he hath mercy on whom he will, and whom he will he hardeneth.**] The mercy and the hardening must be interpreted

in harmony with the history of the case. The mercy is clearly the gracious dispensation of the gifts of the election, including in the case of Moses an extraordinary revelation of God. As to the hardening, there are two terms used in the Hebrew text, each translated by the English "harden." The first is used where it is said that the Lord hardened Pharaoh's heart, eight times in all. It signifies to make strong or bold and courageous. The second is used, with one exception, where it is said that Pharaoh hardened his own heart, and signifies to make heavy or dull and obtuse. It is the Septuagint translation of the first of these terms which Paul uses in our text. In the case before us the meaning is clear God could have broken the courage of the obdurate sinner at a single blow. That would be of no moral benefit whatever to him, for a forced submission is no submission; it would merely have ended the contest. But it was God's will that the true disposition of Pharaoh should be manifested and openly punished, and therefore he so tempers his judgments that they do not break the courage of the obdurate sinner. And thus it is said that God strengthened his heart. But meantime he was blunting all his own moral sense by his repeated refusals to do the right. This process is indeed once attributed to God, as the result of the moral law of our nature which he has ordained. But in that process, while God has ordained the law which punishes sin by moral obduracy, man is the responsible author of his own hardening, and to this the scriptural use of the terms corresponds But courage is something which is not altogether under our control. We can wilfully lose it but not regain it, and hence it is attributed more directly to God. But in the communication of this courage (even taking the strongest aspect of the case) did God interfere with Pharaoh's personal probation? Far from it. He really placed him in the position of responsibility. The man whose courage is utterly broken is hardly a responsible being. He is under a compulsion which deprives him of moral freedom. His acts are the acts of the man with the loaded pistol at his head. In Paul's affirmation of the sovereignty of God in the choice of those through whom he will reveal either his mercy or his judgments we thus find nothing to contravene the law of personal probational responsibility But while Paul has established the fact of the sovereignty of God in election, and has shewn that there is no unrighteousness with God in this, inasmuch as this is not a matter of personal probation, but of much wider consequences, and hence to be determined on a wider basis, there still remains the objection, that if this is a matter of sovereignty then the nation cannot be blamed for the loss of that which God hath taken from them. The removal of the privileges of the election is not their fault but is God's sovereign will. It is to this question that Paul next addresses himself.

19. **Thou wilt say then unto me, Why doth he still find fault? For who withstandeth his will?**] We may paraphrase these questions thus: "If we have no right to find fault with God in his dis-

pensation of the privileges of the election according to his own sovereign will, then certainly he has no right to find fault with us, because he has taken those privileges from us. We have not resisted, nay, are utterly helpless to resist, his will." This question opens up the exceedingly difficult subject of the relation of the privileges of the election to national and individual responsibility. This question Paul deals with to the end of the chapter, affirming, first, the sovereignty of God in assigning to each man or body of men their probational position: and secondly, the responsibility of man for his use or abuse of that probational position.

20. Nay but, O man, who art thou that repliest against God? Shall the thing formed say to him that formed it, Why didst thou make me thus?] This confirms our interpretation of verse 19, for these questions clearly relate to matters which God hath held in his own power and hath not assigned to human responsibility. It is therefore to interpret Paul in the face of the whole purport of his teaching to make this "forming" the decision of eternal destinies. These, he has expressly declared, depend upon personal probation (ch. ii. 6-10). The "forming," or creative sovereignty, must therefore be that which precedes personal probation, and lays the foundation for it, *i.e.*, the assigning to each man the sphere of his life and his individual gifts and endowments. This is of God's sovereignty. No man has a right to say unto God, Why hast thou made me thus? but should thankfully make the most of that which God has given him. This broad creative sovereignty includes the special sovereignty of the election. This broad principle Paul illustrates from the analogy of the potter.

21. Or hath not the potter a right over the clay, from the same lump to make one part a vessel unto honour, and another unto dishonour?] This simile is at once an argument from analogy for, and an illustration of, the creative sovereignty. It does not suppose that the potter acts with an arbitrary disregard of the qualities of the clay. The question is of the choice of the purpose for which it is fitted, or which he may desire to accomplish by means of it. But the Greek terms are scarcely fairly represented by our words " honour " and " dishonour." "Costly" and "cheap" would be nearer the original. This is the general significance of these words when applied, as here, to articles of commerce. Applied to men or to the gods they signify honour or dignity and dishonour or indignity. Although Paul does not here quote from Jeremiah, yet Jeremiah xviii. may be very well compared.

22. What if God, willing to shew his wrath, and to make his power known, endured with much longsuffering vessels of wrath fitted unto destruction:] This is Paul's application of the general principle of creative sovereignty to the instances of election already referred to. In the first case Paul is careful to put forward the just reason of God's choice of " the vessels of wrath." They are " fitted to destruction." His whole teaching protests against the idea that God fitted them for destruction. They fitted themselves; here ap pears their responsibility. God endured them with much longsuffering; here is their distinct probation. But side by side with this God determined to make them an example of his wrath and power to punish the wicked; here is God's sovereignty. He does not make all men such examples. But at the great final judgment there will be "no respect of persons," and "every man shall receive according to his works." Such is Paul's doctrine according to fair interpretation, allowing Paul to explain himself.

23. **and that he might make known the riches of his glory upon vessels of mercy, which he afore prepared unto glory,]** On this side of the question we see at once that Paul speaks much more absolutely. In the dispensation of the privileges of the election man has not the same probational rights. The preparations needed are not within the reach of any individual. They run through the ages, and can only be accomplished by the superintending providence of God. All that is included in the "riches of glory" to be revealed, and in the preparation of the vessels of mercy to receive that glory, Paul alone could unfold. He calls it elsewhere (Eph. i.) "the mystery of God's will" and "the mystery of Christ." The riches of the glory are the successive revelations of God to man. The preparation runs through ages of moral, religious and intellectual discipline, within the chosen people, and collateral to them, and finally expands into the universal dispensation which offers these privileges to all alike.

24. **Even us, whom he also called, not from the Jews only, but also from the Gentiles?]** This final objective point, in which the line of God's electing purpose culminates in the offer to Jew and Gentile alike of the privileges of the election upon the basis of personal faith in Christ, is to Paul's mind the solution of the mystery involved in the election. For all through the ages there was a mystery. Why should God thus favour one little people with privileges withheld from all the rest? The answer is, for *the final benefit of all*. Because "preparation" was needed before the full glory could be revealed. The free and full expansion of the privileges to embrace the whole world is the solution of the mystery. If the world, while waiting for this solution, is dealt with on fair terms of moral probation (Acts xvii. 30), and if when "the fulness of times" has come the result is a richer moral glory for all (Eph. i. and ii.), then certainly no longer is there any dark shadow hanging over God's dealings with man. The unbounded enthusiasm with which this idea filled the mind of Paul is manifest in the frequency with which he returns to it. And such was God's design from the beginning, as is clear from the prophets.

25. **As he saith also in Hosea,**
  I will call that my people, which was not my people;
  And her beloved, which was not beloved.
26.   **And it shall be, that in the place where it was said unto them, Ye are not my people,**
  There shall they be called sons of the living God.

These quotations (Hosea i. 10 and ii. 23) refer originally to the ten tribes. Paul clearly regards them as in the same position as the Gentiles, inasmuch as the line of the election followed the house of David. Other Gentiles had long before been left behind as through Noah, Abraham, Jacob, etc., the chosen seed was marked out by "the promises." But those thus left behind Paul by no means consigns to perdition. Their personal probation continues, and intimations of further provisions of God's mercy will meet us presently. Meantime Paul calls attention to the fact that the sifting of probation was part of God's purpose, side by side with the extension of the privileges.

27. **And Isaiah crieth concerning Israel, If the number of the children of Israel be as the sand of the sea, it is the remnant that shall be saved:**] In this passage (Isaiah x 22, 23) Isaiah is speaking of the judgment and sifting of the chosen people. This is God's "decreed consumption," which (as is evident from the whole course of Isaiah's writings) is no arbitrary matter, but the result of the probation of God's people. With regard to Israel this probation will reduce the number saved, who are here identified with the Christian election, to a very small remnant. Isaiah is thus perfectly in harmony with Paul in combining the idea of personal responsibility and probation with the election. However the outward election, *i.e.*, the nation, might increase, God would sift it down to the righteous remnant. And as by the election of Israel the Gentiles were by no means to be considered as debarred from their rights of probation, so by the election Israel is by no means freed from the re-ponsibilities of probation. But more than that, the question of verse 19 is thus answered. "Why doth he still find fault?" Because the chosen people have been unfaithful to their responsibilities. Paul's answer to the question of verse 19 therefore consists of two parts: (1) God's sovereign right to assign man's probational sphere as seemeth him best, and to use him in that sphere as may best serve his purposes; and (2) God's right in all ages to hold even the chosen people responsible for their privileges, and to cut them off from those privileges for unfaithfulness. And this is in harmony with God's general law of probation.

28. **for the Lord will execute his word upon the earth, finishing it and cutting it short.**] This part of the quotation presents peculiar difficulties both of text and of relation to the original. The shorter text adopted by the revisers has the strongest authorities in its favour, but omits a sentence of the original, which may be rendered as follows:—

"The decisive end is overflowing with righteousness.
For a decisive end is Jehovah the Lord making in the midst of the land."

It is the first line which is omitted in the revised text and combined with the second in the *textus receptus*. Whether Paul quoted the whole in condensed form, or only the last sentence, we may fairly accept the original as expressing his meaning. This is the proclamation through the land of a final short, and yet righteous, "ending up" as between God and his people. The revised text embodies this sense as follows: "The Lord will execute his word" (*i.e.*, his threatened judgments) "upon the earth, making it final and short." The final, summary and righteous judgments of God, therefore, fall alike upon the world and the elect, *i.e.*, both are held to full probational responsibility. This fact of God's probational judgment of the elect appears in Isaiah from the very beginning.

29. And, as Isaiah hath said before,
    Except the Lord of Sabaoth had left us a seed,
    We had become as Sodom, and had been made like unto
    Gomorrah.

There is in this verse again a slight variation from the Hebrew in the substitution of the word "seed" for "remnant." The words are used by Isaiah as equivalent titles of *the sifted elect body*. Here again we find the same doctrine of the probational sifting of the elect body adduced by Paul from Isaiah in proof of his position. The quotation is from Isaiah i. 9. The proof from reason and scripture of the two elements of Paul's answer to the question of verse 19 is thus complete. Why doth he still find fault? Because he hath a sovereign right to assign to each one, even the elect, their probational position, and to hold them to account for their fulfilment of its responsibilities. This concludes Paul's first point—the demonstration of God's sovereignty in the election, vindicating his fidelity under the universal gospel to his covenant obligations on the one hand, and maintaining probational responsibility on the other. He now turns to prove, upon this basis, the justice of the resulting rejection of the great body of the ancient people.

CH. IX. 30–X. 21. APPLICATION OF THE RESPONSIBILITIES OF THE ELECTION TO THE CASE OF THE REJECTED JEWS; OR, THE VINDICATION OF THE DIVINE JUSTICE.

30. What shall we say then?] Paul's formula for directing special attention to a particular point. He has in the main body of the preceding chapter vindicated both the sovereignty of God and the responsibility of man in regard to the election. In verses 22–24 he has put forward the historical result of these two principles in a tentative, hypothetical form, supported by quotations from the Old Testament prophecies (verses 25–29). Fortified by these prefaces he now states the historical outcome directly, making it the basis for a full vindication of the divine justice in regard to the rejection of the Jews and the perdition of so large a number of them.

That the Gentiles, which followed not after righteousness, attained to righteousness, even the righteousness which is of faith:] Paul, with nice delicacy of feeling, to make the subject as little painful as possible, puts the side of God's grace first, and then the side of judgment. "That Gentiles" or "nations." The article is wanting in the Greek, and the term may well be taken indefinitely. "Which followed not after righteousness." We take "righteousness" here, as everywhere in St. Paul's writings, as "rightness with God." Paul here speaks generally. The Greeks, Romans, and other nations to whom God's call came, were not seekers after God as nations, although there were among them some such. "Attained to righteousness"—have grasped it as a prize or precious treasure found lying in their way. When God's electing grace turned to seek his new people among them they eagerly embraced the precious offer. "But the righteousness which is of faith." The Greek conjunction here is not "even" or "also," but the mildest adversative, and may be rendered "but," as there is a slightly antithetic force in the added clause. "They attained to righteousness (not legal righteousness), but the righteousness of faith."

31. **but Israel, following after a law of righteousness,**] Perhaps Paul here puts the zeal of Israel for the law, *i.e.*, the outward Mosaic form or code of ritual and service, into the foreground of purpose. This was indeed a law of righteousness, *i.e.*, intended to lead to right relation to God. But they followed the means rather than the end, and lost the spirit in the letter, and therefore

did not arrive at that law.] Paul here uses a peculiar word which in classical Greek signifies "to come in first" (*prævenire*), but in the New Testament "to go through with," "to follow out to the end," (*pervenire*). The old version is nearer this than the revised. The application of the word here is very clear. *They did not follow the law out to its true result*, else as their schoolmaster it would have led them to Christ.

32. **Wherefore? Because they sought it not by faith, but as it were by works.**] Paul has repeatedly shewn that the true spirit even of the old dispensation was "faith," not "works." Faith represents the moral principle, the spiritual life; "works," merely the outward form. This was the great mistake of the Jews. They were so engrossed in the outward form that they missed all the spirit. Their works (outward forms) filled them with supercilious pride and vain conceits. The spirit of faith is childlike, teachable. Hence

They stumbled at the stone of stumbling;] The stone of stumbling was Christ. In his humble garb and spiritual teachings they knew him not. Had he appeared on David's throne, or even as a great leader of a national party against foreign domination, or perhaps as a great Rabbi teaching the law—in any shape that fitted to the outward forms which they worshipped—they might have received him. But God must sift the true followers of the truth from all who selfishly follow outward and temporal things. So although Christ brought the heavenly kingdom of God's truth, and was indeed the true light which lighteth every man that cometh into the world, "he came unto his own, and his own received him not." And this again was in accord with ancient prophecy.

33. even as it is written,
　　Behold, I lay in Zion a stone of stumbling and a rock of offence :
　　And he that believeth on him shall not be put to shame.
The first of these quotations is taken from Isaiah viii. 14. The sense there is precisely apposite to Paul's purpose. The chosen people then "refused the waters of Shiloah that go softly," *i.e.*, the quiet, unworldly policy dictated by God's prophets, who exhorted them to leave the worldly policy of confederation with the heathen alone, and make the Lord their "sanctuary." To the worldly man and self-conceited statesman of that day this was a stone of stumbling and a rock of offence, and they stumbled over it, and were as a consequence broken in pieces by the Assyrian invasion. The case was in every respect parallel to the one which Paul has in hand. And so was the other side of the picture which Paul takes from another passage in Isaiah (xxviii. 16). The tried foundation of Isaiah was trust in God and adherence to righteousness and equity, in opposition to all covenants and leagues against death, or the overflowing scourge of the Assyrian invasion, such as the leaders of Israel were trusting in. Faith in that foundation should not be ashamed, nor be required to flee away in haste.

1. Brethren, my heart's desire and my supplication to God is for them, that they may be saved.] Paul, having thus gently but explicitly stated the case of the ancient people, pauses a moment to give expression to his prayerful desire on their behalf. This is usually taken as the beginning of a new section of the Epistle. But that verse 1 is actually, if not in form, parenthetical, is evident from the fact that verses 2–4 fall back on chapter ix. 30, 31—the word "zeal" repeating the idea of "following after"; "the law of righteousness" now appearing as "their own righteousness"; and the end of the law which they "did not attain" here appearing as "Christ, the end of the law for righteousness." The connection of thought is thus continuous, and verse 1 is but the passing expression of a desire which Paul has told us (ch. ix. 1) is the continual burden of his heart. This is in harmony with the revised text, which, following the great majority of MSS., reads, "on their behalf," instead of "on behalf of Israel." The noun would be appropriate in the formal beginning of a new section; the pronoun is required in a mere parenthesis. It refers back to the subject of "stumbled" in chapter ix. 32. "They stumbled; but my prayer still ascends on their behalf, that they may be saved. They have as a nation lost the election; but individually they may yet be saved, and find a place in the new election." We do not therefore need, with Prof. Chambers (translation of Godet), to call in Paul's ignorance of their reprobation. He was not so ignorant. Nor need we, with Godet, transfer Paul's prayer to the future. A hopeful reason for this prayer Paul finds in a fact already partially expressed in chapter ix. 31, but which he now expands more fully.

2. For I bear them witness that they have a zeal for God, but not according to knowledge.] Paul was personally cognizant of the nature of this zeal, knowing at once how sincere and yet how blind it was, and how far it was of the nature of that invincible ignorance which places men below the level of responsibility. (Compare 1 Tim. i. 13.)

3. For being ignorant of God's righteousness, and seeking to establish their own, they did not subject themselves to the righteousness of God.] This is at once the proof of verse 2, and a full expansion of chapter ix. 31. For this ignorance they were responsible, inasmuch as the law produced that knowledge of sin which leads at least to a negative knowledge of the true righteousness. He who feels himself a sinner, if he has not positive knowledge of the true righteousness, knows it at least as an object of hope and desire But of all this they were so totally ignorant that they sought to establish a righteousness of their own. How fundamentally opposed any such idea was to the true conception of righteousness Paul has shewn in chapters ii. and iii. They had not only failed to learn the great lesson which it was the province of the law to teach (see note on ch. vii. 13), but they had further made this very law, which, by awakening the knowledge of their own lack of righteousness, was designed to lead to God's righteousness, a means of building up their self-righteous confidence, and therefore the occasion of their refusal to accept God's righteousness. A more complete perversion of God's purpose cannot well be conceived. Observe that to this point Paul has used the historical tense, because so far he is simply stating the facts of the case. He now proceeds to explain those facts on general principles.

4. For Christ is the end of the law unto righteousness to every one that believeth.] The "end" is that to which (in ch. ix. 31) Paul says the Jews "did not come through." The end is the point to which that which prepares the way leads, and at the same time the point in which it terminates. The work or office of the law leads to Christ; it also terminates in Christ. This was true in the relations of the dispensations to each other. It is likewise true in the moral development of each spiritual life. Paul's application here may include both. He asserts the principle in its most universal form as a universal predicate; but as he speaks at the point at which two dispensations meet, it may not be without reference to the futile efforts of the Judaistic party to perpetuate the old dispensation in opposition to God's new order. But his very introduction of the term "righteousness" (the right probational relation of the individual to God) shews that his thought is now fixed, not on the relation of the dispensations to each other, but upon the personal results to the individual Jews in regard to their probation. The reprobation of the nation, in which Paul held that God was sovereign, is at the same time the condemnation of the vast body of individuals through whom this reprobation took place. We are therefore now distinctly on the ground of the personal relation of the Jews to God; and here Paul vindicates no longer the sovereignty but the justice of God. The election was taken from the Jewish nation because, in God's sovereign purpose, the full time for the extension of its privileges to the Gentiles had now come. In this God was sovereign. The Jews were not saved as individuals because they "did not submit themselves to the righteousness of God." In this God was just. Had they so submitted themselves they would have been embraced in the new election, and so have retained all its privileges. Their reprobation was therefore entirely of themselves. The election is entirely of God. But this consequence of their refusal to submit themselves to God's righteousness was not a result of an arbitrary arrangement on God's part. This very principle, so contrary to their Pharisaic spirit, was to be found even in the Mosaic law itself. The words of Moses shall condemn them for refusing to submit to God's righteousness.

5. For Moses writeth that the man that doeth the righteousness which is of the law shall live thereby.] This quotation, which is from Lev. xviii. 5, is not materially altered in sense by the variations of the MSS. It represents the genuine spirit of the Mosaic dispensation—a dispensation of tutelage: "Do this and live." This passage may have been quoted by Paul's opponents as against his doctrine of faith. If so he is quite willing to concede its full force. This doing, even there, was not the self-righteous doing of the Pharisee, but the humble doing of God's servant. Even there the idea of mercy and the principle of faith existed, as witness the following (also from Moses):—

6. But the righteousness which is of faith saith thus,] This quotation, from Deut. xxx. 11-14, is introduced by a peculiar form of expression. Godet notes that Paul no longer says "Moses writes," but "The righteousness which is of faith saith thus." This can scarcely bear any other meaning than that the principle of God's gracious gift of righteousness to obedient and trusting faith runs through the law as well as through the gospel, and that we find it expressing itself in such passages as the following:—

Say not in thy heart, Who shall ascend into heaven? (that is, to bring Christ down:)] This quotation is part of an address of Moses, urging obedience to the law. An argument for this is, that it is not an impossibility. "It is not in heaven," "neither is it beyond the sea," *i.e.*, it is not a thing far off and difficult or impossible. But Paul puts the words of Moses with his own running comment. "Say not in thy heart, Who shall ascend into heaven? (*i.e.*, to bring down to earth that perfect righteousness which cannot be found on earth)." (Compare our Lord's "Thy will be done on earth as it is in heaven.") But Paul expresses this idea of Moses in terms familiar to the Christian mind, *i.e.*, "to bring Christ down." Christ perfectly fulfilled God's will on our behalf. The object, therefore, of bringing down the Christ is to bring to man that which he alone has accomplished.

7. or, Who shall descend into the abyss? (that is, to bring Christ up from the dead.)] The original words of Moses are, "Who shall go over the sea?" This Paul changes to "Who shall descend into the abyss?" This is an exactly identical figure and form of expression, and can be applied again to the Christian idea, as Paul immediately does in his comment. To bring Christ up from the dead is to accomplish *that for which he arose*, viz., "our justification." Paul's thought may therefore be expressed thus: "I grant you that Moses speaks of the righteousness of the law as a living by doing, but not in the absolute self-righteous sense in which you interpret it; for in that same Moses we find the spirit of the righteousness which is of grace by faith speaking, and bidding us not to despair because we cannot do the things which Christ came from heaven and rose from hades to accomplish."

8. But what saith it?] That is, this same spirit of the righteousness which is of faith.

The word is nigh thee, in thy mouth, and in thy heart: that is, the word of faith, which we preach:] The mouth assenting to God's commands and the heart understanding and willing to do them. This Paul identifies with the faith of the gospel, and again by a running comment applies the very words of Moses to the gospel faith as probably professed in baptism.

9. because if thou shalt confess with thy mouth Jesus as Lord, and shalt believe in thy heart that God raised him from the dead, thou shalt be saved:] Confessing Jesus as Lord involved the full surrender of the whole self to him. It was outward separation from the world, or as the gospels put it, "taking up the cross to follow him." When this outward act, in those days so significant in its consequences, was the result of sincere faith of the heart, *the whole essence of Christianity was involved in it*. It could only be the outcome of the new spiritual life. No man could so "call Jesus Lord but by the Holy Ghost." Paul thus finds a perfect identity between the inner spiritual principle of the new dispensation and that of the old. The fact upon which faith lays hold is this, "that God hath raised him from the dead." On the relation of this fact to the Christian faith see note on chapter iv. 25.

10. for with the heart man believeth unto righteousness; and with the mouth confession is made unto salvation.] In this general statement, which is given as a Christian axiom, the whole process of individual salvation is set forth in its historical order. The foundation is laid, the right relation to God attained, by faith: "With the heart man believeth unto righteousness." And then the Christian life follows in the consistent acknowledgment of Christ as the Lord. The man who to the end holds fast this confession is saved. To this axiom he puts a climax by adding the words of scripture already quoted (ch. ix. 33) from Isaiah xxviii. 16.

11. For the scripture saith, Whosoever believeth on him shall not be put to shame.] Here again Paul quotes to the sense. Instead of the simple "He that believeth" of the original, he brings out its universality by adding an "every"—"Whosoever" Faith thus appears everywhere from Moses to the prophets as the spirit of the Old Testament dispensation.

12. **For there is no distinction between Jew and Greek:**] The connection of this verse lies in the "whosoever" which Paul had inserted on purpose to introduce once more his universal gospel. The general proposition that faith is the groundwork of salvation in both dispensations, growing out of the discussion of the personal responsibility of the Jews for their unbelief, has opened the way for this grand, broad enunciation of the universality of God's grace. Whatever may have been the distinctions of the old election there is no difference or distinction here.

for the same Lord is Lord of all, and is rich unto all that call upon him:] The first part of this proposition no Jew would dispute. It was their boast that Jehovah is Lord of all the earth. But the second follows from it; and although it might strike him as new, yet even a Jew would not be disposed to deny it. If he hesitated Paul has scripture at hand to prove his point.

13. **for, Whosoever shall call upon the name of the Lord shall be saved.**] This passage is taken from Joel ii. 32 Peter had already quoted this prophecy on the day of Pentecost (Acts ii. 17). He had taken it as Messianic and universal in its character. In the original connection it can hardly be otherwise interpreted. It predicts in the last days a universal gift of God to man, prior to God's great and final judgment, and an opening up of deliverance in Zion and Jerusalem, and "in the remnant whom God shall call." And with that deliverance, "Whosoever shall call upon the name of the Lord shall be delivered," Paul's quotation is therefore perfectly apposite, and would be so acknowledged by a Jewish Christian; and the "whosoever" of the prophet is as universal as that of the apostle, and therefore proves his point. Paul has therefore fully established his position. Faith is the test of probation. Only by calling upon the name of the Lord can salvation be found either by Jew or Greek. The privileges or prerogatives of the election put no difference in this respect. He now turns to apply all this to the responsibility of the Jew.

14. **How then shall they call on him in whom they have not believed?**] Calling upon God or Christ as Lord is an act of worship involving faith. (Compare Heb. xi. 6.) Without faith the true calling upon the name of the Lord for salvation is impossible.

and how shall they believe in him whom they have not heard?] There is no faith without living contact with Christ, either listening to his own voice or to him through his ambassadors. Faith is not speculative assent to truth *about Christ*. Hence we are not at liberty to translate Paul's accusative by "of whom." It is obedience to his call to be reconciled to God. Rejection of this call is unbelief in Christ. To hear this call is to hear Christ. To obey this call is to believe in Christ.

and how shall they hear without a preacher?] Literally, without a herald, the ambassador of 2 Cor. v. 20, who therefore speaks as the voice or mouthpiece of his Master.

15. **and how shall they preach, except they be sent?**] Holding to the Greek terms we see more clearly the force of the syllogism. "How shall they make proclamation, except they be sent?" The office of the herald implies an authority by which he is sent and whose voice he utters. A universal proclamation by a universal apostolate is the necessary outcome of a universal gospel. And this, too, has been anticipated by the prophets of old.

even as it is written, How beautiful are the feet of them that bring glad tidings of good things!] Quoted freely from Isaiah lii. 7, but in harmony with the prophet's meaning. There, as here, the messenger is an ambassador or herald sent by God.

But while the meaning of this series of questions in verses 14 and 15 is thus clear in itself, we must define its relation to Paul's argument. In verse 3 he asserted that the Jews were missing salvation by their refusal to submit to God's righteousness. In this they were missing the great end of the law, which should have led them to Christ. This he proves by shewing that the spirit of the law is the spirit of the righteousness of faith, and that, so, man's individual responsibility, whether he be Jew or Greek, can only be discharged by faith. "Whosoever shall call upon the name of the Lord shall be saved." The argument by which Paul establishes this universal basis of human responsibility is, from the Jewish standpoint, absolutely unanswerable, confirmed as it is by his many quotations from the Old Testament scriptures. This being made clear and put in its final form in verse 13, he proceeds to apply it by a very skilful series of rhetorical questions from verse 14 to the end of the chapter. These are linked to the preceding demonstration by a "then"— "how then." We think that in each of these questions the persons referred to are the Jews. But Paul approaches the terrible conclusion regarding them by gentle and, as it were, hesitating steps. The great truth at which he has arrived from the Old Testament implies just the provision made in the gospel, as set forth in verses 14 and 15, and this itself was predicted by Isaiah. Now, the form of this provision—a preaching to be responded to by faith—was what the Jews objected to. They wanted some form of outward doing, or at least some outward sign, instead of the inward spiritual faith of the gospel. The preaching of Christ was to them a stumblingblock; but inexcusably so, since both the faith and the preaching were in such perfect harmony with the Old Testament. When therefore Paul adds,

16. **But they did not all hearken to the glad tidings. For Isaiah saith, Lord, who hath believed our report?**] he pronounces their condemnation on the ground of a fact which is as old as the time of Isaiah, who complains of a similar disbelief of God's glad tidings (Isaiah liii. 1). This is, we think, the first point to which Paul

brings his conclusion as the result of his series of questions, and should form the end of a minor paragraph.

17 So belief cometh of hearing, and hearing by the word of Christ.] Paul bases his second point of application upon a repetition in this verse of the principle of verses 14 and 15. This is usually construed as a parenthesis. But why should a writer repeat in the form of a parenthesis what he had just set forth in the boldest rhetoric? Besides, the conjunction here used is not such as would introduce a parenthesis, but one whose office it is to sum up the conclusion of a point already discussed. The conclusion here stated can only be drawn from verses 14 and 15; and if the conclusion were drawn for its own sake it would naturally find place at the end of these verses. But Paul there places, not this logical conclusion, but, what was to his purpose, the moral application. When therefore he here appends the conclusion we think he does it solely as the introduction to another application founded upon it. The conclusion itself was so obvious from the rhetorical questions of verses 14 and 15 that Paul only weakens it by stating it formally; and he would not have done so except in this new paragraph, where it is made the basis of a further important factor in his application, which he at once appends.

18. But I say, Did they not hear? Yea, verily,
    Their sound went out into all the earth,
    And their words unto the ends of the world.
This is the *second* application. *First*, they did not hearken, *i.e.*, did not believe or obey. *Secondly*, they *did hear*, *i.e.*, the proclamation of the gospel was so fully presented to them that their outward ear was reached, and thus the unwillingness of unbelief was left without excuse. The quotation here is purely literary. Paul adopts the beautiful language of the nineteenth psalm, not as a proof-text, but as an elegant and suitable expression of his present thought, which is, that the gospel had been so publicly and extensively preached as to have reached the outward ear of the whole Jewish nation even in their wide dispersion over the face of the earth. Paul has but one point more to add in the way of application, *i.e.*, that this unbelief or disregard of God's proclamation of mercy existed in the face of a clear knowledge of what its result must be.

19. But I say, Did Israel not know?] The adversative conjunction "but" with which this third application is introduced does not throw it into antithesis with either the first, in verse 16, or the second, in verse 18. The connection is, we think, rather this: each of the three applications (verses 16, 18 and 19) is introduced by a "but," which throws it independently into contrast with the broad position stated in the rhetorical questions of verses 14 and 15. In verse 16 the first application is made directly—"How shall they hear without a preacher?" "but" to the preacher of the good things "they did not all hearken." In verse 17 the central part of the platform is thrown into the form of a conclusion, "So belief cometh of hearing," and then the antithetic application follows (verse 18), *"but"* they did hear, without faith. Finally, in still stronger contrast to all that was needed for their salvation, *i.e.*, to the whole position set forth in verses 14 and 15, Paul adds, " But I say, Did Israel not know?" What he means by " knowing " here is clear from what follows. It is the understanding of the consequences of their conduct. If they refused to listen to God's offer, and that in the face of the fullest provision that they should hear that offer, and still further, in the face of the knowledge of what the consequence of such refusal would be, then their responsibility was complete. Their blood must be upon their own head. This last point, which most of all aggravated their guilt, Paul forbears to put as a direct assertion, but simply recites three passages from the Old Testament which leave no possibility of mistake as to what the fact was.

First Moses saith,
I will provoke you to jealousy with that which is no nation,
With a nation void of understanding will I anger you.

This quotation, from Deut xxxii. 21, is the first Old Testament proof that Israel possessed the requisite knowledge. A simple reference to the original passage shews that these words describe the first result of the unfaithfulness of the chosen people to their God. They are not therefore a mere prediction " that the gospel would go forth into all the earth," but that the election would be taken away from God's once elect and given to those who have been "no people," and this in punishment for their sin. What they ought to have known, therefore, was this very result of their unbelief.

20. And Isaiah is very bold, and saith,
I was found of them that sought me not;
I became manifest unto them that asked not of me.

This quotation, from Isaiah lxv. 1, is of the same purport as the preceding one from Deuteronomy. The second part of the verse, "I said, Behold me, behold me, unto a nation that was not called by my name," shews clearly that the prophet is speaking of the transfer of the election to a new people. The following verse, which Paul immediately quotes and applies to Israel (as it properly applies in the original), shews that this transfer is the penalty of the prolonged unfaithfulness and disobedience of God's ancient people. The boldness which Paul here ascribes to Isaiah is the peculiar emphasis with which he sets forth this course of the divine judgment. This manifestation of himself on God's part to those that asked not of him was on account of what Paul now adds, also from the very same prophecy of Isaiah:

21. But as to Israel he saith, All the day long did I spread out my hands unto a disobedient and gainsaying people.] The proof of their responsibility, and hence of God's justice in taking from them the privileges, is thus complete. In closing up this proof, however, Paul has once more brought them back from the standpoint of their personal salvation to that of their national election.

Before proceeding with the exposition of Paul's final theme we must prepare the way by the consideration of the relation of these two important matters (so interwoven by Paul) to each other.

EXCURSUS ON THE RELATION OF THE ELECTION TO INDIVIDUAL
SALVATION AND RESPONSIBILITY.

First of all we must bear in mind that the fundamental error of the Jew lay in the idea that (total apostasy perhaps excepted) the election absolutely secured personal salvation, so diminishing the sense of personal responsibility. John the Baptist attacked this idea in his preaching (Matt. iii. 9). Several generations before his time we may find the beginning of this doctrine in the second book of Maccabees. There all the Jews who are dead are "dead under God's covenant of everlasting life" (2 Macc. vii. 36), "and to them alone belongs the hope of the resurrection" (vii. 14). If they sin they shall be chastened for their sins, but not forever, for God "will yet be at one again with his servants." In the days of our Lord this doctrine, which in its Maccabean form somewhat resembles the doctrine of the Roman Catholic church, had degenerated into the antinomianism of the Pharisee, so keenly exposed in the second chapter of our Epistle. But it will be seen at once that the doctrine of election, which thus contravenes the idea of personal probational responsibility, is not *a secret counsel of God* in regard to the bestowal of his grace on *individuals*, but a *declared counsel of God* in reference to certain privileges conferred upon *a people*. The error of the Jews did leave room for personal responsibility in one direction, *i e.*, for the observance of outward conditions of the national covenant, the badges of their national prerogatives. The foundation of all these was circumcision, and to despise this ordinance was the most heinous of all sins, and the prime accusation against St. Paul (Acts xxi. 21). This led, as elsewhere, to a complete reversal of God's order of moral law, exalting the ceremonial and ritual far above the moral and spiritual. As the maintenance of ethical principles and of a sense of personal responsibility in opposition to the antinomian tendencies of this Jewish doctrine is Paul's great design in writing this Epistle, it would be extremely improbable that we should find him introducing a doctrine still more thoroughly antinomian as a substitute for that which he has overthrown. A secret, irreversible personal election could scarcely be more conducive to the sense of personal responsibility than the old Jewish idea of the national election. And we cannot find that Paul anywhere objects to the national idea of the election, or proposes to substitute for it a personal election in the secret counsel of God. He everywhere speaks of the national election as a fact. The election belonged to Israel. But he maintains, in opposition to two false views of the Jews, (1) that in that national election God is sovereign, and can reverse or change it as it pleaseth him; (2) that even under the election God holds men to strict personal account, and that failure to meet this responsibility renders the election void so far as the individuals are concerned, and may even result in the complete reversal of the election or its transfer to others so far as concerns the body. This establishes perfectly both individual and national responsibility, side by side with the election. An election which is not an immutable decree binding both God and man, but a wise and benevolent choice of such instruments as may be best fitted for God's gracious purpose, is perfectly consistent with the idea of probation and responsibility. And when there is added to this the idea that personal probation absolutely determines the benefits of the election as to the individual, and that conditional or collective probation decides the question of the continuance of the election as to the body, then the election becomes a mighty motive to the highest moral earnestness. We may thus gather from the teachings of Paul the following propositions as to the relation of the election to probation:—

1. The election does not supersede probation by absolutely securing individual or personal salvation.
2. Unfaithfulness to the responsibilities of the election may result in the loss of individual salvation.
3. Election is not immutably, but only probationally, assured to the body.
4. Unfaithfulness of the great body of the elect may result in the transfer of the election to a new body.

From these four propositions we may deduce a fifth—
5. The election itself thus involves a *personal* as well as a collective *probation*.

Two questions thus remain to be answered—
1. Is there a distinct moral probation in virtue of which the great end of their being may be secured or lost by those who are not included in the election?
2. How far is the probation of the election identical with that personal probation in the case of the elect?

The first of these questions Paul does not touch in the present discussion, but the answer of it is plain from the first three chapters of the Epistle. "These, having not the law, are a law unto themselves" (ch. ii. 14). "The law" was the distinctive privilege of the elect people (ch. iii. 2). Responsibility therefore continues in virtue of a universal form of law, *i.e.*, of test or condition of probation, even with the non-elect; and in chapter ii. 14 Paul assumes, to say the least of it, *that some of them may meet the requirements of that probation and attain its results.* That a large part of the world was without the pale of the election did not therefore discharge them from responsibility or *preclude their salvation.*

The second question must be considered under two categories—
(1) The old election of Israel. The basis of this was descent from Abraham along the chosen line of Isaac and Jacob. The immediate personal condition was circumcision, to which was added, on the

exodus from Egypt, the full Mosaic law or covenant Now, the essential difference between Paul and the Pharisees lay in the interpretation of the terms of this Mosaic covenant, and further, of the circumcision which lay behind it. He extends circumcision to the heart, and finds even in the law of Moses the spiritual principle of the righteousness of faith. The conditions of God's covenant with his elect, as Paul interpreted them, covered the whole ground of man's moral probation, and lifted that probation to an altitude of ethical obligation unknown in all the outside world. *All those who finally stood in the election under these conditions were without doubt saved in Paul's estimation.* He thus does not quarrel with the Jewish belief that all the finally elect were saved, but only with that cast-iron and external view of the election which made it a matter of outward *prerogative*, and which disregarded *God's probational sifting of the election until only the holy remnant remained*.

(2) As regards the Christian election Paul without doubt regarded its one condition as being *that faith in Christ in virtue of which we are accepted as righteous before God*. He found the spirit of that faith speaking even in the Mosaic law. The condition of personal salvation and that of the probation of election are, under the Christian dispensation, perfectly one, and entirely inward and spiritual. It might be supposed that baptism, as an outward form of initiation into the visible elect body, would take the place of the old covenant sign of circumcision But Paul speaks comparatively little of baptism, except as the renunciation of sin, and regards the elect body as *the body of believers*, united to each other by common faith in Christ Jesus. The true probational conditions of the election thus include, under the Christian dispensation, the entire ground of man's moral probation in the highest form yet assigned to the human race.

As regards individual probation the election becomes thus one phase of that varied distribution of probational advantages which a wise God has seen fit to make to men.

CH. XI. 1-10. GOD'S CONTINUOUS FAITHFULNESS IN THE ELECTION.

1. I say then, Did God cast off his people?] In this question and in that of verse 11 we have the two final theses of Paul on this subject. The present question raises the point of God's continuous fidelity to his covenant. This Paul vindicates by explanation of the present crisis in the history of Israel as a sifting rather than a reprobation. This was the peculiar doctrine of Isaiah, to which we have already been referred in chapter ix. 27. There he introduces it for the purpose of proving the responsibility of the elect people, and hence the justice of God in rejecting such as were unfaithful. Here it is introduced for the purpose of distinguishing between the faithful election who constitute the body to whom God's covenant belonged, and the unfaithful who alone are cast off. This doctrine of

probational sifting explains both difficulties—God's justice in rejection and God's faithfulness in saving the remnant.

God forbid. For I also am an Israelite, of the seed of Abraham, of the tribe of Benjamin.] The "God forbid" is Paul's answer. This makes the question equal to "Has God utterly or arbitrarily cast off his people?" Had that been the case Paul himself must have been reprobated. The present is not a case of any absolute arbitrary rejection of the ancient people. Large numbers of them were saved and included in the new election, of whom Paul himself was an example.

2. **God did not cast off his people which he foreknew.**] The point of difficulty here lies in the phrase "which he foreknew." Is it a limiting adjunct? or is it a condensed syllogism? As a limiting adjunct it would admit that the nation was cast off as a nation, but that the secret election of God was saved out of it. This secret election was designated as the "people which God foreknew," as distinguished from the outward people who appeared to the eye of man. This view might be harmonized with a certain interpretation of the verses immediately following, but does not fall in with the scope of Paul's complete view which finally identifies the nation, all Israel, with the elect, and predicts their restoration and salvation. As a condensed syllogism the clause "which he foreknew" may be expanded thus: "When God chose this nation he chose them with a perfect knowledge of their entire history. To suppose that now he casts them off entirely as a nation would argue fickleness in God's plan. Therefore we cannot suppose that God has cast them off."

Or wot ye not what the scripture saith of Elijah? how he pleadeth with God against Israel,] The disjunctive conjunction with which this question begins always implies an alternative question. (See note on ch. iii. 29.) The alternative here is, we think, to be found in the preceding part of the verse. That thrown into the form of a disjunctive question would run thus: "Whether is this a case of God's casting off his people, whose whole history he foreknew? or is it a case of there still being a remnant to represent them, as in the time of Elijah?" The force of the Greek disjunctive may thus be given as equal to "on the contrary." The phrase "in Elias" may be paraphrased as "in the history or record concerning Elias" "when he pleadeth with God against Israel." (See 1 Kings xix.) This last clause defines the particular occasion referred to. With this construction the verb "saith" is to be taken indefinitely as equal to "what lesson the scripture teacheth." This seems best to harmonize with the summary way in which Paul has reproduced the leading points of the passage referred to, using sometimes the words, sometimes the thought, and condensing a lengthy narrative into a few sentences.

3. **Lord, they have killed thy prophets, they have digged down thine altars: and I am left alone, and they seek my life.**] The analogy in the present case is very complete. From Paul's point of

view, as he saw the Jewish nation, including many who called themselves Christians, united in fierce opposition to himself as a representative of the universal gospel, he might well feel as did Elijah of old. But God had given him a faith to see further. Hence he adds,

4. **But what saith the answer of God unto him?**] "The answer of God" is literally the divine or oracular response, a word used only here in the New Testament.

I have left for myself seven thousand men, who have not bowed the knee to Baal.] The verb here used by Paul corresponds in tense and person to the Hebrew, and represents in the active voice of the Greek the "hiphil" of the Hebrew. The root is that of Isaiah's chosen term "remnant." It might be translated, "I have caused there to be a remnant of," etc. But was this divine causing, as Moule supposes, "a sovereign act of grace" withholding them from idolatry? Does not the context rather plainly point to God's providence in protecting and saving his faithful worshippers from the persecuting rage of Jezebel? These God had left, *i.e.*, caused to remain for himself as his witness in Israel. They are known as ones "who have not bowed the knee to Baal," literally "to the Baal," which is probably an abbreviation for "the image of Baal," or else an expression of contempt, the article being feminine.

5. **Even so then at this present time also there is a remnant according to the election of grace.**] Paul's combination of the adverb and conjunction expresses the argument from example or analogy. We might expand it thus: "In like manner we conclude that there has been at this present time a remnant according to the election of grace." The phrase "according to the election of grace" has, we think, been misapprehended. First of all, we note that in the Greek the article is wanting. Paul has not therefore used the phrase here as a title or definition of the election at large, as it is generally taken to be. Again, the phrase is used but in this one passage It has not thus acquired by frequency of use the force of a titular phrase. We think therefore that there is no justification for departing from the precise rendering, and that we should translate "a remnant on the basis of election of grace." While the adjunct is not so unmistakably attached to the noun as in chapter ix., yet we think that gives the clearest sense, especially as the verb is not the substantive verb. Paul therefore we take to affirm that God's remnant now existing is defined or described as "according to election of grace," *i.e.*, are elected "of grace." Paul's use of the term "of grace" is so frequent in the former part of the Epistle and elsewhere that its meaning is very clear. It signifies that mercy which God bestows on man through faith in Christ Jesus. "Election of grace" thus describes the Christian phase or form of election which is determined, *not on the basis of national lineage, but of the calling of all who are of the faith of Christ Jesus to the privileges of God's elect.* On this basis, Paul says, the elect remnant now exists, and of this number he was one. This remnant, consisting of all

Jews who believed, Paul regards as now representing the ancient chosen people.

6. But if it is by grace, it is no more of works: otherwise grace is no more grace.] His Christian readers would readily agree with Paul that there was a remnant, and that these consisted of such Jews as had been saved by grace through faith in Christ. These continued the election instead of the entire body of the circumcised seed, and hence were called, as distinguished from the old election, "the election of grace." But if the election is thus no longer defined by the outward circumcision, but by the saving grace of God in Christ through faith, then it is "no more of works." But what works are here referred to? Most certainly the old works of the law which were the *signs, seals and conditions of the old covenant*. These works, foremost among which stood circumcision, were what the Judaizing party maintained to be essential to God's elect and to salvation. If now, says Paul, the election is marked out by the operation of the grace of Christ through faith, and includes only those so distinguished, then the old principle of the works of the law (such as circumcision and all its attendant obligations) has become worthless. If this is not so, if election is still on the basis of the legal works, and only personal salvation of grace, then there is *no grace even in personal salvation*, since the election itself includes *as a matter of covenant right* all that belongs to salvation. In this line of interpretation we take Paul to use the phrases "of works" and "by grace" as abbreviated expressions already well understood by his readers. "Of works" expresses the sum total of the old conditions of the Jewish covenant, *by the observance of which they maintained their rightful place as God's elect people*. "By grace" expresses the gospel condition of salvation through Christ, which has been so fully vindicated as God's truth in chapters i.-v. that Paul takes it now as indisputable truth. His argument is that this work of grace now marks out the election, since, if they are still marked out as the elect by the old conditions or badges of works, even their salvation is no more of grace since it is included in their election. This seems to us the obvious meaning of Paul's language in the light of his previous use of these terms and in view of the entire historical circumstances under which he writes, being engaged in conflict with an external and immoral legalism against which he has introduced the principle of grace in the interests of true morality. This interpretation of the verse is in harmony with the rejection of the latter half, which has been done by the revisers on the best critical authority. It is altogether unnecessary, and indeed unsuitable, if our interpretation be correct.

7. What then? That which Israel seeketh for, that he obtained not;] The form of introductory question gives emphasis to this new thesis. The conjunction "then" marks it as a conclusion from the preceding discussion. "That which Israel seeketh for, that he obtained not." This is merely the introductory part of the conclusion, and in fact a repetition of what he had before stated as a main proposition (ch. ix. 31). "They sought a law of righteousness," *i.e.*, a rule or covenant condition by which they might be accepted before God. And they did not "light upon it," or, as Paul previously put it, *did not make their way through to it*. Nor must we here lose sight of Paul's reason, not any decree of God, but because "they sought it not by faith."

but the election obtained it,] How? By virtue of their election? Paul nowhere says so. They, like the Gentiles, attained to righteousness, the thing sought for, "by grace through faith." And their election was founded on this very grace, and so was an "election of grace."

and the rest were hardened:] Not by any arbitrary decree of God but by their own acts. Paul has put it elsewhere (ch. ix. 32), "They stumbled at the stone of stumbling." (See notes *in loco*.) In the past history of Israel there had been repeated examples of judicial hardening as the penalty of sin even among the chosen people. To these our attention is now called in attestation of the conclusion just drawn.

8. **according as it is written, God gave them a spirit of stupor, eyes that they should not see, and ears that they should not hear, unto this very day.**] This passage sums up in one the expressions of two Old Testament passages. In Deut. xxix. 4 Moses *lays it to the charge of Israel* that to this day God had not given them eyes to see nor ears to hear, notwithstanding the wonderful works wrought before their faces. This charge implies responsibility on their part. The withholding of this grace was because of some *fault* of theirs. In Isaiah xxix. 10 the prophet represents God as "pouring out upon his people the spirit of deep sleep," and this again evidently as the penalty of their sins. Both quotations are thus in perfect harmony with Paul's well-defined doctrine of probational responsibility.

9. **And David saith,**
  Let their table be made a snare, and a trap,
  And a stumblingblock, and a recompense unto them:
10. **Let their eyes be darkened, that they may not see,**
  And bow thou down their back alway.

This quotation is taken from Psalm lxix. 22, 23, following in part the variations of the Septuagint. The precise historical interpretation of the psalm is not easy, but the most probable reference is to some period such as that of Isaiah, in which God's poor but holy people were shamefully entreated by their brethren, and cry out to God for judgment. If so then the purport of the quotation will be, Let the very gifts of thy bounty be turned into means of punishment for their sins. This quotation shews how thoroughly the idea of moral recompense was before the mind of Paul, for such a quotation would be a monstrous thing if applied to men on any other basis than that of the recognition of perfect probational responsibility.

Ch. XI. 11—32. GOD'S UNIVERSAL PURPOSE OF MERCY IN THE ELECTION.

11. **I say then, Did they stumble that they might fall?**] This question introduces Paul's second concluding thesis on this great subject. The question here put inquires into the divine purpose. First, mark the force of the two verbs used. The first, rendered "to stumble," expresses an act which is the result of carelessness or wilfulness, hence an act of responsibility; the second, "to fall," designates an involuntary act, the consequence of the stumbling, and here, we think, denotes, not the fall of individuals into perdition, but the fall of these people from the proud position of God's chosen people. The conjunction "that" is the word which designates purpose. Paul's argument clearly defines this to be God's purpose. The stumbling of the Jews was occasioned by God's change in the terms of salvation. "The preaching of the cross" was the stumblingblock of the Jews. When therefore God placed the new election upon the basis of grace through faith he caused a universal stumbling of unbelieving Jews. Was God's purpose in *thus* causing this stumbling merely judicial, *i.e.*, to remove his unfaithful people from their ancient position of exaltation? To this Paul answers,

God forbid:] God does not order the terms of his covenant of election for purposes of judgment, but of mercy and salvation. Those terms ever work out probational justice toward individuals, and the good are saved and the bad are cast away. But the end of the election both to the body and to the whole world is mercy and salvation. This Paul now proceeds to shew.

but by their fall salvation is come unto the Gentiles,] A temporary fall from their high privileges is here conceded, not as God's purpose, but as *incidental* to that purpose. Their temporary fall is their own fault, but through it God's purpose of salvation to the Gentiles, and finally of the restoration of the Jews themselves, is being accomplished. This final purpose of God toward the Jews appears even in the previous purpose regarding the Gentiles.

for to provoke them to jealousy.] From the very outset the ingathering of the Gentiles must have had a strong moral effect upon the mind of the Jew, and Paul evidently counts on it as a powerful chastening influence to bring them to reflection and repentance. Here is God's mercy even in judgment.

12. **Now if their fall is the riches of the world, and their loss the riches of the Gentiles; how much more their fulness?**] The first two clauses are parallel with verse 11: "by their fall salvation is come unto the Gentiles." The idea presented in these three parallel forms of expression may be conceived of in three ways: (1) Their fall has turned out to the incidental enriching, etc., as if God, requiring to fill up the number of his elect, turned to the Gentiles. (2) That it was the necessary preliminary to the enriching, etc., as

if before the Gentiles could be admitted the Jews must be excluded. Both these points of view must, we think, be rejected, and therefore (3) we take it that Paul's true idea is, that if out of the circumstances which brought about their temporary fall and their reduction to a mere remnant God has brought salvation and riches to the Gentiles, what might have been the result, and what may we yet expect, when the whole body are found working into God's purpose? This idea Paul now proceeds to expand, but in such a way as directly to profit his Gentile readers.

13. **But I speak to you that are Gentiles. Inasmuch then as I am an apostle of Gentiles, I glorify my ministry:**
14. **if by any means I may provoke to jealousy them that are my flesh, and may save some of them.]** In the first clause of verse 13 the word "Gentiles" is in apposition to the pronoun "you," not as a limiting epithet but as a descriptive epithet. It does not mean, "to those of you who are Gentiles," as if a part were Jews. But for a logical purpose which appears immediately, the apostle calls the attention of his readers to their Gentile nationality. It is as if he had said, "Now ($\delta\varepsilon$ continuative), you (to whom I speak) are Gentiles, and hence *to you* I may say what follows." The "what follows," *i.e.*, the special communication which he has to make to the Gentiles, as if whispered in their own private ear, is contained in the balance of verse 13 and in verse 14, and may, we think, be rendered and punctuated as follows: "To whatever extent I am an apostle of the Gentiles I magnify mine office, if by any means I may provoke to emulation my brethren in the flesh and may save some of them." That is, Paul *took pains to place before the Jewish nation the full success of his ministry as apostle of the Gentiles*, for the purpose of bringing to bear upon them this spirit of emulation, hoping thus to turn their earnest attention to the claims of Christ, and so win them to saving faith. This intention of his he could communicate to his Gentile brethren, but to have even hinted it to the Jews would have foiled his very purpose. As an example of his thus magnifying his office see ch. xv. 17, etc.; Acts xv. 12; 1 Cor. iii. 10; Gal. ii. 8, 9. This interpretation accords with the readings and punctuation of the revised version, except in placing a comma at the end of verse 13, bringing verse 14 into immediate connection. The two verses have thus somewhat of the nature of a parenthesis for the private ear of the Gentile church, but at the same time form an ingenious device by which he introduces, in continuance of his main theme, some very wholesome lessons for those very Gentiles to whom he is thus speaking in confidence. This second phase of this confidential communication is suggested by $\mu\varepsilon\nu$ in verse 13, and introduced by a corresponding $\delta\varepsilon$ in verse 16. But before introducing this second point he glances once more at the grateful idea presented in verse 12, introducing it as an additional reason for his earnest desire and effort for their salvation.

15. **For if the casting away of them is the reconciling of the**

world, what shall the receiving of them be, but life from the dead ?] A temporary rejection of the Jews is thus taken for granted as having already taken place, but that it is only temporary appears from the confidently expressed hope of their reception again. Both parts of this question are predicated without an expressed verb—the indicative mood must be supplied, and the conjunction "if" taken as introducing the premise of an argument, equivalent to "since their rejection has proved to be, etc., their reception will surely be," "but life from the dead," *i.e.*, a more glorious spiritual life and power of the church than any heretofore experienced. This sense is in harmony with the apostle's line of thought, and with the increasing glow of his feeling which is already rising to the sublime outburst with which he closes this chapter. The literal interpretation, "resurrection from the dead," does not seem so apposite.

16. **And if the firstfruit is holy, so is the lump: and if the root is holy, so are the branches.**] We have already suggested that the introductory δε of this verse should be rendered by "but" to correspond with the μεν of verse 13. To translate the conjunction here by "and" (continuative) necessitates that we interpret what follows as an expansion or confirmation of verse 15. We must thus seek what is a somewhat far-fetched sense for the apostle's figures of "firstfruits" and "lump," "root" and "branches." But Paul elsewhere uses the term "firstfruits" of the *first converts*, except in 1 Cor. xv., where it is used of Christ the firstfruits of the resurrection. (See ch. xvi. 5 and 1 Cor. xvi. 15.) This would be the most natural meaning here. If the little remnant of saved, of whom Paul himself was one, are holy, so is the entire mass of the whole people from whom it is taken. This little remnant still holds the whole body for God, and prevents entire rejection. (See verse 1 and also Isaiah i. 9.) So also this term "root" turns our thoughts back to Isaiah vi. 13 and xi. 1, where the "holy seed" is the living root or "substance" which preserves the whole organism from utter extinction, and is the living root out of which new branches may spring, or into which they may be grafted. This gives a scriptural and Pauline idea. The little salt saves the whole mass. The branches may be ready to die; but while the root to which they belong lives they may still live, or even if cut off may yet be grafted in again. On the other hand, the interpretation which makes the patriarchs the roots and firstfruits gives us the very idea which Paul is combatting, *i.e.*, of hereditary claim or birthright holiness. But why does Paul thus affirm the still continued holiness of the entire body of the Jewish people in virtue of their connection with a sanctified first-offering and a living root? Not, we think, to confirm his hope of the glorious results of their final restoration, but as the basis of a gentle admonition to his Gentile readers, and which constitutes the second part of what he has to say to them apart, and which by this "but" he throws into the antithesis, delicately couching it in the figurative language which he has just adopted.

17. But if some of the branches were broken off,] "But"— better, with Godet, "now," as the antithesis has already been commenced in verse 16, of which this is the continuation. "If some of the branches were broken off"—Paul puts the case in the gentlest form, partly to promote the right spirit among the Gentiles, and partly to avoid needlessly wounding the Jews. But this "breaking off" is a real reprobation of some individuals, as not these same individuals, but those who may hereafter represent them, are the ones restored. But mark that the reprobation is only of those who once, externally at least, belonged to the elect.

and thou, being a wild olive, was grafted in among them, and didst become partaker with them of the root of the fatness of the olive tree;] "A wild olive"—better "being wild olive," as the word in the original is without the article, and hence adjective in function. But what does Paul mean by saying that the Gentiles were "wild olive"? The expression certainly cannot be taken as equivalent to the dead branches cut off and gathered for the burning. The Gentiles were not, by natural position, reprobates. The term does not imply any such idea. It denotes nothing beyond the absence of those covenant advantages possessed by the chosen people which, while increasing their privilege, increased their responsibility. The "wild olive" was capable of faith and salvation, and in virtue of that faith was graciously grafted in among the natural branches, *i.e.*, those who had previously enjoyed the covenant privileges, and so "made a joint partaker of the root of the fatness of the olive tree." If the root is the living body of the church or chosen people of God, then the fatness of which the Gentiles become joint partakers is nothing else than the privileges and promises of the covenant (Eph. iii. 6). This is Paul's own explanation of this grafting, and it drops out of sight the fact that the scion ingrafted is usually of a kind to bear better fruit, and emphasizes the fact that the stock chosen is always vigorous, full of fat young life. This transition from the low plane of moral probation of the heathen world to the lofty responsibilities, privileges and hopes of the covenant people was indeed a glorious transfer; but it did not place them beyond probation, although it brought them a present assurance of salvation. Therefore

18. glory not over the branches:] *i.e.*, "Despise not the branches." (Godet.) The branches certainly are primarily the rejected body of the Jewish people. This is clear from verse 19. Even the omission of the article there in the revised text does not make it any less evident that in the apostle's mind the "breaking off" was likely to lead to this despising.

but if thou gloriest, it is not thou that bearest the root, but the root thee.] The form in which Paul puts his hypothetical clause implies a possible if not an actual case. He throws into sharp juxtaposition with this possible or actual contempt the fact which made it unreasonable. "Thou bearest not the root." If the root were the patriarchs how could such a supposition be entertained? But if the root be the living church of God the Gentiles might easily begin to feel as if they were now the very root, or at least as if their accession maintained its vitality, as if they "bare up the pillars of it." But Paul reminds them that this is not so; that the church is still the Jewish root, as theirs are the covenant, and the promises, and the divine revelation, and the Messiah; and that the Gentiles are, to change the figure for another of St. Paul's, built in upon their foundation (Eph. ii. 19, 20).

19. **Thou wilt say then, Branches were broken off, that I might be grafted in.**] The apostle, by omitting the article, makes it clear that only *some* branches were broken off. The conjunction "that" denotes purpose. The Gentiles might be disposed to say that the very object of the exclusion of the Jews was the admission of the Gentiles. To this Paul replies καλως, "truly," or "granted," but with a limiting clause:

20. **Well; by their unbelief they were broken off,**] This limiting clause at once puts the cutting off on the basis of responsibility. "Truly, they were cut off by unbelief that thou mightest be grafted in." This limitation of the apostle, therefore, admits only this and no more, *that the exclusion of the unbelieving Jews was necessary that the Gentiles might come in.* Why? Because the admission of the Gentiles required that the covenant should be placed on the new principle of faith. Only thus could the door be freely opened to the Gentiles (Acts xiv. 27). But once this new basis was adopted *all unbelieving Jews must be cut off.* The cutting off of the unbelieving Jews was thus the necessary accompaniment of the admission of the Gentiles, but necessary only upon probational, and not upon arbitrary, grounds. Against the latter Paul has carefully guarded us by this interjected clause. But this implies also the probational tenure of the Gentiles.

and thou standest by thy faith.] The new election is universally and solely dispensed on principles of probation; therefore

Be not highminded, but fear:] The probational principle of faith makes it of pure grace, and therefore excludes boasting; but still conditional grace, and therefore excludes antinomian security.

21. **for if God spared not the natural branches, neither will he spare thee.**] This fact is at once a demonstration and a warning of the justice with which God's judgment will determine every individual probation, national or personal, Jew or Greek. The natural branches are the birthright members of the church in its old form. As Paul maintains the unity and continuity of the church, he sees the new elements not built into a new body but into the old.

22. **Behold then the goodness and severity of God:**] "Then" sums up the special address to the Gentiles; and "behold" calls emphatic attention to the conclusion. It is twofold and in both directions. The goodness is God's *grace;* the severity is his judgment. The judgment has fallen upon the Jews, but is without respect of persons, and so may light on the Gentiles either individually or col-

lectively. The grace has come to the Gentiles but will yet find out the Jews, for all are still under probation.

toward them that fell, severity;] This word "severity" is the act of the execution of justice, literally the "cutting off." Those that fell are those who have fallen away from their ancestral privileges. It seems to denote, not so much the moral act which determines probation, as the result of that act, though the two can scarcely be separated. But in the term *a probation* is implied, and also that the probation has been *terminated* by such an act as necessitated the intervention of judgment, and the "cutting off" is the execution of that judgment.

but toward thee, God's goodness, if thou continue in his goodness: otherwise thou also shalt be cut off.] The term in antithesis to "cutting off" here used signifies mercy or goodness in the sense of "helpfulness." It is therefore as appropriate to the beginning of probation as the "cutting off" is to the end. This same benignity had been extended to the Jews at the outset and all through their national probation, and was no other than the *chesed* of the Old Testament. But then as now it was probational. They continued not in his goodness, and so were "cut off"; and so, if thou continue not in his goodness, "thou also shalt be cut off." This absolute statement by Paul of the probational conditions both of the old election and of its new Christian form should prevent all possibility of misunderstanding his doctrine.

23. **And they also, if they continue not in their unbelief, shall be grafted in: for God is able to graft them in again.**] The conjunction might be translated "but." It is not a strong antithesis, but there is a contrast in the new thought thus introduced. The cutting off is not yet final. The change in the dispensations, great as it was—implying the ending up of one great world age, and thus in itself a foreshadowing of the final judgment—still left room in the coming age for renewal of national, as well as continuance of individual, probation. The terms here used may apply to either. The individual Jews, from their lower probational position outside of the covenant, may regain the privileges of the covenant through faith, just as the Gentiles have received them. Nay, more, their past probational training favours them.

24. **For if thou wast cut out of that which is by nature a wild olive tree, and wast grafted contrary to nature into a good olive tree: how much more shall these, which are the natural branches, be grafted into their own olive tree?**] Paul is not afraid to recognize the moral forces of nature in this matter. The long history of the Jews as God's chosen people had given them a natural relation to, and fitness for, God's moral purposes in the election. It was only their unbelief that excluded them. This unbelief removed they could, even more readily than the Gentiles, be incorporated in the chosen body. Meyer, on the other hand, makes the "how much more" refer, not to the congruity, but to the certainty of the restora-

tion. But this certainty must arise either from the congruity of the case or out of an idea of persistence of God's love, as if they had a special right to it. This latter idea seems so contrary to Paul's well-established doctrine of the universality and impartiality of both the love and the justice of God that we prefer the other line of interpretation. The "much more" in any case must refer to man, for so far as God is concerned there is nothing easier or more difficult, more certain or less certain, in his purposes. We can therefore read it only as "how much more readily *may we conclude* that the natural branches," etc., or "how much more *readily* may the natural branches." If we adopt the first method of supplying the evident ellipsis, our "more ready" conclusion can only be drawn from the fact that for God's purposes the long history of the chosen people had given them special advantages over the Gentiles, advantages which their unbelief alone had made of no avail. And this is one of God's purposes still in the future, as Paul proceeds now to shew.

25. For I would not, brethren, have you ignorant of this mystery, lest ye be wise in your own conceits,] A mystery with Paul is something now being or still to be revealed. The mystery here is God's purpose touching his ancient people. This, while yet not fully unfolded, was, even in Paul's day, in part clear, at least to himself, from the ancient prophets as he read them in the light of the New Testament inspiration. This he unfolds for the benefit of the Gentiles as a safeguard against the supercilious spirit already referred to.

that a hardening in part hath befallen Israel, until the fulness of the Gentiles be come in;] As to the nature and method of this judicial hardening see note on verse 7. The expression in part is, as Godet observes, defined by "the rest" in verse 7, and by "some" in verse 17. It is therefore numerical and in contrast with the "all" of the next clause. As to the time of this hardening, its continuance is clearly defined in the adjunct "until the fulness of the Gentiles," etc. But here two difficulties present themselves. First, as to the force of the conjunction, we think it means, not "as long as," but "up to the time at which." The term "fulness of the Gentiles" will thus mean "the full complement of the Gentile church." What this will be, whether a majority of all nations or what might be called practically all men, Paul does not here define; and the word "fulness," meaning simply the full measure, *i.e.*, God's full measure, measured on just and merciful conditions of probation, does not define it. Until then the times are "the times of the Gentiles" (Luke xxi. 24); but this does not imply that God hath left his ancient people "without a witness." Their blindness has thrown them into a lower plane of probation, in which they will be "judged every man according to his works." But at the end of these times of the Gentiles the ancient people are to be restored to a position of at least equal glory. This Paul now adds.

26. and so all Israel shall be saved:] The word "so" expresses

manner and not time, and it would seem that it here indicates an instrumental relationship of the fulness of the Gentiles to the salvation of the Jews. Godet conjectures that they may be brought to faith in Christ by the fulfilment of the ancient universal prophecies in the Christian church. This it was which convinced the Rabbi Jacob Freshman. The "all Israel" must mean Israel as a people; still, it is worthy of attention that the "all" is distributive, as if "every one of Israel" (like the Hebrew *kōl* with the construct state). This glorious consummation at the end of the times of the Gentiles is confirmed to Paul's mind by prophecy.

> even as it is written,
> There shall come out of Zion the Deliverer;
> He shall turn away ungodliness from Jacob:
> 27. And this is my covenant unto them,
> When I shall take away their sins.

This is generally taken to be a quotation from Isaiah of two distinct passages, the first, as far as the word "them," from Isaiah lix. 20; the last line from Isaiah xxvii 9. But we doubt the correctness of the latter reference. It seems quite as probable that the quotation refers but to the one passage, the latter part of which Paul has abridged in part in words borrowed from Isaiah. If so we must interpret the whole passage as one; whereas if there were two distinct quotations each must be interpreted in its own historical connection. The quotation of the main passage is exact from the LXX., with the exception of the substitution of "out of" for "on account of." This may have arisen from the mistake of an early transcriber misunderstanding an abbreviation. But in a very essential point our present Hebrew text differs from the LXX. It reads "and to those who turn away from iniquity in Jacob." The whole passage in the Hebrew stands thus: "There shall come a Deliverer to Zion, and to those who turn from iniquity in Jacob, saith the Lord. And as for me, this is my covenant with them, saith the Lord; My spirit which is upon thee, and my words which I have placed in thy mouth, shall not depart out of thy mouth, nor out of the mouth of thy seed, nor out of the mouth of thy seed's seed, saith the Lord, from this time and to the world age." In the first place, we see that the prediction is clearly Messianic. Again, it implies a perpetual relationship of God's ancient people to himself. But so far as the Hebrew text goes there is no prolonged interruption of the covenant relation. The Deliverer comes to a people who are turning away from iniquity, and to them the covenant is perpetual. In the Septuagint, on the contrary, the Deliverer comes "for the sake of Zion," or as Paul has it, "out of Zion"; and, finding Jacob in iniquity, one great work which he surely will accomplish will be to turn away this iniquity, and so the covenant of God with them will be perpetual. Now, the point of Paul's argument requires the adoption of the reading of the LXX. instead of the Hebrew text; and there is no reason that the LXX. may not be correct. According to that reading the Deliverer shall accomplish his work, and will yet make the covenant perpetual. The whole passage so admirably suits Paul's purpose that we think he has summed up the latter part of it in the words "this is my covenant unto them, when I shall take away their sins," only because he knew the passage to be perfectly familiar to his readers, and that a summary reference was quite sufficient.

28. **As touching the gospel, they are enemies for your sake: but as touching the election, they are beloved for the fathers' sake.**] We have in this verse three pairs of contrasted terms: the "gospel" and the "election"; "for your sake" and "for the fathers' sake"; and "enemies" and "beloved." The terms must be interpreted in harmony with each other. The gospel is a *dispensation* or method in which God deals with men for their salvation. The election must therefore be taken as the divine *dispensation* in which God chooses a body of men for the maintenance and dissemination of his saving grace among men. It cannot therefore, with Moule, be taken to mean "the elect body or people." The preposition κατα would here seem to designate the rule or principle by which the ancient chosen people were tested. According to the gospel standard they are enemies, *i.e.*, condemned. "He that believeth not is condemned already." But according to the scope of God's election purpose, in which he chose their fathers as the vessels of honour through whom salvation was to come to the world, they are beloved, *i.e.*, still within the reach and purpose of God's mercy. The new universal probational terms of the gospel by which the Jews are condemned, and for the time being their privileges forfeited, were introduced into God's purpose to meet the wants of the Gentiles. But the far-reaching promises of the ancient covenant were given to the fathers, and for their sakes will yet surely be fulfilled.

29. **For the gifts and the calling of God are without repentance.**] It must be first of all remembered that these words are spoken, not of an individual, but of a people. We have no right, therefore, to transfer them from their original application. The gifts of God consisted in that prominent position of moral and religious advancement to which, at an early period in the world's history, the Hebrew people were raised. Paul referred to them in the beginning of the third chapter, and again more fully in chapter ix. The calling was to the responsibility of holding these gifts in trust both for their own salvation and for that of the whole world. As Paul has shewn in verse 2, these gifts and calling were bestowed with the whole history of the world in view, and as part of a purpose of the ages which never moves backwards. For a time, while the Gentile line is being brought up, the old Hebrew line may stand still; but God will take it up again. God's order of progress in his work is ever upwards.

30. **For as ye in time past were disobedient to God, but now have obtained mercy by their disobedience,**] These are historical facts the meaning of which Paul has already thoroughly explained (verses 11, 12, 19, 20, 28). They are here adduced anew with an

emphasis on the order, *first disobedience, then mercy,* toward the Gentiles. They are also presented from a special aspect, that of disobedience and mercy. The term "disobedience" has reference to probational requirement. It is sometimes rendered "disobedience" and sometimes "unbelief." Its special nature is determined by the nature of the probation. The Gentiles were disobedient to moral law, but not without an element of unbelief. The Jews were unbelieving towards the gospel, but not without an element of moral disobedience. But the end in view in both is mercy.

31. **even so have these also now been disobedient, that by the mercy shewn to you they also may now obtain mercy.**] The conjunction "that," expressing a purpose or end to be reached, implies that there is something in the disobedience which prepares the way for the mercy. It may not be a necessary way to the end, and yet actually prove to be the way by which the end is reached. The Jews, without this preliminary experience of disobedience, with its accompanying judgment of rejection and humiliation, might have obediently accepted God's mercy; but they did not do so. Hence the gospel conditions, which put them on a level with the Gentiles, and which served to bring their proud disobedience to the light. Bye-and-bye, when, under the protracted discipline of separation from God which this disobedience entails, their pride is subdued, then will they be prepared to accept of *the Gentile way of mercy, i.e.,* will obtain mercy through the very same mercy which God has shewn to us. We may therefore paraphrase verses 30 and 31 thus: "As when the Jews by disobedience placed themselves on a level with the Gentiles, God made their disobedience the occasion for opening, even to the disobedient Gentiles, the doors of his mercy on the same conditions as to the Jews, so now God has brought into manifest light the disobedience of the Jews, humbling them to the level of the Gentiles, that they may accept the same merciful way of salvation." Paul has thus at last brought side by side the dispensation of the Gentiles, the dispensation of the Jews, and the common dispensation of the gospel. He has pointed out the end of each of these. The dispensation of the Gentiles has proved all to be under sin. The Jews, by circumcision and the law, have proved to be but transgressors of the law. The earlier dispensations both brought universal condemnation. To meet the common moral want thus clearly manifest God hath offered a free salvation through grace in the gospel. This has proved a ministry of mercy to the Gentiles, but still of condemnation to the Jews. But as the previous ministry of condemnation finally resulted in mercy, so will this. Hence at last the universal law of God's dealing with sinful man, whether Jew or Gentile.

32. **For God hath shut up all unto disobedience, that he might have mercy upon all.**] In these words we reach the grand culmination of Paul's argument. This is the *goal of the dispensations,* the ultimate result of God's purpose in the ages, to which the succes-

sive elections of Jew and Gentile are all subordinate, and to which the historical reprobations and moral distinctions of mercy and judgment are also subordinate. But we must bear in mind that Paul has here in view the race relations rather than the individual—the solidarity of man. In the progress of the world towards this goal, in which "the fulness of the Gentiles" and "all Israel" shall unite in the common mercy of God, each man of all the generations shall be judged according to his works. He may have been one of the elect, an Hebrew of the Hebrews, but he cannot escape the judgment of God. He may have been one of the Gentiles without law, but still God's judgment measures his righteous deserts. Paul has made it abundantly clear that all men are equal in this one thing, that "We must all be made manifest before the judgment seat of Christ, that each one may receive the things done in the body, according to what he hath done, whether it be good or bad." This is the theme of all his opening chapters. But when he touches the broader question of why, in the course of human history, there has been a difference in God's dealing with this common humanity—a difference as between the people of the same generation; exalting some and passing others by, dealing out to some wrath and to others mercy; a difference as between successive generations: visiting a people, once highly favoured and chosen, with long ages of reprobation and wrathful judgment, and exalting those who once were suffered to walk in their own ways to the chosen place of privilege—Paul sees running through this mystery a golden purpose of final universal mercy, in the course of human history meting out to each people and each generation that which best serves their present moral condition, and which in the far-off result will best serve the accomplishment of the grand design. And one principle governs the direction which this golden purpose takes as it leads us now here, now there—*all must know their sin* that they may receive the mercy. This law governs the solidarity as well as the individuality, and is the key to solve the mysteries of the moral inequalities of human life. The discipline of law which worketh wrath must first come to all that the way of mercy may be opened. This Paul had previously applied to the individual. And now to the two great classes of Jew and Gentile, *both alike*, the same principle must be applied by which they are shut up to the consequences of their own courses until the discipline of judgment brings them humbly to receive *the glorious universal mercy*.

Once more, in view of this wondrous thought, the apostle breaks forth into a hymn of ecstatic praise.

CH. XI. 33–36. THE HYMN OF THE DISPENSATIONS OF THE AGES.

33. O the depth of the riches both of the wisdom and the knowledge of God!] The exclamation of the text shews that it was with the mystery of the problem of the divine dispensations that the apostle had been struggling. As we shall see presently, he does not boast of a solution. He sees unfathomable depths yet beyond him. But as far as the wondrous light given him carries his thoughts into the mysteries of God's purpose he finds only riches of wisdom and knowledge—a knowledge which has provided for every eventuality of human freedom in the course of the world's history, and a wisdom which surmounts every difficulty in the accomplishment of God's merciful design. Note that Paul's exclamation of wonder is not at the amazing fulness of the divine mercy. Nothing could enhance the view of that mercy which he had already long since attained, and which in the closing verses of chapter v. he has pictured as triumphing over all sin. But here his entire attention is rapt in the contemplation of the wisdom and knowledge by which that saving love reaches its end.

how unsearchable are his judgments, and his ways past tracing out!] Mark the Hebraistic poetic parallelism which runs through to the end of the chapter. God's judgments are beyond our searching or criticism; only the divine result already experienced or foreseen to prophetic faith can enable us to understand them. And the ways of his mercy, especially when they pass down through the darker and more perplexing mysteries of judgment, are past our tracing out.

34. For who hath known the mind of the Lord? or who hath been his counsellor?] A quotation from Isaiah xl. 13, where these words are used to describe the same divine wisdom and knowledge upholding and directing all things in his providence to the well-being of his chosen servant. The questions *magnify the greatness* of the divine wisdom and knowledge. These are such as could be derived from no finite being. They therefore should be taken as pointing, not to the secret mystery of inscrutable decrees, but to the unfolding light of an infinite mercy which, with a purpose illimitably rich in resources of wisdom and knowledge, is working out its end.

35. or who hath first given to him, and it shall be recompensed unto him again?] Again a quotation (Job xli. 11). It should, however, be interpreted after the Hebrew idiom, in which the second clause in the imperfect tense is subjunctive in force. "Who hath first given unto him. that it should be repaid," etc. It seems inconsistent with the intensity of Paul's emotion, filled as he is with adoring wonder at the wisdom and knowledge of God, to make him turn round to summarize his whole doctrine of grace. It is too sudden a transition from the rapture of the poet to the sharp logic of the controversialist. We should therefore take it rather as a continuation, in words borrowed from Job, of the thought which Isaiah expands at length in the passage just quoted. Of such wisdom and knowledge human mind could not conceive; it is due to no finite counsellor; none hath lent it unto God. It cometh only from the immeasurable fulness of his own nature.

36. For of him, and through him, and unto him, are all things.]

"Of him are all things," and so are these riches of wisdom. "Through him are all things," and so shall be the execution of this divine plan. "Unto him are all things," and so its final issue is *the unveiling of his universal mercy.*

To him be the glory for ever. Amen.] And let all God's people, joining in this sublime contemplation, say also, *Amen!*

CH. XII. 1, 2. GENERAL EXHORTATION BASED UPON THE COVENANT MERCIES OF GOD.

1. I beseech you therefore, brethren, by the mercies of God,] Paul, having thus established to the Gentile Christian church the right to all the mercies of the covenant, in two comprehensive statements sums up the obligations flowing from their possession. This gives us, not in distinct terms, but in the entire point of the preceding chapters, a basis for the "therefore" of this verse. The expression "the mercies of God" sums up that which the preceding discussion had vindicated as the right of the Christian church. That the term "mercy" was in the Greek that which represented the "*chesed*" or "*chanan*" of the Hebrew, a designation of the grace of the covenant promises, appears from Luke i. 54, 55, 72, 78.

to present your bodies a living sacrifice, holy, acceptable to God, which is your reasonable service.] This is the first duty imposed by the obligations of the covenant. The chosen people were an holy priesthood, and therefore must offer sacrifice; they were God's peculiar possession, and therefore that sacrifice must be themselves. On the body as the instrument of all righteousness compare chapter vi. 13. The presentation of the body is thus the presentation of the whole outer life. The sacrifice is an offering of living "energies" (Moule), holy, *i.e.*, set apart to God, and cleansed from all defilement of sin by the sprinkled blood of Christ (compare the corresponding use of the terms "holy" and "cleansed" in the Epistle to the Hebrews), and so "acceptable to God." This constitutes the true "service" or "worship" which God delights to receive from his chosen priesthood. Further, this worship or service is not of outward forms or ceremonial offerings, but is a worship of a spiritual God in spirit and in truth. The Greek word $\lambda o\gamma\iota\kappa\eta\nu$ denotes, not so much what is fair and just in the judgment of reason, as what reason, or spiritual intelligence, renders. The holy work of the Christian life is the true and highest worship which can be offered by rational intelligence. The presentation of all the active energies of our bodies is thus the outward expression of the worship of the spiritual being who dwells in the body.

2. And be not fashioned according to this world:] This constitutes the second and negative side of the covenant obligation—separation from the world. This was the most prominent idea of the Mosaic dispensation (Luke xx. 24). On Paul's projection of this characteristic of the ancient people into the Christian dispensation

see 2 Cor. vi. 17. The separation is, however, not "out of the world," but from the sinful customs and habits of the world, the fashion of their godless life. The world from which the Christian chosen people are thus called to be separate is "this age," which, however, is not merely the present godless generation in the midst of which Paul wrote, but it includes the whole course of human history outside the sanctifying influence of the chosen people. The kingdoms of this world are, however, to become the kingdoms of our Lord and of his Christ. Then shall the church and the world be one. Till then the church must maintain her separation as the bearer of God's vessels of service. But such separation is possible only by an inward transfiguration of the church itself.

but be ye transformed by the renewing of your mind,] The word used to denote worldly conformity points to the outward life; the one used here rather to the inward ideal, that which shapes the outward life from within, the organic or organizing form. It is an inner power of new life which makes the fashion of our outer life to differ. There is here no prescription of a puritan fashioning from without. This inward power of Christianity manifests itself through a renewing of the mind, *i.e.*, that moral and religious understanding which directs the life aright. (Compare the law of the mind, ch. vii.) This mind, however, must be renewed, *i.e.*, restored to its original power to discern and "approve of" and "delight in" the right, and so "serve" God. By nature it is weak through the flesh; but through grace it is renewed,

that ye may prove what is the good and acceptable and perfect will of God.] This clause depends directly upon the word "renewing"—"renewing of the mind so as to prove," or "for the proving" —εις of purpose. "The will of God, the good, the well-pleasing and the perfect," is thus the sum total and perfection of all moral obligations from the Christian standpoint. The "proving" of this is not the putting of it into practice but the clear discernment of it, its exploration and verification. This is the purpose of the renewal of the mind, and the renewed mind so transforms all the outward life. The practical result of regeneration thus lies in the power of the Christian conscience or moral judgment to apprehend with clearest certainty every aspect and the full extent of moral obligation. Such is the grand foundation which Paul lays down for the ethics of God's people.

CH. XII. 3-21. SPECIAL EXHORTATIONS TO PARTICULAR CHRISTIAN DUTIES.

3. For I say, through the grace that was given unto me, to every man that is among you,] "For" is here explicatory, the unfolding in particular precepts of the general ethical exhortation. This Paul does "through the grace given unto him" as the apostle of the Gentiles. (See ch. xv.•15, and compare 1 Cor. xv. 10; Eph.

iii. 8; Gal. ii. 7-9.) In virtue of this apostolic authority to the Gentiles—an authority peculiar to Paul, as at the time at which he writes even Barnabas falls out of sight—Paul can thus address the whole Roman church as being throughout a Gentile church.

not to think of himself more highly than he ought to think; but so to think as to think soberly,] Paul begins, as was to be expected, in the very heart of the religious duties and exercises devolving upon the covenant people. As God's people they had received the wonderful gifts of God's Spirit. The very possession and exercise of these gifts exposed them to the moral danger of pride, already referred to as against the now rejected Jew (ch. xi. 18), and of unholy rivalry as between themselves. That the tendency here referred to was a common accompaniment of the *charismata* would appear from 1 Cor. xiv. 26, etc. In opposition to such tendencies Paul urges humility and a sober mind. This expression, already used by Paul in chapter viii. to designate the practical aim or aspiration of life (see note, ch. viii. 5), does not denote mere pride or ambition, but rather an aiming at things too great for us, beyond our measure. Our aim in our individual Christian work must be regulated by sobriety, or as Paul puts it in the next clause,

according as God hath dealt to each man a measure of faith.] The aim or effort of each man is to be directed by a sober estimate of God's gift to him of faith. It is very evident that the apostle is thus not speaking of self-conceit or self-confidence, but of the *too-great-attempts* which arise out of overweening confidence in our gifts or powers. Our attempts must be moderated to the measure of God's gift *of faith*. The true God-given faith, which is ever humble and sober-minded, and not the carnal self-confidence, which is ever proud, and headstrong, and rash, is to be the measure of our aspiration to work for God. The man to whom God has given the gift of faith which may make him mighty in prayer, may not have the gift which will make him mighty in preaching. This Paul proceeds to illustrate.

4. **For even as we have many members in one body, and all the members have not the same office:]** For the very full Pauline expansion of this illustration compare 1 Cor. xii. 4-31.

5. **so we, who are many, are one body in Christ,]** The glory of the one body in Christ is thus compatible with the most perfect humility and sobriety of the members.

and severally members one of another.] The mutual interdependence and the mutual sharing in the common honour and joy which this relation implies are beautifully expanded in the passage of the Epistle to the Corinthians already referred to.

6. **And having gifts differing according to the grace that was given unto us,]** The older commentators make this the beginning of a new sentence, with a hortatory ellipsis as in our English versions, and, as Meyer has shewn, rightly so. These gifts in the apostolic church were sharply defined as to the time of reception, hence the aorist. This manifestation of the gifts at the time of conver-

sion does not, however, exclude the natural basis, which was also a prior gift of God.

whether prophecy, let us prophesy according to the proportion of our faith;] Prophecy was a speaking from the depths of the inner consciousness of the things of God. Its value depended upon the clearness with which faith apprehended the unseen and spiritual. Prophecy beyond this became wild raving. The faith is the God-given intuition of moral and religious truth. Faith apprehended what prophecy uttered. The prophet must speak out of the full assurance of this faith. (Compare 1 Cor. ii. and xiii. 8, 9, etc.)

7. **or ministry, let us give ourselves to our ministry;]** The ministry referred especially to the care of the poor, the sick and the afflicted. This required a peculiar gift. It was the least ambitious of the services of the church; and to give one's self entirely up to it indicated a noble perfection of Christian character. It often takes the spirit of a hero to be faithful, kind, patient and self-forgetful in the sick room.

or he that teacheth, to his teaching;] This was also a very important function in the early church, as it is to-day, and not as attractive to the natural mind as some others. Hence the exhortation "to his teaching." If that is your gift from God faithfully and patiently use it.

8. **or he that exhorteth, to his exhorting:]** This exhortation was especially the giving of comfort to those in distress and to all the feeble-minded. This duty was discharged, not in large public assemblies, as at present, but in private, and in the humble and almost private gatherings of the Christians. It is to be distinguished from such an address as that of the day of Pentecost; hence, as in the case of ministering and teaching, the apostle contents himself with urging its faithful discharge.

he that giveth, let him do it with liberality;] We here see that the gifts had a natural basis. The charism of giving was founded in the possession of means. The call to such was to "singleness," which seems to imply that motive which seeks only to accomplish the good. To such a motive there will be no lack of liberality.

he that ruleth, with diligence;] The term here used refers to the oversight or direction of any part of the work of the church. The duty here is whole-souled devotion, and perhaps the force of the word here is that energetic earnestness in the work which the leader may impress upon all who labour under him.

he that sheweth mercy, with cheerfulness.] Some duties already touched, such as ministering, comforting and giving, may reappear under this head. We see that thus the apostle has not in view specific offices so much as classes of work which may fall to the lot of any Christian. The cheerful spirit often blesses more than the outward gift.

This closes the apostle's first specialization of duty—duties arising out of the functions of the church as a body, and which were distributed by the variety of God's gifts. He next turns to duties common to all Christians as individuals.

9. **Let love be without hypocrisy.**] This love "unfeigned," out of a "pure heart," is the foundation of all mutual discharge of duty.

Abhor that which is evil; cleave to that which is good.] Truly sincere love is pure. It compromises none of its fidelity in its love. Such a foundation of love, sincerity and fidelity can alone sustain the perfect Christian character.

10. **In love of the brethren be tenderly affectioned one to another;**] Implying the thoughtful, self-sacrificing consideration of members of a perfect family circle or brotherhood.

in honour preferring one another;] This translation doubtless gives the spirit, if not the literal sense, of the apostle's words. The honour, however, is probably not that which we seek but that which we pay; the verb thus has its ordinary meaning of "taking the lead"—"Taking the lead of each other in rendering to each other loving honour and respect." The most perfect brotherly affection is impossible without such *honour of each other*.

11. **in diligence not slothful;**] The "diligence" is the earnestness of spirit with which we address ourselves to work. In this we are not to be slack.

fervent in spirit;] The warm glow of spiritual life sustains the ardour of Christian toil. And so

serving the Lord;] With the devotion and fervent spirit just expressed.

12. **rejoicing in hope; patient in tribulation; continuing steadfastly in prayer;**] These three are again united. That blessed hope was the only abiding source of the Christian's joy, while the frequent tribulations demand patience and perseverance in prayer. (Compare 1 Thess. v. 17.)

13. **communicating to the necessities of the saints; given to hospitality.**] The mention of the tribulations calls up these needed duties. In times of persecution the churches free from the scourge were often called to send to the relief of their suffering brethren; while it became a sacred duty to open their doors to those of them who were driven from home. It is easy to see the association of thought which leads to the next verse. Persecution may also fall to their own lot, and hence he adds,

14. **Bless them that persecute you; bless, and curse not.**] The words of our Lord are probably here before the apostle's mind. Christ's precept he leaves without further expansion, as probably the Roman church had not yet passed into the furnace of persecution, and turns to other forms of Christian sympathy easily associated with his line of thought.

15. **Rejoice with them that rejoice; weep with them that weep.**] A beautiful antithesis, implying, as Chrysostom has it, the highest nobility of soul. The highest joys and the deepest sorrows were the portion of the church in those days of the martyrs; and the bond

of Christian fellowship made these the common heritage of all. This perfect unity of Christian feeling leads to the next precept:

16. Be of the same mind one toward another.] That is, "Have the same aspirations," or as Godet puts it, "Aim at the same things for each other as for yourselves." This follows from the perfect fellowship in their joys and sorrows. But even here humility reigns.

Set not your mind on high things, but condescend to things that are lowly.] The verb in the first clause is still the same, and designates the ambition, aspiration or aim of life—that which attracts our earnest thoughts and desires. The "high things" are the high things of the world, which we are to covet neither for ourselves nor for our brethren. But on the contrary, we should let our sympathies follow out with the lowly, whether persons or things. Paul sees in these the line in which God's will is most frequently found.

Be not wise in your own conceits.] The pride of superior wisdom was a natural outcome—in fact, one form—of the spirit against which Paul is here guarding (1 Cor. viii. 1, etc.).

17. Render to no man evil for evil.] The participles and infinitives so frequently used in these exhortations belong to the gnomic, or aphoristic, form, and hence may be rendered as principal verbs. The humble and the forgiving spirit are near akin. Hence the juxtaposition, though we have here the introduction of a new line of thought—the duties that "make for peace."

Take thought for things honourable in the sight of all men.] The first clause and the last belong to each other. "Provide in the sight of all men, for things morally noble." We have already found Paul using this grand old Greek word to express that in virtue which commands our admiration. The class of duties upon which Paul is dwelling—the cultivation of unity between man and man—would be naturally promoted by the spirit of this last precept.

18. If it be possible, as much as in you lieth, be at peace with all men.] This adds a third to the duties of peace. The first is negative, counteracting the worldly spirit of "an eye for an eye, a tooth for a tooth," etc., the spirit which breeds endless contention. The second takes away all occasion to the world for offence as against us. If everywhere the honourable is maintained before all men they have no just cause of quarrel with us. This third precept contemplates the possibility of offence even where not intended, and that some unreasonable and ungodly men will not suffer peace. Hence "if it be possible" is expressed as a condition. The second clause, however, is not of the nature of a condition. "As much as in you lieth" is not "to the extent of your ability" to restrain yourself, but "to the extent of your ability" to take away or obviate all occasion for quarrel. It calls out on our part every effort and every sacrifice in the way of conciliation except the sacrifice of truth and right. But notwithstanding all this the offences will come, and hence the tenderly pressed exhortation which follows—

19. Avenge not yourselves, beloved,] When all conciliatory efforts fail still the Christian must maintain the passive spirit of meekness, possessing his soul in patience.

but give place unto wrath:] Not our own wrath but the wrath of God, which will surely visit those who sin against the unoffending, and who proudly trample upon all those who meekly seek to maintain peace. For this divine wrath we are to "leave room," not forestalling it by taking our cause into our own hands.

for it is written, Vengeance belongeth unto me; I will recompense, saith the Lord.] In this quotation, from Deut. xxxii. 35, Paul gives at once the reason for, and the confirmation of, the precept just advanced, "Avenge not yourselves."

20. **But if thine enemy hunger, feed him; if he thirst, give him to drink:**] The "but" is equivalent to our "on the contrary." It is not merely negatively but positively opposed to the course forbidden. This precept is likewise in the form of a quotation from Prov. xxv. 21, 22, the quotation extending through the following clause—

for in so doing thou shalt heap coals of fire upon his head.] Neither in the original nor as here quoted by Paul is this to be taken as describing the spirit in which we are to return good for evil, but as simply stating its result. But what result? Some say a fiercer divine wrath; others, the burning shame and confusion which must at last conquer the evildoer; others carry this result up to true penitence. But are not all included? If the "coals of fire" work not a truly penitent shame they surely will bring the fiercer burning of divine wrath in an eternal remorse.

21. **Be not overcome of evil, but overcome evil with good.**] Wherever our meekness of spirit, our love and our Christ-like compassion are displaced by the spirit of wrath, there are we overcome. But the steady, manly maintenance of the Christian spirit of well-doing, of calm, patient love within, and of active beneficence without, is the most sublime of all moral victories.

CH. XIII. 1–10. FURTHER PRESENTATION OF CHRISTIAN DUTY, INCLUDING DUTIES TO CIVIL AUTHORITY AND TO OUR FELLOWMEN GENERALLY.

1. **Let every soul be in subjection to the higher powers:**] In this one precept is enforced the whole duty of civil obedience. The grounds of this duty are, however, expanded at length in the very important ethico-dogmatic statements which follow. The connection of this precept with the preceding would seem to lie, as Tholuck points out, in the fact that the civil power was soon to be the persecuting power. Paul perhaps already anticipated the danger of this; and when pressing upon the church the importance of guarding against every possible ground of offence, he could scarcely fail to warn them on the point where their Christian principles were shortly to be tested to the utmost. The phrase "higher powers" may be

somewhat misleading. It might well be rendered "the powers exercising sway." It includes all proper civil authority, higher or lower, and the qualifying adjunct refers simply to the exercise of that authority.

for there is no power but of God; and the powers that be are ordained of God.] This is the universal ground of Christian submission, and is twofold, in relation to each of the two words used in the preceding clause to describe the power: (1) All power or civil authority is of God. This refers to the general institution of government. Paul recognizes government in human society as a law instituted of God. This has reference to the noun or common term $\dot{\epsilon}\xi o v \sigma \iota a$. (2) This general authority of government is specifically represented to us by that particular form which at present exists over us ($\dot{v}\pi\epsilon\rho\epsilon\chi o v \sigma a \iota \varsigma$). And this Paul says "has been ordered of God," *i.e.*, his overruling providence has brought these particular men, or this particular form of government, into power at the present time and over us. Therefore both in the general institution of civil government and in the existing forms we are to recognize the hand and authority of God.

2. **Therefore he that resisteth the power, withstandeth the ordinance of God:**] The two verbs chosen by Paul for this sentence are emphatic. The first might be rendered "he that is insubordinate to the power." It points not only to organized rebellion but also to individual disobedience or transgression. The second might be rendered "stands opposed to God's ordinance." Such an one is guilty, not only of disobedience as towards the authority, but of presumption in setting himself against the order which God's providence has permitted or established.

and they that withstand shall receive to themselves judgment.] This judgment is that both of God and man. The man who puts himself into opposition to established, or existing, authority, challenges the judgment of human society and the judgment of God's providence. He may be claiming what he regards as his personal rights. But society and God's providence in the final event will determine whether it is right or best that order should be disturbed or that individual rights should suffer. It is to be noted that Paul does not use the strong term $\kappa a \tau \dot{a} \kappa \rho \iota \mu a$ (condemnation), but $\kappa \rho \iota \mu a$, which signifies a moral or a legal judgment and its results, whatever these may be. The judgment may thus be that of the rulers, or it may be that judgment with which the laws of society and God's providence visit all who sin against the common order.

3. **For rulers are not a terror to the good work, but to the evil.**] If the two clauses of verse 2 are co-ordinate, and both alike dependent on $\ddot{\omega}\sigma\tau\epsilon$ (so that), then the "for" with which this verse begins may be best referred to the latter part of verse 1. It assigns the reason for, or the proof of, the statement that civil power is an ordinance of God. The logical connection is thus much clearer than when it is joined with the last clause of verse 2. "Rulers" (which

in the Greek has the article) is to be taken thus as generic. The class of rulers are a terror, not to the good, but to the evil. This is the general principle upon which civil authority is established by God. From this general principle our general course of conduct toward them is clear.

And wouldest thou have no fear of the power? do that which is good, and thou shalt have praise from the same:] This is the logical duty arising from the principle upon which God's ordinance is based. "Do that which is good" is the universal rule. This entitles us to the praise of the power.

4. for he is a minister of God to thee for good.] Paul recognizes even in the case of the Christian the necessity and advantages of this ministry. The world has not yet seen the people capable of living without external law and its ministry for good.

But if thou do that which is evil, be afraid; for he beareth not the sword in vain:] This is the other alternative. Instead of saying "thou shalt be punished," as the correlative to "thou shalt have praise," Paul says "be afraid, for he beareth not the sword in vain." The meaning is the same ("expect thy just desert"), though couched in an elegant phrase which has passed into the literature of all Christian lands.

for he is a minister of God, an avenger for wrath to him that doeth evil.] The ministry is thus two-fold—a ministry for the promotion of all good, and a ministry for the suppression and punishment of all evil. This last point is of special importance. In Paul's theory of civil penalty the consideration of absolute moral desert had a place. He was not a mere utilitarian, even in the administration of civil law.

5. Wherefore ye must needs be in subjection, not only because of the wrath, but also for conscience sake.] This is the final precept on civil obedience, founded on a full consideration—(1) of the divine institution of government; (2) of its twofold office of the promotion of virtue and the punishment of crime. Paul has thus given us both a succinct Christian theory of civil government and a threefold precept of duty in relation to it: (1) The general duty of submission; (2) the duty of aspiring to the honour of good citizenship; and (3) the duty of doing this, not from the common or lower motive of fear, but from a high sense of right. The sanctions of religion guard the duties of citizenship. To the important circle of precepts thus completed Paul adds a reference to a supplementary duty. This he appends, not as a command—for the tax gatherer does not wait for moral considerations—but as founded upon the broad doctrine of government already announced. What to the world was an exaction or a necessity he thus elevates to the dignity of a conscientious act, without putting it as a direct command.

6. For for this cause ye pay tribute also;] The conjunction "for" ($\gamma\alpha\rho$) may here be taken, not as adducing a reason or proof of what goes before, but in its primary meaning ($\gamma\epsilon\ \alpha\rho\alpha$) "yea further" or "in fact" (see Winer, p. 558 (a)), adducing a supplementary fact of the same purport. If the duty of paying tribute is thus supplementary to the duty of subjection to civil authority, being a fact which further affirms that duty, then the adjunct "for this cause" points back to the same ground as lies at the foundation of that duty. This ground, however, is repeated in the next clause with a γαρ, which repeats the διὰ τοῦτο (for this cause), and with such variations as suits its new application.

for they are ministers of God's service, attending continually upon this very thing.] The fulness of this clause, as well as what follows, shews clearly that in the first clause there was implied a new precept, and that it is not to be taken merely as a dependent adjunct of verse 5. The Greek word translated "ministers of God's service" is very emphatic as expressing Paul's high estimate of the moral and even religious dignity of the duties referred to. They are ministers, as priests in the temple.

7. **Render to all their dues:**] The last implied precept suggests this, which opens up before us one of the grandest summaries of relative duty as between man and man to be found even in the New Testament, being only surpassed by those which our Lord himself has left in the golden rule and the second great commandment. This last it embraces, expands, and finally generalizes in verse 10. The best authorities favour the rejection of the conjunction "therefore." The argument which Meyer bases on this conjunction, against the view we have taken of the preceding verse, thus disappears, and we have here the distinct independent beginning of Paul's final resumé of general duty to our fellowman. "Render to all their dues" recognizes the social duties of the varied ranks which in the providence of God may exist among men. These are next presented in detail.

tribute to whom tribute is due;] Tribute was a direct tax levied on the whole country or upon each individual or property, and represented an external power or authority.

custom to whom custom;] This was a toll upon goods or other commerce passing through some point over which others were supposed to hold rights. These may not be our superiors, but their rights are to be respected.

fear to whom fear;] This is the reverence due especially to magistrates, but generally to all superiors. "Tribute where tribute was due" was a corresponding outward duty. He had already fully expanded the idea of submission.

honour to whom honour.] This was the respect due to our fellowmen in every station in life. In chapter xii. 10 Paul had enjoined the same feeling as between the members of the Christian church. (Compare 1 Peter ii. 17 for a striking parallel in which this honour is enjoined, not only toward the king, but toward all men.)

8. **Owe no man any thing,**] This is the exact counterpart of "Render to all their dues," and there seems no good reason why the

first should be limited to the state and its officers while the latter is taken as universal. We think that already, in verse 7, Paul has extended his thought from the authorities of the state to the whole extent of society which they represent. "Render to all their dues," and thus "owe no man any thing" except that universal debt which can never be paid in full, *i.e.*,

save to love one another:] That this was a debt universally due, and in its very nature ever due, Paul shews in the next clause. It might be thought that the duty of the church to the outside world was purely defensive, as already set forth in chapter xii. But not so, for even negative duties are only fulfilled in the spirit of love.

for he that loveth his neighbour hath fulfilled the law.] Paul thus, in enjoining this spirit of charity, incorporates the whole moral law into Christianity, not in an external legal way, but as the essential spirit of Christianity.

9. **For this, Thou shalt not commit adultery, Thou shalt not kill, Thou shalt not steal, Thou shalt not covet,**] Here are four commands of the second table rehearsed, three in order, then the last, followed by an expression including all else—

and if there be any other commandment,] *i.e.*, "whatsoever other commandment there is." These clauses from the beginning of verse 9 constitute the subject of which the remainder of the verse is the predicate. The reproduction of the subject in the neuter pronoun in the middle of the sentence obscures the sense and breaks Paul's construction, which may be represented thus (beginning with the article το, which takes as its substantive the whole collection of clauses to εντολη, which entire substantive expression is the subject of ανακεφαλαιουται):—"For the precepts, Thou shalt not commit adultery, Thou shalt not . . . . and whatsoever other commandment there is, are summed up," etc. This assertion proves Paul's thesis, that "he that loveth his neighbour hath fulfilled the law."

it is summed up in this word, namely, Thou shalt love thy neighbour as thyself.] There is no pronominal subject expressed or understood in the Greek, the subject of the verb "summed up" being the entire substantive rehearsal contained in the preceding part of the verse and thrown into the substantive form by the neuter article preceding. This construction could not be imitated by an English translation, but is paraphrased above. The Greek verb is scarcely expressed by our term "summed up." The verb signifies to bring under a general head or category, a comprehensive expression, formula or principle which includes all individual details. Paul therefore affirms that in that which our Lord had already pointed out as the second great command there is contained the fundamental principle of all duty to our fellowmen. Nor is this true as a philosophical formulary merely; it is true in practical life and morals as well.

10. **Love worketh no ill to his neighbour:**] The negative is contained in the positive as the less in the greater. The life filled out

with the blessed activities of love finds neither time nor place for evil. The good excludes the evil.

love therefore is the fulfilment of the law.] The law of the Old Testament was largely in the negative form, "Thou shalt not." This was suited to the world's infancy, and was likewise suited to the design for which the law was given, *i.e.*, to give to man the knowledge of his sin. But for the advanced work of filling the world with righteousness a higher and positive moral principle was needed. And this positive principle fulfils even the negative law, *i.e.*, accomplishes all required by its precepts. With this universal principle Paul closes up his general presentation of Christian ethics, and adds

CH. XIII. 11-14. AN EXHORTATION TO ALL DUTY, BASED UPON THE NEW RELATION OF THE CHRISTIAN TO HIS MORAL ENVIRONMENT.

11. **And this,**] That is, "And do all this." The demonstrative points back to the entire presentation of Christian duty in these two chapters. It recapitulates every imperative, and adds the common incentive to them all.

knowing the season,] This word "season" always signifies a passing period of opportunity and of consequent obligation. It here designates the season pre-eminently of Christian probation. The ordinary interpretation refers that probation to the church as extending to the second advent. Paul has, however, been expounding personal duties; the season, therefore, of which he speaks must apply to the individual. It is therefore either *the entire season of their Christian probation* as individuals or some peculiar crisis of that probation then upon them. But we must let Paul define his own meaning.

that now it is high time for you to awake out of sleep:] In accordance with the classical idiom this sentence may be rendered thus: "It is now time that ye awoke out of sleep." But this is capable of a twofold interpretation. According to the ordinary classical use of the aorist infinitive depending upon ὥρα, the infinitive is to be taken conceptually, not as that which has already been done, but as that which ought to have been done already or should be done at once. But in this idiom the infinitive is generally used without the subject accusative. The other interpretation would take the infinitive with its subject accusative historically as implying what had already actually taken place. The use of the subject accusative favours this, as the infinitive with the accusative is usually used in accordance with the historic force of its tense. There are several considerations which point to that signification here: Paul has used this form of exhortation in two other passages closely resembling the present. In 1 Thess. v. 5 he says, "Ye are all the children of light, and the children of the day: we are not of the night, nor of darkness. Therefore let us not sleep, as do others; but let us watch and be sober." Here it is clearly expressed that the awakening *had already taken* *place*, and the obligation is to the watchful, wakeful attitude of mind suitable to the day. In Eph. v. 8, etc., the illustration is expanded at still greater length: "For ye were sometimes darkness, but now are ye light in the Lord: walk as children of light." Then follow warnings against the licentious works of darkness, ending up, as he here begins, with the injunction to "redeem the time." It is evident, therefore, that in Paul's use of this, to him, familiar illustration, he conceives of the Christian church as already awake from sleep, and out of darkness into the light, and that his injunction is to that watchful, wakeful moral earnestness which is intent upon making the most of the light while it is day. And this same conception here gives us the best interpretation of the clauses following.

for now is salvation nearer to us than when we first believed.] The word "now" is a different one from that used in the preceding clause. That designates time fully up, equal to our "already"; this designates the time now passing, and in contrast with or dated from a time past. The meaning thus may be paraphrased as follows: "We have not to wait for the time of our earnest, wakeful Christian life, for already it is here; for even at the present time 'our salvation is nearer than when we believed.'" A part of our "season," or probational opportunity,'is thus already over. But what are we to understand by "our salvation nearer than when we believed"? The last words clearly denote that act of faith by which we first became accepted in Christ. Of this faith salvation is the end, and with Paul includes, not only the spiritual blessings received in this life, but also the resurrection and the final glory. Salvation is already in part realized in the initial act of faith, so that, as here it is regarded as coming nearer from the day of believing onwards, it must mean the fulness of salvation which shall be revealed in the resurrection. We are moving forward to meet it, and hence are already in the region of the light and of wakeful watchfulness. There is nothing in this which implies the speedy approach of the second advent. In Paul's conception each man reached the goal of his full salvation at the end of his life; and if the Lord hath not already come, the crown of life which the Lord will give at his coming is thenceforth laid up for him (2 Tim. iv. 8).

12. **The night is far spent, and the day is at hand:**] This is not a translation but a paraphrase or interpretation. The verb in the first clause signifies to move forward to its fulness. But the tense is not present or perfect but aorist. The period of the night's thus spending itself is a past time, and may be rendered "the night was spent, and the day has come near," the present perfect tense. The present perfect tense of this verb is indeed used in the sense of "is now on." What is this night and this day? In each of the other passages in which Paul has used the same illustration the night is the old heathen life, to which belonged the works of darkness. This corresponds with the use of the aorist tense here. And the day is the light of the Christian life which has shined already upon these

Roman Christians. This is also in accord with the tense here used. The passage is thus parallel with Eph. v. 8 and 1 Thess. v. 4, 5, and hence is followed by the same exhortation.

let us therefore cast off the works of darkness, and let us put on the armour of light.] Here all acknowledge that the darkness is moral darkness, as in verse 11 the slumber was moral torpor. It seems, therefore, the more inconsistent to take the night of verse 12 as the night of sorrow of human life, and the day as the day of Christ's glorious second coming. The casting off is that of an old garment that we may be clothed in the armour of light. But why should we put on armour for the day of Christ's second coming? The day of Christian life with its moral light is a day of conflict; the other is the day when our warfare is over. (Compare the reference to the armour in 1 Thess. v. 8, where it is the armour required for the day of Christian life, as contrasted with the darkness and moral slumber of the heathen life. See also the fuller reference to the armour and conflict in Eph. vi. 10, etc., in continuation of the preceding chapter.)

13. **Let us walk honestly, as in the day;**] The word "honestly" is here used in the old sense of seemly or honourable, equivalent to the "good report" of Phil. iv. 8. The contrast is with the works of darkness which immediately follow.

not in revelling and drunkenness, not in chambering and wantonness, not in strife and jealousy.] Here are three pairs of sins, each pair inseparable, and all characteristic of the heathen life, and, alas, too common fruits of fallen human nature in every age, and even in Christian civilization. On the extent to which the Greco-Roman civilization was at this time given up to all these vices, drunken brawls, carousals and midnight orgies, shameful, abandoned sensuality, and social, political and personal jealousy, and envenomed bitterness, compare the not always obscure references of Horace and the Satirists. (See also Eph. v. 3, etc.)

14. **But put ye on the Lord Jesus Christ,**] As the "works of darkness," the old habit of life, was a garment put off and forever cast aside, so here "the Lord Jesus Christ" is the new habit of life which Christ enjoins, of which his own life was the most perfect exemplar, and into which his Spirit leads all his believing followers. This same idea is spoken of as the "new man" (Eph. iv. 24), *i.e.*, the new course of life, which we are exhorted to put on as a garment.

and make not provision for the flesh, to fulfil the lusts thereof.] It might be supposed that this last injunction was but a repetition of the preceding. But in reality it is much more. It enjoins a moral principle which strikes at the very root of all forms of sensual sin. It forbids, not proper provision for the wants of the body, but all provision for the mere gratification of our lower nature. It is the utter abnegation of our lower nature as an end of life. It is this making the flesh and its gratification in any way and to any extent an end of life which brings the flesh into conflict with the spiritual life. The flesh is but the servant, and must never be the master. With this sweeping precept Paul closes this part of his exhortation. On the relation of this passage to the spiritual life of St. Augustine see Confessions viii. 12.

CH. XIV. 1-XV. 7. DISCUSSION OF THE DUTIES ARISING OUT OF THE EXISTENCE OF PARTIES IN THE CHURCH.

1. **But him that is weak in faith receive ye,**] The rendering of the conjunction δε by our distinct adversative "but" is, we think, a mistake. The δε serves simply to mark the transition to a new subject. But who are designated by the phrase "him that is weak in faith"? It certainly cannot be fairly applied to the adherents of any Jewish or heathen sect. Nor does it, we think, properly apply to the Judaizing party. They were certainly very far from being of weak faith; and Paul would be just as far from encouraging the church at Rome to receive them. There is therefore no fair parallel between the present passage and the Epistle to the Galatians. That deals with subverters of the Christian faith and with those who had been subverted; this, with persons of weak or not yet fully enlightened or established faith. The remaining alternative is, that Paul here deals with a class who have been unsettled by the teachings of the Judaizers, and affected by their superstitions, but not wholly subverted. They still retain true though weak faith. Paul says receive such, *i.e.*, admit them to the fellowship and privileges of brethren in Christ. Contrast this with his language in regard to the Judaizers (Gal. i. 8. 9). It is not necessary to suppose that the persons here referred to were members of the church at Rome, as does Meyer; nor even to suppose that they were Jewish Christians. The word "receive" implies, perhaps, that they were visitors, and we know that Gentiles as well as Jews were affected by these scruples.

yet not to doubtful disputations.] Better with the margin, "to decisions of doubts." The preposition "unto" has its usual meaning of "design" or "end": they were not to be received by the Church for the purpose of discussing the questions of doubt. The original meaning of the words, as well as the connection of thought, seems to suggest this interpretation. By this we do not understand that the officers, especially the teachers of the church, were not to seek to enlighten and strengthen these brethren; but that when they were welcomed into the assemblies of the church their entrance was not to be made the occasion for a wrangling controversy. For the spirit which would easily fall into this sin see 1 Cor. viii. 1, etc.

2. **One man hath faith to eat all things:**] Compare 1 Cor. viii. 4-6, which fully sets forth the apostle's meaning here. The verb translated "hath faith" might be translated "hath confidence."

but he that is weak eateth herbs.] That is, so strong are his scruples that rather than eat any thing unclean, especially any thing offered to idols, he abstains from animal food entirely.

3. Let not him that eateth set at nought him that eateth not;] This would be the natural result of the pride of superior knowledge, referred to in 1 Cor. viii. 1. But conscience is a grander thing than any mere enlightenment of the understanding, and should be honoured even when associated with narrow intelligence.

and let not him that eateth not judge him that eateth:] This is the opposite danger, the disposition to narrow the standard of moral obligation to our own conscientious scruples, and judge our fellows by our own subjective standard. True charity distinguishes between essentials in morals and matters of opinion. But for this class Paul has an argument the force of which they will feel more readily—

for God hath received him.] The verb is in the aorist, and points to a definite historical fact and to something about which there could be no dispute. We take this to be the divine testimony of the Spirit given at conversion, the extraordinary manifestations of which were evident to all men. The argument is therefore that to which Peter appealed in the case of Cornelius (Acts xi. 17), and to which he subsequently refers (Acts xv. 8). The fact that God received men who, according to Jewish scruples, were unclean, is in these instances indisputable. To refuse to fellowship with them is thus to put our judgments above that of God. Such a feeling Paul rebukes, and that even sharply.

4. Who art thou that judgest the servant of another? to his own lord he standeth or falleth.] The man who has no scruples and who freely eats all things is God's servant. The scrupulous brother who presumes to judge him is not his master; and in passing his narrow judgments upon him is transcending both propriety and equity.

Yea, he shall be made to stand; for the Lord hath power to make him stand.] The "standing" here is the standing of the preceding clause as contrasted with the "falling," and would there be most readily taken as "stands in, or falls from, his master's favour." But what then is the meaning of the present verse? The difficulty thus raised induces Meyer to interpret both verses of "standing fast in the Lord—perseverance in the Christian life and character." But the difficulty is solved by remembering that the one who makes him stand is *the Lord* (not God, as in the Text. Rec.). It was needful to remind these persons afflicted with Jewish scruples that they stood in the merits of Christ, and not by ritual observances. If they, the Jews, stood in God's favour only through faith in Christ Jesus, this same Lord Jesus could place even the uncircumcised in the same position of favour. (Compare Gal. ii. 15, 16.)

5. One man esteemeth one day above another: another esteemeth every day alike.] This constituted another point on which scruples arose. This point was probably not so prominent as the preceding, as it is not referred to in Acts xv., and is openly condemned by Paul (Gal. iv. 10) as representing the extreme folly of the Jewish error. With the scruple touching things offered to idols he deals more gently, except where it is forced upon those whose enlightened conscience rises superior to it. However, here even this scruple he does not condemn, but places it along with the other under a broad general rule which should guide us as regards ourselves.

Let each man be fully assured in his own mind.] This is the universal rule as to all matters of mere opinion. Let each man seek for the clearest light and the most perfect assurance possible, and act accordingly. This precept at once corrects unnecessary scruples and guards the sacredness of conscience. It is to be a matter of rational intelligence (νους). Hence all possible light must be sought. Yet it must be a matter of full assurance. Hence, as Paul points out presently, if doubt remains conscience must have the benefit of the doubt. Thus conscience is kept sacred.

6. He that regardeth the day, regardeth it unto the Lord:] It is for the Lord's sake (as God's command) that he regardeth it. This was too clear to need proof.

and he that eateth, eateth unto the Lord, for he giveth God thanks;] This second example required proof, which was ready at hand. The act of thanksgiving which accompanied every meal made it an act of worship (1 Cor. x. 31), as indeed the old heathen meals frequently had been.

and he that eateth not, unto the Lord he eateth not, and giveth God thanks.] It is quite clear that his refusal to eat is for God's sake, supposing that such food is displeasing to God, and hence Paul adds, "and giveth God thanks," not as a proof but as an accompaniment of his good conscience. That he is acting in the fear of God and in the name of Christ is confirmed to us by the thanksgiving which goes up to God over his meal of herbs.

7. For none of us liveth to himself, and none dieth to himself.] The "of us" is of the members of Christ's church. Paul does not assert of the wide humanity that none liveth to himself. That may be true as a social law, but it is not true of their aim or intention of life, which is often supremely selfish. But of the true Christian it can be said that he does not live to himself. This general principle which governs the Christian life Paul adduces as a ground of that charity which recognizes religious motives even in the scruples of our weak brethren. As we act out of regard to God, so should we credit others with the same motive. But at the same time this principle is recited for its own sake.

8. For whether we live, we live unto the Lord; or whether we die, we die unto the Lord: whether we live therefore, or die, we are the Lord's.] This expansion of the foregoing precept shews that, introduced apparently incidentally, it has its independent importance, and is thus emphatically repeated as a broad principle governing all inward motive of Christian life. We live, act and feel as those who, in every contingency of our being, in life, in death, are the Lord's property. This is not a command, to regulate our inward state, since inward feelings cannot be regulated by commands. But it has for our inner life the force which a command has for our outward life. It describes that which ought to be, and which actually exists wherever the great foundation truth of redemption has its proper effect upon us.

9. **For to this end Christ died, and lived again, that he might be Lord of both the dead and the living.**] Here we have the fact upon which the state of mind described is founded. This is not to be taken that Christ died to become the Lord of the dead, and lived again to become the Lord of the living; nor even in the more general form of Godet, "that by traversing all the domain of existence himself he has so won them that, in passing through them in our turn as believers, we never cease to be his." Such an interpretation lays too much stress upon the mere play of the words, which is not as prominent in the original as in our version. The death and resurrection of Christ have been repeatedly referred to by Paul as the essential elements of his redeeming work. By virtue of that work he claims the lordship of all, living and dead.

10. **But thou, why dost thou judge thy brother?**] The "but" throws into contrast with this common relation to our Lord the spirit which judges, on the one hand, and the spirit which despises, on the other. In this first clause the scrupulous man is addressed, who applies in adverse judgment his own scruples to his brother's life

or thou again, why dost thou set at nought thy brother?] Here the other party, the man of broad, advanced freedom of thought, is addressed. To each his own error is brought home, both alike opposed to the spirit which lives to Christ.

for we shall all stand before the judgment-seat of God.] God, not man, is the judge who hath authority; and as we are to be judged we should abstain from judging others.

11. **For it is written,**
As I live, saith the Lord, to me every knee shall bow,
And every tongue shall confess to God.] (Isaiah xlv. 23.) This passage in the original does not imply on the part of the prophet a clear knowledge of a final judgment such as Paul here speaks of. But it does imply that God brings every man into probational account with himself. Both the "submission" of the first clause and the "confession" of the second clause imply that, if not at the bar of the great final day, yet at the bar of our own conscience, we must answer and submit. This Paul sums up accordingly.

12. **So then each one of us shall give account of himself to God.**] This verse summarizes that which was proved by the quotation. The "bowing" and "confessing" of Isaiah Paul interprets as "giving an account." In this passage he leaves it as Isaiah does, undecided as to when and where this account is to be rendered. But he emphasizes Isaiah's affirmation of universality—"each one of us"—of himself individually.

13. Let us not therefore judge one another any more:] A concluding exhortation commending itself to any mind fully impressed by the great truth just uttered. A due sense of the omnipresent divine judgment excludes the carping, fault-finding spirit towards others.

but judge ye this rather, that no man put a stumblingblock in his brother's way, or an occasion of falling.] The word "judge" in Greek expresses the act of moral discrimination between right and wrong. This may be exercised upon the acts of others or upon our own. It may be exercised after the act or in anticipation of it. Here the right moral judgment of our own conduct in advance, discriminating our true duty, is contrasted with the wrong moral judgment passed upon the conduct of others. This part of the precept is for both the strong and the weak, but especially for the strong, as appears from what immediately follows. The "stumblingblock," or "occasion of falling," refers to the weak. The two Greek words seem to be nearly synonymous, though in the first may lie the idea of accident, in the second that of intention. The result is the same in both cases—a fall into sin. The second term applied to the cause of the sin presents it as wrong in more forcible language. The "stumblingblock" is the free conduct of the strong brother. The application to this of the somewhat strong word "scandal" leads Paul into explanation as follows:—

14. I know, and am persuaded in the Lord Jesus, that nothing is unclean of itself:] By this very full enunciation of Christian liberty Paul guards against all misapprehension. He is not encouraging superstitious scruples. He agrees with the strong in their judgment. A touch of reason and common sense sweeps away all artificial distinction of a supposed moral character. Moral distinction has its foundation, not in arbitrary or artificial prescriptions, but in immutable principles. The phrase "in the Lord Jesus" reveals the fact that Paul arrived at this clear cognizance of the true moral discrimination by virtue of the Spirit of Christ. As a Jew he once was bound by "ordinances" as firmly as any.

save that to him who accounteth any thing to be unclean, to him it is unclean.] The exception which Paul here makes to his general principle is of the highest moment, both practically and as throwing light upon the whole question of subjective ethics. His general principle has asserted that moral distinction belongs to the spiritual, not to the external or material. It is therefore apprehended by the inner, and not by the outer, eye. Its discernment is by that moral understanding which Paul has designated as the (νους) mind. It cannot be apprehended by touch, taste or smell; by eye or ear. It is not, therefore, uncertain. No man held to the reality of moral distinctions more firmly than Paul. But moral distinctions reveal themselves to the inner eye in that subjective sphere which we call conscience. And in the passage now before us Paul asserts that for each individual his conscience is *for the moment* the final appeal. If conscience is violated, not this, that or the other particular precept is broken, but the authority of all right is rejected. Paul grants that conscience may at times be mistaken. But still, as conscience represents the authority of all moral obligation it must always be obeyed. The individual mistake is a matter of trifling moment; the authority of moral law is life. The practical rule must therefore be universally observed—"Obey your conscience." To you your conscience is the expounder of moral law. Disobedience to conscience is rejection of moral law as such, and hence is sin even where conscience may be mistaken as to the particular act.

15. **For if because of meat thy brother is grieved, thou walkest no longer in love.**] According to the reading adopted in the revised version verse 14 is to be taken as a parenthesis, explaining why the somewhat harsh term "scandal" has been applied to the free acts of some of the Gentiles. Verse 15 then connects directly with verse 13, giving a reason for the precept in the second clause: "Make it a matter of conscience not to put a stumblingblock in the way of thy brother, for it is a breach of charity to grieve another for the sake of meat." The grief here refers to the wound to his conscience. This follows if he imitates your example. It follows in another form if he resists that example, and so in his own mind condemns you.

Destroy not with thy meat him for whom Christ died.] Even Meyer admits that the danger against which this warning is directed is that of final perdition. Hodge, too, admits that this is "more consistent with the common meaning of the original word." To those who have followed the thoroughly ethical drift of Paul's entire doctrine no argument on this point is needed. The heart of Paul's gospel is individual *probational responsibility*. Sin against conscience may therefore bring destruction even to those for whom Christ died. This last phrase is here introduced as a contrast to the selfish lack of charity which will not even forego its favourite meats for the sake of a brother's soul. Christ gave up his life.

16. **Let not then your good be evil spoken of:**] That is, do not so thrust forward your liberty (a good thing in itself, as Paul will again shew presently) as to give rise to reproach. The evil report would be that arising from unseemly contentions between brethren in Christ. (Compare 1 Cor. iii. 3.)

17. **for the kingdom of God is not eating and drinking, but righteousness and peace and joy in the Holy Ghost.**] "The kingdom of God" is here clearly the kingdom within, the rule of grace in the heart. "Eating and drinking" represent the ritual precepts of the old law. These are excluded, and the true fruits of the kingdom are "righteousness," right relation of the individual conscience to God; "peace" with our fellowman, and especially with our brethren in the church; and "joy in the Holy Ghost" as the outcome of these right relations to God and man. This conforms at once to the context, and to the use of the word "righteousness" throughout the Epistle. These three comprehensive terms summarize the entire extent of Christian life, inward and outward.

18. For he that herein serveth Christ is well-pleasing to God, and approved of men.] "Herein" according to the revised text is "in this" (singular). In what? Difficulties present themselves in regard to all the answers. But the phrase "in the Holy Ghost" just preceding, and Paul's doctrine of the Holy Ghost in relation to the entire Christian life, incline us to refer to that. "As many as are led by the Spirit of God, these are the sons of God." "Serving Christ" expresses the practical relation of the believer to his Lord. Every man who in his daily life serveth Christ in the Holy Ghost is "well-pleasing to God, and approved of men." (Compare ch ix. 1.) The "well-pleasing" and "approved" thus correspond to "righteousness" and "peace." The "service of Christ in the Holy Ghost" is presented, not as the ground, but the proof, of the relation to God and man.

19. So then let us follow after things which make for peace, and things whereby we may edify one another.] Another exhortation deduced from the principles just enunciated. Throughout this chapter the apostle proceeds by the enunciation of great moral or religious truths, deducing from them his practical precepts as he proceeds. The principles thus incidentally presented as the foundation of the precepts are of great value both in Christian ethics and dogmatics.

20. Overthrow not for meat's sake the work of God.] The edification of the preceding verse suggests this form of the exhortation. It is not, we think, a repetition of verse 13. The apostle has moved on to the thought of peace in the church. The edification is thus best taken in the sense of building up—strengthening the church by the unity of its members. (Compare Eph. iv. 12.) The pulling down of God's work is then the distracting and weakening of the church by these divisions. Paul takes it that the strong Christian is quite at liberty to abstain for the sake of charity. If he does not do so it is because of appetite; and to put his appetite for a particular form of food above the interests of Christ's church is indeed a sin.

All things indeed are clean;] The $\mu\epsilon\nu$ is here concessive: "I grant you all things are clean." This should, we think, be taken as the beginning of a new and final paragraph in which are stated the conclusions of the whole discussion. The $\mu\epsilon\nu$ corresponds to $\delta\epsilon$ in chapter xv. 1, where the proposition is concluded. The broad statement here made, however, needs a guard, which is immediately introduced as a parenthesis with $\alpha\lambda\lambda\alpha$.

howbeit it is evil for that man who eateth with offence.] If our interpretation of the clause preceding is correct, then this statement must refer to the case of the strong brother. It is not an explanation of how the weak brother may be destroyed, as Meyer argues, for that would give us a mere repetition of verses 13 and 14, but a parenthetical assertion of the moral wrong of the sin against the unity of the church, introduced to limit and guard the general statement preceding. Even the use of clean things may become evil or sinful if we use them so as to give occasion of sin to others. We think this interpretation is also more suitable to the peculiar phraseology of the original; διά with the genitive would thus express the formal cause, the manner of eating—eating in such wise as to prove a stumblingblock. Compare the phrase "speaking in parables," where the same Greek form is used. "It is evil" may be paraphrased "It is an evil thing."

21. It is good not to eat flesh, nor to drink wine, nor to do anything whereby thy brother stumbleth.] The "good" is here placed in direct contrast with the evil. The evil course gives offence. The noble (beautifully good) course abstains from all cause of offence. The nobility of our moral nature is seen, not in the freedom or impunity with which we can trample under foot unfounded prejudices and scruples, but in the self-denial with which we can meet the weaknesses of others. It is scarcely right to put the question of total abstinence, with the fearful moral dangers with which it seeks to grapple, on the footing of the question here discussed. It cannot be said that alcohol is clean.

22. The faith which thou hast, have thou to thyself before God.] This is not mere permission. The verb expresses active, not mere passive, possession. An enlightened conscience is a great blessing. We should beware of allowing it to fall under the bondage of superstitious scruples. Therefore "hold fast before God, as respects thyself, the faith which thou hast." This verse introduces a second part of the parenthesis, extending to the end of the chapter, and guarding against an incidental danger arising out of the very duty which Paul is enforcing. This interpretation, which is required by the revised reading, is, we think, quite in harmony with this paragraph as a parenthetical admonition. (See on the contrary Godet *in loco.*)

Happy is he that judgeth not himself in that which he approveth.] This follows up the idea just presented, "keep hold of thy faith," because "Blessed is he," etc. The word "judge" must here be taken of a condemning judgment, or at least of a judgment that questions. The "approval" is equal to our word "sanction," and may be rendered "judgeth to be right," or "esteemeth right." Such clear moral discernment as leaves no room for doubting judgment is indeed a great blessing, and should be prized accordingly.

23. But he that doubteth is condemned if he eat, because he eateth not of faith;] The word translated "doubteth" signifies hesitation in judgment, uncertainty. It is not unbelief as opposed to faith, but the absence of clear moral conviction. To such an one "if he eat" there is "condemnation." This word cannot mean less than condemnation in his own conscience. But why positive condemnation when the wrong is still doubtful? "Because he eateth not of faith." Many expositors take "faith" here as in the sense of saving faith. In this entire discussion, however, beginning with the first verse, Paul has used the word faith in a broader sense of clear conviction of truth. The "weak in faith" of the first verse is not one lacking justifying faith, but one who has not yet embraced with full assurance *all the truth* of the gospel. The perfected faith of Christ sets a man fully free from these Jewish scruples. We can scarcely understand the word "faith" in a different sense here. It is also in this sense that Paul says,

and whatsoever is not of faith is sin.] As this is one of the broadest ethical principles set forth by Paul it becomes necessary to examine it very carefully. Faith, as we have just seen, is a full assurance of moral conviction, grounded upon the principles of the gospel of Christ. It is not mere natural subjective confidence, but the assurance arising from the moral illumination of the gospel of Christ. The gospel enlightens conscience. It places it in the true relation of rightness with God. It restores it to that moral confidence before God through which alone it can discriminate the genuine right. And to the man whose conscience is placed in this new relation duty claims the whole life. Nothing can pass without its verdict, *and to act without its clear verdict of approval is sin*. "Whether ye eat or drink, or whatsoever ye do, do all to the glory of God." No higher moral standard than this is conceivable; and yet this is the standard to which Paul holds all Christians. Having completed this incidental but most important explanation of ethical principles Paul now returns to his main theme.

1. Now we that are strong ought to bear the infirmities of the weak, and not to please ourselves.] The conjunction δέ with which this verse begins naturally carries us back to the μεν of verse 20; and this gives an excellent connection: "All things, I grant you, are pure," "*but* we that are strong ought to bear the infirmities of the weak," etc. The parenthesis thus begins with αλλα (verse 20). The objection to this connection is the length, the variety and the importance of the parenthetical matter. But we are not without examples of similar construction in the earlier part of the Epistle. (See ch. v. 15-17, where the parenthetical matter needed to guard a preceding statement is also introduced by αλλα.) "To please ourselves" refers to the indulgence of appetite for meats, etc., and maintains the continuity of thought. The words, like the clause of verse 20 with which we have immediately connected them, are addressed to the strong, and certainly imply what we have found indicated everywhere through the Epistle, that the readers were Gentiles, free from Jewish scruples.

2. Let each one of us please his neighbour for that which is good, unto edifying.] We have here defined the limits and result of this acquiescence in the scruples of our neighbours. It must be for individual good, and it must be such as builds up the church.

3. For Christ also pleased not himself;] The full extent of the self-abnegation of Christ we may learn from such passages as Phil. ii. 1-8. (Compare Matt. xx. 28 and 2 Cor. viii. 9.)

but, as it is written, The reproaches of them that reproached

thee fell upon me.] This passage, taken from Psalms lxix. 9, is part of an inspired complaint, many quotations from which are applied to the Messiah. It is one of the psalms of God's afflicted servant. The indications are that it was written during the captivity, and like Isaiah liii. belongs to that period of prophecy in which, out of the sufferings in which the chosen people were but the type of their Messianic Head, they were given a glimpse of the glory that should follow. Paul quotes it here, not to prove the fact of our Lord's self-sacrifice, but to give expression to his appreciation of it. He quotes it, also, not without a reference to its original historic application to a people or a person who for God's sake endured affliction.

4. For whatsoever things were written aforetime were written for our learning, that through patience and through comfort of the scriptures we might have hope.] This idea of the object of the scripture record was a favourite one with St. Paul. (See 1 Cor. x. 11.) There is a vein of pathos running through these last words of the apostolic admonition. The words "patience," "comfort" and "hope," and the need of these (which is so plainly intimated), point, as in chapter viii., to the time when these Roman Christians will share with their Master and with the chosen people of old in the cup of suffering. So strong is this presentiment in the mind of the apostle that it converts his next words of admonition into a prayer.

5. Now the God of patience and of comfort grant you to be of the same mind one with another according to Christ Jesus:] Every word of this precious scripture grows rich with the tenderness of Paul's heart. God is the God of patient endurance and of comfort. His grace is to give perfect unity of spirit to the church, and that unity is to be based upon the perfect truth of Christ; for this is, we think, the meaning of this last clause. And the blessed result of this is as follows:—

6. that with one accord ye may with one mouth glorify the God and Father of our Lord Jesus Christ.] The "one accord" is the perfect unity of loving desire, and the "one mouth" is the final unity of faith and opinion. Paul prays for both. He is not satisfied with the unity of charity alone. He desires also that they all "speak the same things." (Compare 1 Cor. i. 10.) This will be one blessed result of the perfecting of the saints (Eph. iv. 12, 13). Did Paul foresee how long patience, and how many words of comfort, and what ages of hope, would be needed before this glorious result should be reached? We are here, too, reminded that the unity of the church is the glory of God, especially before the world. (Compare John xvii.)

7. Wherefore receive ye one another, even as Christ also received you, to the glory of God. This closes Paul's admonition and opens the way for another brief but most important passage bearing upon, and in some sense summarizing, the whole theme of the Epistle. "Receive ye one another" refers to the mutual relations of Gentile Christians with their scrupulous Jewish brethren.

In no case was the spirit of Christian unity to be violated by refusal or failure to give them full cordial recognition as brethren in Christ, and this to the glory of God and after the example of Christ, for he "*also received you*," *i.e.*, you Gentiles, into the fellowship of God's people. This had been the one great central theme of Paul throughout this entire Epistle. He began with the declaration of grace and apostleship for the obedience of faith among all the Gentiles, and he here ends by thus introducing a brief but remarkable section on the same great subject. No stronger motive to the duty enjoined of cordial friendliness to their Jewish brethren could be presented than this. What follows is usually taken as a part of the present section, but its great importance and its independent dogmatic character lead us to treat it separately, as closing the didactic portion of the Epistle, to which Paul appends only personal explanations, salutations, and the benediction.

Ch. XV. 8-13. Conclusion of the Didactic Epistle by Emphatic Assertion of the Reception of the Gentiles.

8. For I say] The conjunction does little more than hinge this short paragraph to the phrase immediately preceding. "As Christ also received you, for I assert," etc. "I can use this argument, inasmuch as I assert that." On the use of the phrase "I say" to introduce a new proposition with special emphasis compare ch. xi. 1, 11.

that Christ hath been made a minister of the circumcision] This was perhaps a point urged by Paul's opponents. That Christ was made a minister of the circumcision Paul grants, but not with emphasis either upon the word "minister" (Riddle) or upon the phrase "minister of the circumcision." This entire phrase occupies the unemphatic place. The emphasis is first upon "Christ," then upon the phrase with which the sentence ends.

for the truth of God,] "*Christ* was made a minister of the circumcision for the *truth of God*." So the sentence should read if we found our idea of the emphasis upon the order of the Greek text. What this special truth was which required that our Lord should come as a minister of the circumcision is set forth in the two clauses which are in virtual apposition with, and so explanatory of, the phrase "truth of God."

that he might confirm the promises given unto the fathers, 9. and that the Gentiles might glorify God for his mercy;] These clauses governed by εἰς of result attach directly to the main predicate "was made a minister of the circumcision for the truth," etc. The preceding preposition ὑπερ (for the sake of) gives us the motive of the mission of Christ; the present preposition εἰς points out the direction to which this motive leads, and by which as a result it is satisfied. It therefore explains the motive. The truth of God is maintained by confirming, literally "making strong" (a Hebraism for "giving effect to"), the promises given to the fathers,

But what were those promises? No other than those which Paul proceeds to quote, and which he first summarizes in the next clause— "and that the Gentiles might glorify God for his mercy." This is the Hebraistic parallelism to the preceding. The giving of effect to the promises, the very foundation of which was that in Abraham all nations should be blessed, led directly to their glorifying God. Paul's idea then is that Christ was made a minister of the circumcision, and not sent directly to the Gentiles, because the Gentiles were to be received under the promise given to the fathers. They were to come in as brethren with the chosen people, and so the Messiah should praise God among the Gentiles, and the Gentiles would rejoice with God's people. It was thus for the very unity of Jew and Gentile in the fellowship of Christ, which Paul seeks to promote, that our Lord was made a minister of the circumcision and wrought out his great work from that basis. The tenor of the passages quoted, however, emphasizes the privileges of the Gentiles. The unity with the ancient people is implied, and in one passage expressed. But the quotations impress us with the thought that Paul is here not so much emphasizing a reason for kindly reception of their Jewish brethren by the Gentiles, as giving his last emphatic expression to the great thought of the Epistle that the Gentiles are "fellow-heirs, and fellow-members of the body, and fellow-partakers of the promise in Christ Jesus through the gospel" (Eph. iii. 6).

as it is written,
Therefore will I give praise unto thee among the Gentiles,
And sing unto thy name.

A quotation from Psalm xviii. 49, shewing that even in David's day the Lord's Anointed called the Gentiles to be partakers of the joy of God's people.

10. And again he saith,
Rejoice, ye Gentiles, with his people.

Quoted from Deut. xxxii. 43, where again the world of the Gentiles is called to share in the joy of deliverance of God's people, implying that they have an interest therein, and so a right to this joy. This implies the reading of the LXX. and of Kennicott's variation.

11. And again,
Praise the Lord, all ye Gentiles;
And let all the peoples praise him. (Psalm cxvii. 1.)

This short psalm of two verses is of precisely the same tenor as the passages already quoted. The occasion is the deliverance of God's people, and in their joy the Gentiles are called to share. From all these three passages the inference which Paul draws is clear, that where the Gentiles are thus invited to praise God for the deliverance of his people, the future of that people has an interest for them. The spirit of the olden time, which offered such an invitation to the Gentiles, was the very spirit of Paul's gospel, and in striking contrast to the exclusiveness of the later Judaism.

**12. And again, Isaiah saith,
There shall be the root of Jesse,
And he that ariseth to rule over the Gentiles;
On him shall the Gentiles hope.** (Isaiah xi. 10.)
This passage brings out more clearly the conception already implied in the three preceding quotations. The quotation is from the LXX. The variation from our present Hebrew text is rather in form of expression. Instead of "standing for an ensign," *i.e.*, the banner of a leader, the Septuagint has "ariseth to rule over" the Gentiles. The idea is the same, though the variation from the present Hebrew text sounds like the gloss of the later Judaism, with its idea of subjugating the world, rather than of marshalling it under the banner of the Messianic King. If, however, the Septuagint made a mistake, Paul has not thought it of sufficient importance to require correction. The last clause, "on him shall the Gentiles hope," gives Paul his required resting place. It asserts in direct terms the right of the Gentiles to the same hope which the twelve tribes, serving God day and night, laboured to attain. To the rest of this hope he now commits his readers in a beautiful closing benediction.

13. Now the God of hope fill you with all joy and peace in believing, that ye may abound in hope, in the power of the Holy Ghost.] The interrelation of faith, peace, joy and hope are here beautifully presented. Faith is the foundation. This faith produces "peace with God" and "joy in the Holy Ghost." Out of this peaceful, joyous state of mind "hope" abounds. And all is the blessed work of the Holy Spirit.

Ch. XV. 14-33. A Brief Personal Epistle.

14. And I myself also am persuaded of you, my brethren, that ye yourselves are full of goodness, filled with all knowledge, able also to admonish one another.] This concluding personal address corresponds both in tone and thought with the personal introduction (ch. i. 8-13). Both are designed to obviate any idea of Paul's being unduly pressing of himself in sending this Epistle to a church to him as yet unknown. With the appreciation of the goodness, knowledge and pastoral ability of the Roman church here expressed, we may very well compare his appreciation of their faith (ch. i. 8).

15. But I write the more boldly unto you in some measure,] This should be rendered "I wrote," as the tense is first aorist, and there is no conceivable reason for departing from the historical sense. This certainly implies that the Epistle had been written some time before. It might almost suggest the thought that the Epistle as just closed had been transmitted to Rome, and that after the lapse of some interval this brief note was forwarded to explain the delay of his intended visit (verse 22), and to indicate his present intentions and difficulties (verses 24 and 28, and verses 30 and 31). It may, however, be that this Epistle had not been transmitted through lack of opportunity; and that after his apostolic journey through Illyricum, returning to Corinth just prior to his departure for Jerusalem, he adds this appendix, the opportunity for transmission now presenting itself. The comparative degree points back to the preceding verse, "'more boldly' than might be needful in view of your knowledge," etc. The phrase "in some measure" would indicate that Paul's excessive earnestness appears only here and there. For the great part of his Epistle he needs no apology. This qualifying explanation retracts or weakens nothing of the *matter* of the Epistle; it touches only the personal relations of the writer to his readers.

as putting you again in remembrance,] An elegant and delicate method of presenting this grandest of written treatises to his readers, as if they but needed to be reminded of its contents.

because of the grace that was given me of God,

16. **that I should be a minister of Christ Jesus unto the Gentiles,]** The break is best made here, as here the sense is complete, and in the next word is taken up again for fuller expansion. Paul frequently refers to his commission to be the apostle to the Gentiles in similar terms. (See especially Eph. iii. 8.) This commission justifies his assumed boldness. (See also a hint of this in ch. i. 5, 6.)

ministering the gospel of God, that the offering up of the Gentiles might be made acceptable, being sanctified by the Holy Ghost.] The word here used is not the ordinary word denoting public or religious service or worship, but signifies the work of the priest. It might be paraphrased, "Fulfilling the priestly office in the gospel of God." The word "gospel" denotes, not the subject matter of the preaching, but the entire work of preaching, especially the final result in the salvation of those to whom he preached. It is here that the priestly function appears. These souls, saved through the preaching of the gospel, are so presented to God as an offering acceptable to him, because sanctified, not by ritual ceremonies, but by the Holy Ghost. This verse, as Riddle observes, is not an authorization of a priestly theory of the ministry. It is simply an elegant metaphorical presentation of Paul's evangelistic work.

17. **I have therefore my glorying in Christ Jesus in things pertaining to God.]** Our version does feeble justice to the sanctified modesty of this sentence. There is no possessive pronoun in the original, and the article can scarcely be rendered thus when followed by a limiting adjunct. "I have therefore the boasting which is in Christ Jesus, the things which are with God." "The boasting" is not matter for boasting but the act itself. "Glorying in the Lord" is the only glorying suitable to man, and this is Paul's glorying. The matter of this glorying is the precious oblation made to God of saved souls, a matter laid up "in the presence of God" as an holy and acceptable offering.

18. **For I will not dare to speak of any things save those which Christ wrought through me,]** But of what other things could he speak? Meyer says, "things not done through me as if the Lord

had brought them about through me." To this Godet objects, as if it meant that Paul needed to tell his readers that he did not invent his facts. The true idea will, I think, be found by comparison with 2 Cor., chs. x., xi. and xii. In this passage the subject here merely touched is treated at length. This glorying of Paul is *the assertion of his apostolic authority.* It was the mention of this in verse 15 which called it up here. On this point Paul was continually placed on his defence by his enemies. The "glorying in Christ Jesus" was the seal of his apostolic authority given him by Christ, the precious offering of souls to God. In saying "I will not dare to speak of any thing which Christ hath not wrought through me" he gives a passing allusion to his maligners, who boasted in "another man's line of things made ready to their hand" (2 Cor. x. 12-16). He will not dare to do as they did, in Galatia and elsewhere—pervert the converts of others, and then claim them as his own. The broad seal of the Master on his commission shall be what Christ hath wrought through him; and that is amply sufficient.

for the obedience of the Gentiles, by word and deed,

19. in the power of signs and wonders, in the power of the Holy Ghost;] This was the summary of what Christ had wrought through him. The end and result of all was, the obedience of the Gentiles to the faith. This was effected through the word of his preaching and by work, the toilsome variety of which he describes in 2 Cor. xi. 23, etc.; but the efficient power of this word and work lay in the signs and wonders by which God accompanied this word and work, and in the Holy Ghost. (Compare 1 Thess. i. 5.)

so that from Jerusalem, and round about even unto Illyricum, I have fully preached the gospel of Christ;] That Paul did deliver his testimony at Jerusalem would appear from Acts xxii. 18. "Round about" may be taken to signify the neighbourhood of Jerusalem, including Palestine and Syria. (See Acts xxvi. 20 and Gal. i. 17-21.) From this his labours had already ranged to Illyricum on the north-west, *i.e.*, to the present western boundaries of the Austrian empire. By the highways of those days this was a range of some two thousand miles from south-east to north-west, much of it traversed repeatedly, and for hundreds of miles in lateral extent. Over this extent he had "fulfilled the gospel," by which we may fairly understand, not had perfectly made known the gospel, but had extended the gospel toward what, in God's purpose, was its full measure.

20. yea, making it my aim so to preach the gospel, not where Christ was already named,] Literally, "making it my pride," my ambition, not to occupy the comfortable, well-tilled fields, but to take up new ground,

that I might not build upon another man's foundation;] Paul's foundations were the doctrines which he preached (1 Cor. iii. 10). He was fully aware of the special nature of these doctrines, and preferred that his work should stand out distinctly by itself, and be tested by its power to endure (1 Cor. iii. 13). This ambition of his he sets forward in the beautiful words which Isaiah used of the ministry of the Lord's servant,

**21. but, as it is written,
They shall see, to whom no tidings of him came,
And they who have not heard shall understand.**
Quoted from Isaiah lii. 15, where they clearly refer to the extension of the Messiah's kingdom. Paul thus regards his work as a fulfilment of the purport of this prophecy.

22. Wherefore also I was hindered these many times from coming to you:] Paul thus naturally hinges on the second topic to which he wished to call attention in this personal Epistle, i.e., his proposed visit to Rome, which occupies his thought as far as verse 29. This he had also referred to in his personal introduction (ch. i. 10, etc.). The present passage explains the cause of the delay, possibly of the delay which had occurred since he wrote chapter i. If so the visit to Illyricum may have occupied the interval.

23. but now, having no more any place in these regions,] The expression "any place" evidently signifies any room for extension, any new opening. We are thus brought into contact with Paul's spirit and manner of work, ever watchful for the calls of God. Possibly such a call led him to Illyricum, as previously to Macedonia.

and having these many years a longing to come unto you,] On Paul's desire to visit Rome compare chapter i. 11 and 15, where see notes.

24. whensoever I go unto Spain] The repetition of this intention in verse 28 renders interpolation of the full clause here improbable. At the same time there has been serious disturbance of the text. Some texts have inserted "I will come to you." Others have omitted "for" in the next clause. Either of these changes makes the grammatical construction easy (and hence both have been rejected by the critics, though Meyer adopts the latter, and so solves the difficulty). Accepting the revised text we have a broken grammatical construction of which the only solution is that offered by the revised version. Godet and the Syriac version agree with Meyer and render thus, "whensoever I go unto Spain, I hope to see you in my journey." This makes the grammatical structure complete, making ἐλπίζω the principal verb, and does not change the sense, even if not representing the exact form of the primitive text. The verb "I go" is subjunctive, expressing uncertainty, not removed by the subjective phrase which follows.

(for I hope to see you in my journey, and to be brought on my way thitherward by you, if first in some measure I shall have been satisfied with your company)—] Godet and Meyer, as above, make this the principal clause, omitting the conjunction "for," and thus removing the long and awkward parenthesis. The pleasure which Paul anticipated from this visit he has already set forth in chapter i. 11, 12.

25. but now, I say, I go unto Jerusalem, ministering unto the

saints.] The conjunction "but now" is taken as repeated from verse 23 to complete the construction there interrupted. This is expressed in the translation by adding the phrase "I say"; but see above on verse 24. On the ministration in which Paul was now engaged see Acts xxiv. 17; 1 Cor. xvi. 1-4.

26. For it hath been the good pleasure of Macedonia and Achaia to make a certain contribution for the poor among the saints that are at Jerusalem.] This contribution would seem to have been a systematic part of Paul's organization of his work. (See 1 Cor. xvi. 1; Gal. ii. 10.) Yet it came from a cheerful spirit, and so Paul here speaks of it as the voluntary offering of the churches (2 Cor. viii. 1, 2, etc.; ix. 2, etc.) Yet a duty as well as a gift.

27. Yea, it hath been their good pleasure; and their debtors they are.] Paul had already touched this point (ch. xi. 18), which he now expands more fully.

For if the Gentiles have been made partakers of their spiritual things, they owe it to them also to minister unto them in carnal things.] The presence of these two verses in the Epistle to the Romans may well be taken as suggesting the performance of a similar duty on their part. The reasons presented are more than a suggestion; they have the force of a moral imperative.

28. When therefore I have accomplished this, and have sealed to them this fruit, I will go on by you unto Spain.] This carries us back to the thought suspended at verse 25. The ὅτι sums up verses 26 and 27 in the two participles. The verb "to seal" has been variously understood in this passage. Most expositors take it in the general sense of confirming or making sure. Some say, "when I have officially delivered," and find a reference to a sealed discharge. Paul's use of the word looks, we think, in another direction. He speaks of the foretaste, or firstfruits, as the seal of the fulness. This gift was the seal to the Hebrew church of all fruits of goodness and brotherly love in the time to come. It was that which was, so Paul hoped, to ratify the bond which had been so strained by the diversity of opinion which existed. Paul and the Gentile churches were sealed to them as brethren, or sealed themselves to them as loving brethren, the seal being this fruit of their love. The force of the middle voice may lie here, "When I have made this fruit a seal to them on my behalf."

29. And I know that, when I come unto you, I shall come in the fulness of the blessing of Christ.] Paul, as we have already seen in chapter i. 11, anticipated benefit to the church at Rome from his visit. He is confident that no other apostle can bring to them gifts beyond what the Lord has ministered through him.

30. Now I beseech you, brethren, by our Lord Jesus Christ, and by the love of the Spirit,] In these words, indicative of deep emotion and of a great burden of anxiety, Paul opens the last of these personal thoughts. "The Lord Jesus Christ" and "the love" which the Spirit works in the hearts of all God's children, are the motives by which the apostle seeks to move his readers. Had he used the word "entreat," or "beg," or "ask," then he would say, "for the sake of." But with the verb here used, often translated "exhort," "by" is the appropriate preposition.

that ye strive together with me in your prayers to God for me;] Paul believed in the power of earnest prayer—"strive." He believed in unity of faith and prayer—"together with me." And he believed in intercessory prayer—"on my behalf." There were four topics (in pairs) which lay upon his heart—

31. that I may be delivered from them that are disobedient in Judæa,] The disobedience here referred to was clearly the disobedience of unbelief, the rejection of the gospel. How deeply this burden was laid on Paul's heart in this journey appears from Acts xx. 22.

and that my ministration which I have for Jerusalem may be acceptable to the saints;] Even Paul's fond hope that his offering might be the seal of a covenant of love with the Hebrew church had its misgivings. These could not have been less trying to his heart than the direct opposition of the unbelieving Jews. As Moule well observes, they give us an insight into the lifelong struggle of this noble man. He worked for Christ under the cold distrust of what was, apart from his own labours, the whole Christian world.

32. that I may come unto you in joy through the will of God,] All through there is the shadow of what voiced itself at Ephesus, "not knowing the things that shall befall me there." But he has high hopes of Rome. To that church, so thoroughly in sympathy with his own faith in Christ, he can turn with joy.

and together with you find rest.] In their sympathy and love he hopes at last to find rest from false accusers and false brethren. How little could he foresee that the rest would be in the cold vault of the Mamertine prison, and at last on the headsman's block and in the tomb by the Ostian Way!

33. Now the God of peace be with you all. Amen.] The brief benediction, the outpouring of a loving heart, closes this minor epistle.

CH. XVI. 1, 2. A LETTER OF COMMENDATION.

1. I commend unto you Phœbe our sister,] From 2 Cor. iii. 1 we learn that such letters of commendation, or as we would say, introduction, were common, and that the verb here used supplied the formulary with which they opened. Of Phœbe we know nothing except what is here stated. She may have been, as the later tradition states, the bearer of this Epistle. The title of "sister" here used by Paul was an honour indeed.

who is a servant of the church that is at Cenchreæ:] The title "servant" may very well be here taken in the official sense—a deaconess. This office was probably still, as in its origin, one of ministering to the sick and the poor. It was therefore quite appropriate for a woman. The letter of introduction of course implies that she was travelling from Cenchreæ, the port of Corinth, to Rome. It gives us thus internal evidence of the place from which this Epistle was written, and so of its date.

2. that ye receive her in the Lord,] On the meaning of this term "receive" see note on chapter xiv. 1. To the Christian society only accredited members were admitted. They were received "in the Lord," *i.e.*, welcomed into the fellowship of the household of Christ.

worthily of the saints,] Paul bespoke for this sister a right royal, as well as a right hearty, welcome.

and that ye assist her in whatsoever matter she may have need of you:] This was a draft at sight, and to unlimited extent, upon the liberality, hospitality and kindly aid of the church at Rome, indicating the full confidence of Paul in this holy woman. It illustrates the brotherhood of the early church, and that the spirit of the period immediately following the Pentecost had extended with the spread of the gospel. The clause which follows rather discountenances the idea that the assistance was in a legal matter.

for she herself also hath been a succourer of many, and of mine own self.] The word "succourer" here used is cognate to the verb rendered "assist" above. As it would be out of the question to refer it to legal assistance here, such application becomes unlikely above. She had been at her own home, where she had means and influence, a patroness of many a needy Christian, and even of Paul himself. Now, in the great strange city, Paul places her under the protecting care of the church of Christ.

Ch. XVI. 3–16. Salutations.

3. Salute Prisca and Aquila my fellow-workers in Christ Jesus,] Our information regarding these saints is found in Acts xviii.; in 1 Cor. xvi. 19, where we find them apparently at Ephesus (compare Acts xviii. 18); and in the present passage, where, a little later, we find them at Rome, whence they came at first. In Corinth and Ephesus they had been Paul's fellow-workers in the gospel. Perhaps when Paul left Ephesus they returned to Rome.

4. who for my life laid down their own necks;] Both in Corinth and in Ephesus Paul's life had been in danger (Acts xviii. 12; xix. 26; 1 Cor. xv. 32; 2 Cor. i. 8, 9). When and how these friends had thus shewn their love we know not.

unto whom not only I give thanks, but also all the churches of the Gentiles:] Paul feels that had his work been cut short it would have been a loss to the whole Gentile world. The Jewish world was otherwise provided for, but the cause of Christianity among the Gentiles was bound up with the life of Paul.

5. and salute the church that is in their house.] The Christian assemblies of a great city were as yet without a public place of congregation, and hence must have met in detachments, which is probably the meaning of the expression used here.

Salute Epænetus my beloved, who is the firstfruits of Asia unto Christ.] A convert either during Paul's short visit to Ephesus or during the subsequent labours of Prisca and Aquila. If the latter, he may, as Godet suggests, have accompanied them to Rome. Paul plays lovingly with the names, "the praised one" and "my beloved one." The reading of "Asia" instead of "Achaia" is supposed to point to Ephesus as the destination of this part of the Epistle. It is not, however, sufficient, even in connection with the third verse, to establish the probability of such a theory.

6. **Salute Mary, who bestowed much labour on you.**] The use of the aorist tense and the reading "you," well-established instead of "us," suggest that this woman had occupied an important place in the work of evangelization at Rome, in fact, in founding the church. In reference to works of charity the aorist tense would scarcely be used. It would not stand out as a fact of the past.

7. **Salute Andronicus and Junias, my kinsmen, and my fellow-prisoners, who are of note among the apostles, who also have been in Christ before me.**] Few passages are more tantalizing to mere curiosity than this. What was the relationship of these persons to Paul? When and where were they his fellow-prisoners? How comes it that men so well known are not elsewhere mentioned? We only learn from the whole the fragmentary character of our knowledge of the apostolic age.

8. **Salute Ampliatus my beloved in the Lord.**] This, as a definite Latin name, brings us nearer to Rome.

9. **Salute Urbanus our fellow-worker in Christ, and Stachys my beloved.**] The designation points to evangelistic work, in which Stachys may have been an assistant, as Mark with Paul and Barnabas.

10. **Salute Apelles the approved in Christ.**] A Christian who had passed through the furnace of trial.

Salute them which are of the household of Aristobulus.] Slaves or freedmen in the household of a man of wealth who himself is not saluted, either because dead or because not a Christian. The whole house seem included as all Christian.

11. **Salute Herodion my kinsman.**] This personal designation tells us less than either of the others. Kinsman or countryman.

Salute them of the household of Narcissus, which are in the Lord.] Here the Christian portion of the household is distinguished. It can only be conjecture as to whether this Narcissus was the freedman of Claudius, executed before this date, or the bad favourite of Nero.

12. **Salute Tryphæna and Tryphosa, who labour in the Lord. Salute Persis the beloved, which laboured much in the Lord.**] The mention of these three women, with Mary and Prisca and Phœbe preceding, shows us how prominent was the part taken by women in the work of the gospel, and how fully their work was sanctioned by

Paul. Meyer notes the delicacy indicated by the fact that Paul does not say "my beloved," as of the men. Hers was the universal esteem of the church. Her work was now finished, and the fruit of it remained in this precious title.

13. **Salute Rufus the chosen in the Lord, and his mother and mine.**] A Rufus is mentioned in Mark xv. 21. Was this the same? The intimate acquaintance of Paul with so many at Rome may be explained by the fact that to the great capital the stream of travel and commerce converged from all parts of the world. See also the greeting of Paul at Appii Forum (Acts xxviii. 15).

14. **Salute Asyncritus, Phlegon, Hermes, Patrobas, Hermas, and the brethren that are with them.**] A group, perhaps, forming one of the divisions of the Christian church at Rome, as the assembly in the house of Prisca and Aquila was another.

15. **Salute Philologus and Julia, Nereus and his sister, and Olympas, and all the saints that are with them.**] Here is another group, the fifth so mentioned. If each of these represented a church or assembly of Christians, then we may perhaps regard them as branches of the central assembly to which the Epistle was more especially directed, and to which the next and final salutation is presented.

16. **Salute one another with a holy kiss.**] A custom observed in the primitive church. See Tertullian, De Oratione, xiv.: "Having fasted, and prayer being offered, they bring in the kiss of peace with the brethren, which is the seal of prayer, since the more peace prevails among the brethren the more acceptably does prayer ascend."

·**All the churches of Christ salute you.**] That is, return in spirit the kiss of peace just given to each other. This final clause thus becomes, not a message from all the churches to that at Rome (these are delivered further on), but an expression of the universal brotherhood expressed by the kiss of charity.

CH. XVI. 17-20. FINAL AND SPECIFIC WARNING AGAINST THE FALSE TEACHERS.

17. **Now I beseech you, brethren, mark them which are causing the divisions and occasions of stumbling, contrary to the doctrine which ye learned:**] We must first of all define the parties here referred to. They were teachers, inasmuch as their work is here contrasted with the *didactic* form of teaching or doctrine which the church at Rome had learned. We have already seen good reason to believe that the church at Rome had been evangelized under the Pauline form of doctrine. The teaching of the Judaizers would therefore answer to this part of the description. The application to their work of the term "scandal," so prominently used in chapters xiv. and xv. of the results of the Jewish perversion of the gospel, also points in the same direction. The term "divisions" is also used in 1 Cor. iii. 3 of the dissensions there sown by the Judaizing teach-

ers; and although the word does not occur in chapter xiv., yet the fact itself is there. Further, in our text the article is used without a limiting phrase. "The divisions and the scandals" can only mean some well-known divisions, etc. And as the apostle refers to these in general terms, and does not say that they existed at Rome (among you), we must take them of a widespread schism and offence in the church. The Judaizing faction alone corresponds to this description. If so then the short section now before us is a specific, almost personal, warning of the believers at Rome against the danger of these Jewish teachers. It does not imply that they were as yet at work in Rome. It does imply that they were at work in the church at large; the present participle, used without limitation of time or place, would indicate this. In the preceding Epistle Paul had laid bare every possible aspect of this great error, but had done so without reference to the persons who taught. He kept his great exposition and defence of the universal ethical gospel free from all complication with personal controversy, such as appears in the Epistle to the Galatians. The personal warning against the false teachers (needful in itself) is therefore thrown into this brief appendix amid personal matters. The verb which Paul here uses, "*look out for*," implies that they had not yet come to Rome. It is the vigilance of the sentinel.

and turn away from them.] The very opposite of the "receive" of chapter xiv. 1. It implies refusal to admit them to the freedom and courtesies of the Christian assembly, where, as in the synagogue, a visiting brother was free and even invited to speak.

18. **For they that are such serve not our Lord Christ, but their own belly;**] But how could this be said of the Judaizers? To answer this we have only to remember that their doctrine maintained the old sacrificial feasts, which had been the delight of the well-fed priest in every age. On Paul's rigid self-restraint in this matter see 1 Cor. ix. and 2 Cor. xi., etc., where there are not obscure hints that others made gain of the Corinthian church.

and by their smooth and fair speech they beguile the hearts of the innocent.] Compare 1 Cor. ii. 1; 2 Cor. vii. 2; x. 10, 11; xi. 13.

19. **For your obedience is come abroad unto all men.**] Compare chapter i. 8. "Obedience" expresses the ready faith with which they had received the gospel. This clause should, we think, be connected directly with παρακαλῶ, verse 17, "I exhort thus because your obedience to the pure faith of the gospel is so well known."

I rejoice therefore over you:] "as partakers with me in the full liberty and privileges of the gospel." This rejoicing would thus express the fellowship and unity of the church at Rome with Paul in his doctrine, as the next expresses his desire that it should not be broken in upon by false teaching.

but I would have you wise unto that which is good, and simple unto that which is evil.] δέ here, without a μέν preceding, may be rendered "and." It is continuative. "'I exhort you,' for your obedience has come abroad to all. I therefore rejoice over you, and would have you," etc. The play upon the word "simple," in the authorized version, is not found in the Greek, and has tended to mislead as to the connection. There may be in the word "wise" a reference to the assumed wisdom of the false teachers. They alone possessed the knowledge of the true teaching of Christ and of the true apostles. The word translated "simple" signifies "unmixed," hence pure, unmixed with evil. Paul desires his readers to be possessed of all true wisdom, but uncontaminated by the admixture of false teaching.

20. **And the God of peace shall bruise Satan under your feet shortly.**] Literally, "shall bruise the Opposer under your feet in a little time." The God of peace is opposed to those who cause dissension. On the reference to Satan here compare 2 Cor. xi. 13-15, where the same false teachers are called the "ministers of Satan." "Shortly" is not to be taken, we think, of date, as if the day of judgment were near at hand, but of manner. A speedy victory will be gained over such opposing power of Satan. It is perhaps the thought with which this brief warning concludes which calls in here the shortest form of benediction,

The grace of our Lord Jesus Christ be with you.] See a similar brief benediction at the close of the longer personal postscript (ch. xv. 33).

Ch. XVI. 21-23. Salutations from Paul's Associates.

21. **Timothy my fellow-worker saluteth you;**] See Acts xx. 4. The same term is applied to Prisca and Aquila, and to Urbanus.

and Lucius and Jason and Sosipater, my kinsmen.] These names appear in Acts xiii. 1; xvii. 5; and a similar one in xx. 4, but we cannot affirm the identity.

22. **I Tertius, who write the epistle, salute you in the Lord.**] The aorist participle may be taken substantively as equal to "the writer," *i.e.*, the amanuensis usually employed by Paul. (See 1 Cor. xvi. 21 and Gal. vi. 11.)

23. **Gaius my host, and of the whole church, saluteth you.**] We meet this name four times elsewhere in the New Testament: Acts xix. 29, Gaius of Macedonia; Acts xx. 4, Gaius of Derbe; 1 Cor. i. 14, almost certainly the same as here; and 3 John 1. He was distinguished for hospitality in that age of Christian hospitality.

Erastus the treasurer of the city saluteth you, and Quartus the brother.] The mention of this important officer gives us an idea of the influence of Christianity in this great Greek city.

The *textus receptus* inserts a brief benediction after this verse as verse 24, which is omitted in the revised text.

Ch. XVI. 25-27. Doxology.

25. Now to him that is able to stablish you according to my gospel] This closing doxology resembles the opening address in the skilful condensation of an epitomized argument into a series of adjuncts and relative clauses. The doxology itself is contained in the opening article and participle and in the concluding line, in which there is a broken grammatical construction, caused by the introduction of the relative. All else is the epitome of a grand argument in adjuncts of the opening participle.

"To him that is able to stablish you." This was, in fact, the purpose of the Epistle. The word denotes the perfect settlement of the religious life on the foundation of truth. This truth was the gospel which Paul preached, and of which he has just given us so full an exposition.

and the preaching of Jesus Christ,] "The preaching" generally signifies the truth preached, and is used by Paul with "gospel" to designate the entire form of truth for the world's salvation with which he was put in trust (1 Cor. ii. 4 and xv. 14). This gospel and preaching is to be the rule according to which they are to be established. But this itself has had an antecedent rule with which it accords.

according to the revelation of the mystery which hath been kept in silence through times eternal,] Of the various constructions of this adjunct we prefer on the whole to connect it directly with τὸ κήρυγμα. We should then translate and punctuate as follows: "According to my gospel, and to the preaching of Jesus Christ which is according to the revelation of the mystery," etc. "My gospel" is a definite phrase needing no further definition. But by describing it by the parallel expression, "the preaching of Christ which is according to the revelation of the mystery," Paul at once opens out the full grandeur of this gospel. It is the line of God's *development* of his great design. In this word ἀποκάλυψις Paul anticipated the true doctrine of religious development. For the full expansion of this thought consult the Epistle to the Ephesians in the first three chapters.

26. but now is manifested,] In emphatic contrast with "the silence of the ages." On the relation of the "manifestation" to the "revelation" compare chapter i. 18, etc. The manifestation is the culmination and result of the long revealing process which fills the ages. The mystery is the truth still in part concealed in God's silence, but in part revealed.

and by the scriptures of the prophets,] Better the margin, "through means of." We have had abundant illustration of Paul's use of the prophetic scriptures in bringing to light his gospel. This adjunct modifies "made known."

according to the commandment of the eternal God,] A second adjunct of "made known." No point was clearer in Paul's mind than this, that in this proclamation of the universal gospel he acted under a divine commission, by divine command. This command is that of the *eternal* God, who through the *eternal* ages hath unfolded his design.

is made known unto all the nations] "Unto" is not the mere dative of "to" or "for." It expresses destination, purpose. God's purpose as *to extent* reaches "all nations."

unto obedience of faith;] The same preposition of purpose, but now purpose of efficiency. But in both purposes God commits the accomplishment of his will to man.

27. to the only wise God,] A parting glance at the theme of the of the hymn of the ages (ch. xi. 33).

through Jesus Christ, to whom be the glory for ever. Amen.] The ancient authorities who omit "to whom" are at least right in interpretation. In the gospel of our Lord Jesus Christ Paul has shewn us the wisdom of God, as he had proved in experience the power of God; and now he calls upon the church of all ages to join with him in ascribing "to the only wise God the glory" of this great salvation. And to the end of the ages the church will still say, "Amen!"

www.ingramcontent.com/pod-product-compliance
Lightning Source LLC
Chambersburg PA
CBHW032108220426
43664CB00008B/1178